U0049498

[海外客家研究叢書01]

東南亞客家及其周邊

張維安◎主編

中央大學出版中心 ｜ 遠流

目錄

《海外客家研究叢書》總序 / **蕭新煌**　　　　　　　　　　　　　i

序：從互動中浮現客家文化特色 / **張維安**　　　　　　　　　　iii

廟宇策略與新加坡閩客族群的發展：以天福宮和望海大伯公廟為例 /
黃賢強、賴郁如　　　　　　　　　　　　　　　　　　　　　1

馬來西亞檳城海珠嶼大伯公的族群性格：客家與福建人之間 / **張維安**　23

新加坡中藥業的族群分工與族群意象 / **張翰璧**　　　　　　　　45

性別、族群與宗教之交織：印尼亞齊客家女性改信伊斯蘭教的經驗與
過程之初探 / **蔡芬芳**　　　　　　　　　　　　　　　　　　67

馬來西亞柔佛州古來縣新村客家社群的民間信仰考察 / **黃文斌**　　105

One Deity, Many Ways: A Comparison of Communal Rituals in Two
Chinese Settlements, Sarawak /
Elena Gregoria Chai Chin Fern（蔡靜芬）　　　　　　　　145

Hakka in Engkilili, Sarawak: Community and Identity / **Daniel Chew**　177

The Hakka in Sabah before World War Two: Their Adaptation to New
Environment, Challenges and the Forging of New Identity /
Danny Wong Tze Ken（黃子堅）　　　　　　　　　　　　235

《海外客家研究叢書》總序

蕭新煌

　　中央大學客家學院獲得李誠代校長的大力支持於2012年底正式成立「海外客家研究中心」，在中心的工作目標裡，明列出版《海外客家研究叢書》，以貫穿教學、研究和出版的學術三大宗旨。

　　「海外客家」，顧名思義是以原鄉中國和本國台灣以外的客家族群和社會做為研究對象。就客家族群歷史淵源來說，台灣客家也算是中國原鄉的「海外」移民客家，但客家在台灣經歷三百年的本土化、台灣化和國家化之後，已與台灣的新國家社會形成有機體。如此的國家化和「去離散化」的經驗乃構成台灣客家與其他全球客家很不同的族群歷史和政治文化樣貌。基於此，如果將台灣客家與其他海外客家進行比較研究的著作，當然也可以列入此一叢書。

　　到底「海外客家」有多少人？一直是人人有興趣、大家有意見，但彼此都不太確定的「事實」。偶爾會聽到的猜測竟高達8,000萬到1億，但根據1994年「世界客屬第十二次懇親大會」所公布的統計是6,562萬，似是比較嚴謹和實在的數字。在這6,562萬當中，中國原鄉大概有5,290萬、台灣有460萬，剩下來的812萬客家人口嚴格說來，就是本叢書系列著作要去探討研究的「海外客家族群」對象。

　　如何在這812萬海外客家裡，去做進一步的分類、理解和比較，恐怕也是見仁見智。我認為，至少也做以下的初步分類嘗試：

　　第一群是所謂海外華人集中的社會，即香港（125萬）、澳門（10萬）、新加坡（20萬）。在這三個社會裡客家族群（共155萬）如何形成、演變，並與其他華人族群如何相同相異，當是很有意義的研究主題。

　　第二群是亞洲和太平洋的海外客家，其總人數有360萬，僅次於

台灣的460萬，包括印尼（150萬）、馬來西亞（125萬）、泰國（55萬）、越南（15萬）、緬甸（10萬）、澳大利亞（4.3萬）、印度（2.5萬）、太平洋各島嶼（1.7萬）、日本（1.2萬）、菲律賓（6,800）和汶萊（5,000）。這些身處少數的亞太客家族群的變貌和如何維繫客家族群認同，及其與在地本土社會、族群和國家的種種生成、矛盾、辯證關係，即是有價值的探討課題。

第三群是北美洲和中南美洲的海外客家，共60萬。其中美國有28.4萬、加拿大有8.1萬，其餘的23.5萬則分散在秘魯、牙買加、古巴、圭亞那、巴拿馬和巴西等國。這些算是少數中的少數之海外客家族群經驗中，最難能可貴的恐怕就是如何去延續什麼程度的客家文化傳統和習慣的「微觀族群生活經驗」。

第四群是其他的海外客家，共28萬，包括歐洲的20萬和非洲的8萬。其中歐洲的英國有15萬、法國3萬，再次是瑞士、荷蘭、比利時，北歐的瑞典和丹麥也有少數客家人的蹤跡。至於非洲的模里西斯有3.5萬，算是可觀，南非有2.5萬，留尼旺約有1.8萬。

本叢書的目的就是計畫陸續出版有關上述這些分散五大洲，多達80個國家和社會海外客家族群之移民史、在地化歷程、「離散經驗」和維繫並延續客家文化認同的奮鬥和努力。

以上就是我做為本叢書總主編的出版想法和期許。

序：從互動中浮現客家文化特色

　　自在族群與自為族群之別，在於後者有比較清楚的族群意識，自在的客家早已存在，自為的客家則是近代的產物。族群意識之產生，往往發生在族群互動之中。長時期以來，客家文化一方面經營著自身的特色，但也同時從與周邊族群的互動中形塑新的面貌。以世界客家作為分析單位，將會發現客家族群內部驚人的異質性，不論是語言、建築、飲食，甚至信仰儀式，各地的客家族群都可以找到彼此之間的差異性。多元異質的客家如何形成，而其又如何構成一個族群，學界已有不少研究，其中遷移及與周邊族群的互動應是一個不可忽略的因素，因與周邊族群互動，有時彼此影響相互吸納，有時更加清晰的區別彼此的族群界線。

　　在全球客家族群中，東南亞客家是一塊最關鍵的拼圖，要了解東南亞客家必須對其歷史、社區、經濟、產業、宗教信仰多所了解，而與周邊族群互動的部分則顯得更加重要。由於在中國或台灣原鄉，各地客家之間可能已經有所差別，對於一個移民海外的客家族群而言，其周邊更包括了不同地區的客家人、客家人以外的華人（可能是福建人、廣府人、海南人、潮州人）、移入地的原住民、移入地的他國移民等等。因此，對東南亞客家的了解，除了探索客家社群內部之外，客家及其所生活的歷史脈絡與人文生態之了解是不可或缺的一環，族群生態、政治生態、經濟生態、文化信仰的生態環境，都屬於本書的「周邊」範圍。

　　本書八篇文章分別從不同的案例進行探索，期能對東南亞客家族群這塊拼圖有更清晰的理解。在廟宇的策略方面，黃賢強和賴郁如的論文分析客家人與福建人因為不同的生態而有不同的方式，閩幫企圖利用天福宮作為團結閩人和建立領導整體華社力量的策略，尤其是以後者為主要取向；而客幫則是運用望海大伯公廟促進客家人之間的凝

聚力。這兩種不同的目標取向其實和兩幫群的人數多寡及經濟實力息息相關。在廟產使用的競爭方面，張維安在海珠嶼大伯公廟個案中所處理的客家人與福建人關係是為一例，從寶福社正月初十四將金身送入海珠嶼大伯公，初十五晨請火，清晨往市區送香火給會員，初十六在寶福社犒軍（十六實際上沒在海珠嶼伯公廟進行活動），初十七送回五德宮的大伯公金身等，分析客家與福建人對於海珠嶼大伯公廟的競爭。

　　以上兩篇文章討論的客家族群周邊是其他華人──福建人。張翰璧的論文，也是以客家和其他華人為分析架構，在族群產業獨占與分工方面，例如福建人多為開設銀行、保險業主要在廣府人手中、金銀業中則是潮州人和廣府人分庭抗禮、典當業多以客家人為主要經營者等。甚至是中藥業內還區族群而有不同，例如中等成藥的生產領域以客家人為多，尤其是永定的客家人，但是在貴重藥材的部分，則是以潮州人為主要經營的族群。

　　客家族群的周邊不一定是客家以外的人群，有時候只是另一群客家人，不同群體因為在地化的關係而有不同的儀式，蔡靜芬的兩座大伯公儀式研究，說明了這個現象。有時候是因為與不同一個地方的客家相遇，因而帶來宗教上的影響，黃文斌所分析的古來縣則是另外一例，這裡的客家可進一步細分為河婆、惠州、豐順及鶴山人。他們的信仰中，有一些是直接與客家原鄉民間信仰相關的，如河婆客家人的三山國王（粵東區）及惠州客家人的譚公，但是也有一些神明不專屬於客家人，卻成為了客家村里流行的共同信仰。

　　除了不同地區的客家人與華人之外，周丹尼的論文處理的是客家和當地原住民（伊斑人）的互動，客家人學習伊斑語言並與之通婚等，但卻保留客家話和國語。黃子堅對於沙巴客家的研究，則可以看出客家移民在當地各方面的適應策略，通過客家族群周邊人文生態的互動來解釋。蔡芬芳的性別、族群與宗教的「相互交錯分析」有助於我們了解族群間的互動，刻板印象、相互融入等客家與周邊族群之間

的複雜關係。

　　本書的出版，緣於不同的研究計畫與許多好友的支持，行政院國家科學委員會、蔣經國國際學術交流基金會、國立清華大學人文社會中心、國立中央大學出版中心分別在研究計畫、學術交流、工作坊以及出版方面提供了大力的協助，另外清華大學黃一農院士、中央大學李誠代理校長、中央研究院蕭新煌所長、中央大學張翰璧教授、徐幸君小姐、清華大學人社院陳英惠秘書、陳麗華博士、張容嘉博士生，以及清華大學人文社會中心行政同仁等在各方面的協助，使本書能夠順利出版，謹致上謝忱。

張維安

2013.1.20

國立交通大學客家文化學院

廟宇策略與新加坡閩客族群的發展：
以天福宮和望海大伯公廟為例[*]

黃賢強、賴郁如[†]

一、前言

在早期新加坡方言幫群社會裡，各個幫群的人數規模和擁有的財力資源不同，影響到他們在新加坡的幫群發展策略及目標。位於幫群人口數量極端值兩端的閩幫（即閩南幫，當地習慣稱為福建幫）和客幫，有一個共同的發展策略模式，那就是以廟宇作為整合社群或幫群的機制。廟宇不只是一個實踐信仰的所在，人們還可以利用廟宇來進行幫群社會整合，希望促使幫群勢力的擴張或是凝聚。本文欲探究廟宇在幫群發展的過程中所扮演的角色和具體實踐方式。兩個幫群的目標取向不同和其人數規模與財力脫離不了關係，所以當目標設定相異時，其廟宇策略的具體實踐方式也會跟著不同。如果我們以歷史回溯的方式來看閩客幫群的發展目標，會發現閩幫企圖利用天福宮作為團結閩人和建立領導整體華社力量的策略，尤其是以後者為主要取向，而客幫則是運用望海大伯公廟促進客家人之間的凝聚力。

---

* 本文初稿發表於「季風亞洲華人社會文化流動與多元文化」國際學術研討會（台灣新竹，國立清華大學，2012年6月16-17日）。作者要感謝評論人陳祥水教授和李元瑾副教授的評論和意見。

† 黃賢強，新加坡國立大學中文系副教授；賴郁如，新加坡國立大學中文系博士生。

二、新加坡華人社會概況

新加坡是一個典型的移民社會，從1819年英國人建埠開始，大量華人先後從馬六甲、檳城和中國閩粵等地移入該島。[1] 十九世紀中葉以來，華人人口已經超過總人口半數，不久更達到四分之三。然而，華人人口內部卻充滿高度的異質性，主要可以分成五大方言群，分別是閩南人、潮州人、廣府人、海南人和客家人。根據1881年的海峽殖民地人口統計資料，閩南人占所有華人移民的28.8%、潮州人占26.1%、廣府人占17.1%、海南人占9.6%、客家人占7.1%。到了1947年，各個幫群人口數互有消長，還是以閩南人居多，占42.8%；客家人最少，占5.5%。[2] 到了2010年，族群比例略有變動，但是閩南人依然是多數，客家人還是維持少數，但已經超過海南人（見表一）。用方言或籍貫來將人群區分，進而建立幫群是新馬地區華人社會的基本現象。不少研究都指出「幫群」是新馬地區華人移民社會的基本結構，[3] 顯示幫群組織是新加坡華社的重要特徵。

學者陳育崧以新加坡殖民地時代的華文碑銘為分析基礎，並且以中國傳統社會文化的角度來看這些組織，他認為初期的幫群形成是因為方言的差異，並且是中國傳統社會文化的一種延伸，中國傳統社會結構就是以地緣、血緣和業緣交織而成。[4] 麥留芳則使用人口普查資

1　有關新加坡的華人移民和發展史的基本敘述，可參閱崔貴強，《新加坡華人──從開埠到建國》，新加坡：新加坡宗鄉會館聯合總會、教育出版有限公司，1994；有關新加坡建國前華人社會的專題討論，則可參閱Hong Liu & Sin-Kiong Wong, *Singapore Chinese Society in Transition: Business, Politics & Socio-Economic Change, 1945-1965,* New York: Peter Lang, 2004。

2　李恩涵，《東南亞華人史》，台北：五南圖書出版有限公司，2003，頁272。

3　文崇一，〈新加坡華人社會變遷〉，收錄於李亦園、郭振羽主編，《東南亞華人社會研究（上冊）》，台北：正中書局，1985，頁2。蕭新煌、張維安、范振乾、林開忠、李美賢、張翰璧，〈東南亞的客家會館：歷史與功能的探討〉，《亞太研究論壇》28(2005): 185-191。有關「幫」的定義的討論，參閱吳龍雲，《遭遇幫群：檳城華人社會的跨幫組織研究》，新加坡：新加坡國立大學中文系、八方文化創作室，2009，頁10-13。

4　陳育崧，〈緒言〉，收錄於陳育崧、陳荊和編著，《新加坡華人碑銘集錄》，香港：香港中文大學，1970，頁15-22。

華人族群	人數	百分比
福建人（閩南）	1,118,817	40.0
潮州人	562,139	20.1
廣東人（廣府）	408,517	14.6
客家人	232,914	8.4
海南人	177,541	6.4
其他（福州、興化等）	294,054	10.5
總數	2,793,980	100

資料來源：作者根據新加坡2010年人口普查資料整理。"Census of Population 2010 Statistical Release 1: Demographic Characteristics, Education, Language and Religion", http://www.singstat.gov.sg/pubn/popn/c2010sr1.html，2010年10月9日瀏覽。

料和碑文資料證實在新馬地區華人方言群意識的存在，他認為方言群認同是早期新馬地區華人分類幫群的方式。他也是將這種現象置於殖民地時代的背景來看，各個方言群因為工作機會和移民程序等的介入，必須作最表面化的社會接觸，語言上的差異便被體現出來，促成內外群的觀念產生。[5] 這些依據不同身分認同所成立的華人幫群組織，並不是完全處於對立或是互不往來的狀態。因為生存的需要，可以看見各個幫群或是其下較小組織之間角力、合作、分裂或是整合的例子。[6] 因此，在研究新加坡華社的發展和演變時，必須將幫群發展的過程考慮進去。本文希望從廟宇策略的角度來觀察閩客幫群發展的過程。

---

5 麥留芳，《方言群認同：早期星馬華人的分類法則》，台北：中央研究院民族學研究所，1955，頁192-197。
6 有關新加坡早期華人幫群間的競爭與合作，參閱林孝勝，《新加坡華社與華商》，新加坡：新加坡亞洲研究學會，1995，頁28-62。

三、天福宮與望海大伯公廟

（一）天福宮

　　供奉天后媽祖的天福宮位於直落亞逸街（Telok Ayer street），馬來語「Telok Ayer」是海灣之意，可以得知當時天福宮是臨海，此廟築於臨海處對華人來說有一種地利之便。舊時華人抵達新加坡後，一上岸就是到此祭拜媽祖，答謝媽祖保佑航行安全，讓他們安全抵達；或是華人要回中國時，也會到此祈求平安歸去。但是，現在的天福宮已經不再瀕海。天福宮所在的直落亞逸海灣岸邊低淺，經常遭受海潮侵蝕和造成水患，也容易堆積泥沙，不利船隻之停泊，西元1865年殖民政府開始進行填土工程，之後又陸續進行幾次大規模的填海活動，這片海埔新生地讓天福宮成為遠離海岸的市區廟宇。[7]

　　天福宮的初期歷史可以從西元1850年（道光30年）的〈建立天福宮碑記〉一窺，石碑記載此宮是在西元1840年建成。這份具有歷史價值的碑記全文如下：

> 新加坡天福宮，崇祀
> 聖母神像，我唐人所共建也。自嘉慶廿三年[8]，英吏斯臨。新闢是地，相其山川，度其形勢，謂可為商賈聚集之區。剪荊除棘，開通道途，疏達港汊，於是舟檣雲集，梯航畢臻，貿遷化居，日新月盛，數年之間，遂成一大都會。我唐人由內地帆海而來，經商茲土，惟賴 聖母慈航，利涉大川，得以安居樂業，物阜民康，皆 神庥之保護也。我唐人食德思報，公議於新加坡以南直隸亞翼之地，叨建天福宮，背戌面辰，為崇祀聖母廟宇。遂僉舉總理董事勸捐，隨緣樂助，集腋成裘，共襄

---

7 杜南發主編，《南海明珠：天福宮》，新加坡：新加坡福建會館，2010，頁40-41。
8 即西元1819年。

盛事，卜日興築，鳩工庀材，於道光廿年造成。宮殿巍峨，蔚
為壯觀，即以中殿祀 聖母神像，特表尊崇，於殿之東堂祀 關
聖帝君，於殿之西堂祀 保生大帝，復於殿之後寢堂祀 觀音大
士，為我唐人會館議事之所，規模宏敞，棟宇聿新，神人以
和，眾數悅豫，顏其宮曰天福者，蓋謂神靈默佑如天之福也。
共慶落成，爰勒貞石，誌其創始之由，並將捐題姓氏列於碑
陰，以垂永久，俾後之好義者得所考稽，以廣其祀於無窮焉。
是為記。[9]

　　另有一個說法認為天福宮是在西元1842年落成。[10] 兩者略有出
入，但是不論是西元1840或是1842年，可以肯定1840年代初期天福宮
已經建成。雖然天福宮是一座廟宇，卻也是福建會館的前身，負責統
籌閩幫事務，致力於閩幫內部團結，建立幫權。以天福宮創始的三名
大董事來看，三名依序為陳篤生、薛佛記和葉光傳，他們都是當時華
社的頂尖富商，活躍於新馬社會，所以在1840年代閩幫在新加坡華社
裡已經是一股財大勢大的勢力。沒有明顯的證據顯示是否閩幫領導階
層在天福宮建立之前，就將之視為超越幫群的「跨幫服務組織」，但
是從該碑文來看，立碑之時已經形成超越幫群藩籬的視野。碑文中是
用「唐人」，而非「閩人」自居，將天福宮視為「我唐人會館議事之
所」，試圖表達天福宮不只為閩人服務，這是屬於所有華僑的廟宇。
如果比較大約同時期的廣客兩族群合建的福德祠的重修碑文，就可見
閩人和其他族群的企圖心的確有別。該重修碑文刻於西元1854年，
曰：「……茲我廣、惠、肇府人等，羈旅於此，環居一埠，敬立福德
神，建廟以壯神威，設祀以崇祀典，由來尚矣。」[11] 顯然，廣惠肇三

9〈建立天福宮碑記〉，收錄於陳育崧、陳荊和編著，《新加坡華人碑銘集錄》，頁57-58。
10 柯木林，〈古色古香的天福宮〉，收錄於林孝勝等人著，《石叻古蹟》，新加坡：南洋學會，1975，頁
　　49。
11〈重修大伯公廟眾信捐題芳名碑記〉，收錄於陳育崧、陳荊和編著，《新加坡華人碑銘集錄》，頁70-

府人士比較安分，不以籠統的唐人自述，也沒有逾越族群本分。

　　西元1916年殖民政府批准「天福宮福建會館」成立，天福宮福建會館開始逐漸取代天福宮，成為閩幫公認的正式領導機構。在天福宮福建會館出現之前，歷代閩幫領袖都在天福宮處理華人事物、協調商務、籌募賑濟善款，甚至為閩邑族人主持結婚註冊，長期具有完全領導福建族群的權威地位。[12]

（二）望海大伯公廟

　　望海大伯公廟又稱丹戎巴葛福德祠，位於丹戎巴葛（Tanjong Pagar）的Palmer Road。顧名思義，早期大伯公廟瀕臨海洋，從這裡可以望得到海，但是後來就跟天福宮一樣，因為填海造陸，廟宇位置往內陸推進，如今四周圍已經見不到海水的蹤跡。根據廟內文物雲板銘文所記，此廟在西元1844年已經存在。關於望海大伯公廟的起源有兩種口述傳說：一是相傳在未創建之前，有一位客籍的老乞丐在一棵大樹下歸化，後來客家人士就在樹下建起一座小廟，供奉大伯公；[13]第二則是有耆老表示在英國人萊佛士（Thomas Raffles）登陸新加坡時，已經有客家移民在原地供奉大伯公，後來信徒越來越多，於是大家就決定在當地設置祀奉大伯公的福德祠。[14] 現今的大伯公廟外觀是由主祠福德祠以及副祠同德宮（祀有太上老君）組成，主祠的左側供奉虎爺，主祠福德祠重建於西元1861年（咸豐11年），副祠增建於西元1908年。

　　望海大伯公廟是新加坡唯一一座由客屬八邑共同創立和管理的廟

79。

12 杜南發主編，《南海明珠：天福宮》，頁27；吳華，《新加坡華族會館志》，新加坡：南洋學會，1975，頁58。

13 吳華，〈丹戎巴葛福德祠〉，收錄於林孝勝等人著，《石叻古蹟》，頁189。

14 陳波生、利亮時，〈客家人與大伯公的關係：以新馬為例〉，收錄於林緯毅主編，《民間文化與華人社會》，新加坡：新加坡亞洲研究學會，2006，頁64。

宇。[15] 這八邑分成兩個集團，一是由嘉應五屬（梅縣、蕉嶺、五華、興寧和平遠）成立的應和會館，另一是豐永大公會（豐順、永定和大埔）。西元1861年重修廟宇的碑文中刻記有「應和公司」和「豐永大公司」（即為應和會館和豐永大公會之前身）各捐款五十大元，是所有捐款者之最高金額；根據寫於西元1931年的一篇序文來看，兩集團在管理方面是處於平等的地位。從下述碑文記錄透露出，望海大伯公廟是立基於兩大客家方言集團的基礎之上，是屬於客幫的廟宇，不論這些客家人的祖籍地在哪裡，祂是為了促進客幫的集體認同而設立的。[16]

> 董事會由應和會館和豐永大公會各派二十人，設總理、司理、財政各一人、查帳二人，職位由二會館輪值，輪值總理之會館則多派一人共四十一人組成董事會，任期兩年，受託人四名，兩會館各派二人擔任。每年農曆二月十六日大伯公寶誕及七月初一日太上老君寶誕，皆備牲禮，虔誠祭拜。[17]

四、廟宇策略目標不同之原因

首先要說明的是，閩幫和客幫想要建立天福宮和望海大伯公廟的原因，並不是一開始就賦予其功能性的意義，也就是非刻意運用廟宇

---

15 有關望海大伯公廟與新加坡客家人信仰的關係，見利亮時，〈新加坡客家信仰習俗——以望海大伯公廟和客家墳山為例〉，收錄於黃賢強主編，《新加坡客家》，桂林：廣西師範大學出版社，2007，頁195-217。另外一座廟宇「海唇福德祠」，雖然也主要是由客家人（嘉應、豐順、永定、大埔和惠州）管理，但廣州和肇慶府人也參與共同管理。

16 雖然說望海大伯公廟是客家人所立及管理，信奉者也以客家人居多，但是並不代表完全沒有非客家籍的信徒來參拜，現存的匾額還可以見到署名「閩信士陳雲團叩謝」的字樣，刻於西元1923年。但是這位陳雲團到底是否是閩南人，還是來自永定的閩籍客家人，還需待查證。而且，即使是閩南人，閩籍信士畢竟還是少數。

17 高華昌，〈丹戎巴葛客屬八邑福德祠〉，收錄於何炳彪主編，《百年公德被南邦：望海大伯公廟紀事》，新加坡：新加坡茶陽大埔會館，2006，頁9。

來達到族群勢力的擴張或是凝聚。起初，建廟宇絕對是有著神聖性的意義，有信仰上的需求，因為當移民移出原居地時，常常會攜帶著自己原先的信仰到新居地繼續信奉，是為了在不熟悉的環境中求得心安，並且希望在新居地繼續受到神靈的庇佑。遍及台灣甚至是東南亞的媽祖信仰[18]，即是隨著華人移民的腳步從大陸沿海拓展出來的。幫群隨後賦予廟宇世俗性意義，閩幫策略性地選擇用天福宮這個機構將內部勢力凝聚以後，再將影響力伸展到整個華社，而客幫則欲憑藉望海大伯公廟來整合客家族群幫群的向心力，這兩種不同的目標取向其實和兩幫群的人數多寡及經濟實力息息相關。另外，兩廟宇的主神性質對於幫群目標達成也是有舉足輕重的影響，所以當我們要討論廟宇策略目標不同之原因，也是必須著眼於媽祖和大伯公的神明形象。以下將分別討論閩客族群人口與經濟實力以及媽祖和大伯公的神明形象。

（一）閩客族群人口與經濟實力

　　長期研究新加坡幫權社會的林孝勝認為，以十九世紀初新加坡社會的幫權政治來看，大體來說可以分成兩個極端，一端是閩幫，包括漳州府、泉州府和永春州的福建人，另一端是閩幫以外的其餘各幫組成的聯合陣線，包括潮、廣、瓊和客方言群。雖然說各方言群對聯合陣線的投入程度有所差異，但是聯合陣線的出現顯然是針對抵抗閩幫的強大影響力的對策。將潮、廣、瓊和客方言群分開來看，無論在人數或是財富方面，與閩幫相比，他們都是不同程度的少數，所以這種結合是為了在幫權政治下達到勢力均衡的局面。[19] 在競爭有限資源的概念之下，少數族群比多數族群更容易意識到團結的重要性，因為如果少數幫群不團結，其勢力將無法和多數幫群抗衡，最後的結果一定

---

18 有關媽祖信仰的研究論著相當多，可參閱鄭麗航、蔣維錟主編，《媽祖研究資料目錄索引》，福州：海風出版社，2004。

19 林孝勝，〈十九世紀星華社會的幫權政治〉，收錄於林孝勝等著，《石叻古蹟》，頁24-25。

是少數幫群的利益被多數幫群剝奪。由此可見，如果不在聯合陣線的範疇下，客幫是少數中的少數，他們更加需要凝聚向心力，建立起彼此的認同感，唯有如此才能避免自己的勢力被稀釋或是淡化，甚至幫群利益被他群蠶食鯨吞。

相對地，閩幫居於多數，當閩幫勢力發展到一定的程度以後，不需要刻意團結來維護自身的利益，團結與否就不如擴張勢力和影響力重要。在經濟實力方面，閩幫也是凌駕於其他幫群，從天福宮的歷屆領導階層來看，就可以看出閩幫在新加坡經濟實力之雄厚以及企圖心。以閩幫的早期領袖陳篤生為例，他是一名富商，致力於塑造超越幫群的領袖形象。公益形象對於建立超越幫群的領袖形象有十分積極的加分作用，公共事業的參與需要不少資金的投入，他個人的商業事業營利有助於他推動公共事業的進行。在西元1844年，他獨資興建「陳篤生醫院」，嘉惠新加坡所有華社成員，這項義舉讓他在西元1846年獲得海峽殖民地政府的讚賞，被封為「太平局紳」（Justice of Peace），這代表了他的華人領袖地位被政府所承認。他為新加坡華社的領導階層建立起一種模式，想要作超越幫群的領袖必須從事公共事業，服務全體華人，並且要和當權政府有密切溝通。[20] 西元1850年陳篤生去世後，有兩人承接他的領導責任和地位，一是他的兒子陳金鐘，二是與陳篤生家族無血緣親屬關係的陳金聲。陳金鐘繼承其父在閩幫的領導地位，被選為天福宮三大董事之首，持續以天福宮作為總部，處理閩幫和華人事務，也繼續擴建和經營陳篤生醫院。他在西元1865年也受封為太平局紳。另外一方面，陳篤生過世後，陳金聲則被殖民地當局認為是陳篤生的接班人，馬上被封為太平局紳。他也致力於公共事業，例如捐款興建自來水供應系統以及幫助當局平息閩廣會黨械鬥。[21] 後來幾位天福宮的領導人，如陳武烈等人也都跟隨前人腳

---

20 林孝勝，〈十九世紀星華社會的幫權政治〉，頁17。
21 林孝勝，〈十九世紀星華社會的幫權政治〉，頁18。

步，維持前人奠基下來的領導典範。這幾位領導人不滿足於只擔任閩幫領袖，而是以成為新加坡華社領袖為最終目的。在十九世紀的這種領導概念下，天福宮和福建會館的領導階層是高度重疊一起，天福宮自然而然形塑出不是只有服務閩人，同時也是服務和保佑全體華人的形象，這個形象一直延續至今。

　　反觀客幫的經濟實力就不如閩幫強大。早期新加坡的客家人以從事手工業、服務業者居多，也有一些是商人。少數居住在鄉村和外島上的客家人也從事農業和漁業等，以後興起的眼鏡業、中藥業、典當業也主要是由客家人經營。換句話說，客家人在新加坡憑著身強力壯出賣勞動力，依靠一技之長做工謀生，或者積蓄一點資金做小本生意，也有少數人憑著精明能幹經商賺大錢。客幫在早期新加坡社會中的經濟地位，取決於他們從事的行業，因為行業種類會影響財富累積的速度和程度，有些行業如閩幫和潮幫經營的金融業、出入口貿易，大宗米糧買賣等，比較容易有豐厚的利潤，財富可以增加快速。而客幫的行業，比較多是屬於小本經營的行業，影響財富的累積數量和速度，也影響經濟和社會地位。在十九世紀初期，在英殖民地的社會階級上，商人階級高高在上，手工藝技工次之，農耕者漁民排在最後。[22] 既然客家先人早期在新加坡所從事乃手工藝技工和勞力密集的行業，其經濟實力和經濟地位當然也不會太高。甚至有學者認為，那時有一個新興的經濟勢力在當局和歐籍商人的扶持下開始在新加坡華社崛起，這個新經濟勢力就是馬六甲漳泉商人集團，也就是本文中指的閩幫。他們配合萊佛士的經濟政策，在新加坡華社建立一個商業社會。他們的興起也在新加坡華社造成一次大變遷，建立了一種商人集團支配其他行業，使閩幫凌駕其他各幫的新秩序。[23]

　　進入到二十世紀後，從西元1906年成立的新加坡中華總商會（當

<hr>

22 林孝勝，〈開埠初期的新華社會〉，收錄於柯木林、林孝勝著，《新華歷史與人物研究》，新加坡：南洋學會，1986，頁22。

23 林孝勝，〈開埠初期的新華社會〉，頁27。

時稱為中華商務總會）的領導階層更加可以清楚看出，閩幫勢力優於其他幫群的情況。中華總商會是代表新加坡華族最高組織之一，其領導組織大都來自各幫群領袖，要一探客幫和閩幫的經濟和社會勢力，其實也是可以從他們在新加坡中華總商會占有的代表權反映出來。在戰前的新加坡華族社會中，決定領袖地位之首要條件是財富；而擁有財富地位的華人絕大部分為商賈。閩幫一直是最有影響力的群體，總商會成立時，董事會有52席位，規定設「閩幫總理一人，協理四人，議員十六人；粵幫總理一人，協理六人，議員二十四人」，閩幫共占了21席。[24] 總商會在西元1915年改組，閩幫也占32席中的13席，客幫則僅占3席（梅：2席；埔：1席）。[25] 最後，我們可從下表中看到從西元1906年至1983年之間，新加坡中華總商會的歷屆正、副主席中只各出現過一位客家人。所以，在華族的最高組織中的缺席，間接說明了客幫在新加坡華族社群中相對薄弱的經濟實力。以上多少印證並說明了客家人由於鮮少涉足鉅資企業，導致其整體經濟實力遠遜於其他

表二：新加坡中華總商會歷屆正、副主席（1906-1983）籍貫表

幫系	主席	副主席
福建（閩南）	27	24
潮州	12	26
廣東（廣府）	2	2
客家（梅縣）	1	1
三江	0	1
總數	39	48

資料來源：Cheng Lim Keak, *Social Change and the Chinese in Singapore: A Socio-Economic Geography: With Special Reference to Bang Structure*, Singapore: National University of Singapore, 1985, p. 26.

---

24 新加坡中華總商會，《新加坡中華總商會大廈落成紀念刊》，新加坡：新加坡中華總商會，1964，頁145。

25 新加坡中華總商會，《新加坡中華總商會大廈落成紀念刊》，頁146；有關討論，另見甘永川，〈新加坡客家人的經濟生活〉，收錄於黃賢強主編，《新加坡客家》，頁82-83。

方言群（排行在閩幫、潮幫、廣幫之後）。而且，由於整體經濟實力較弱，在許多領域，包括爭取成為華族領袖和擴展族群勢力方面皆形成障礙。從創建望海大伯公廟開始到二次大戰後，客幫的經濟實力和社會地位都是屬於弱勢。弱勢團體如果要免於強勢團體的威脅，就必須團結起來。應和會館和豐永大會館選擇用大伯公信仰作為團結的方式，到現在依然如此，輪流主持，共同管理望海大伯公廟，讓分散在兩個集團的客家勢力結合起來。

（二）媽祖和大伯公的神明形象

　　此部分要討論的並不是媽祖或大伯公是否集中於某些籍貫或是方言群的人崇拜，而是要去討論媽祖和大伯公的形象分別對於「閩幫－擴展勢力」和「客幫－團結內部」取向所提供的助力。

1. 媽祖

　　中國東南沿海一帶，尤其是閩粵地區，因為人地關係的不平衡，人多田少，人們為了生活便往海洋發展，利用漁業和貿易來謀生。古代航海技術不如現代發達，每次出海捕魚或是貿易，人們總是會駭於海洋的不穩定性和不可控制性，希冀能夠靠神靈的力量來保佑自己平安歸來，所以媽祖信仰的產生可謂是一種滿足心理需求的產物。媽祖信仰逐漸在閩粵民間社會形成以後，女海神的形象能夠更快速地深植民心，這和朝廷對媽祖的褒封有關。從北宋開始，歷代帝王都不斷對媽祖進行褒封，有學者統計從北宋宣和五年（西元1123年）到清同治十一年（西元1872年），總共被褒封34次；雖然朝廷對媽祖褒封目的是為了維護其政治統治階級利益的需要，用媽祖信仰來攏絡人心，確立其統治權的穩固，也正是因為朝廷的不斷褒封，也擴大了媽祖信仰在民間的影響力。[26] 媽祖信仰的海外傳播隨著華人到達世界各地，沿

---

26 李天錫，《華僑華人民間信仰研究》，北京：中國文聯出版社，2001，頁13-14。

海人民到國外經商或是從事勞力工作，幾乎都是經由水路的方式到達，新進的機械船隻和航海儀器尚未普遍使用時，航行的平安只能靠祈求媽祖和其他神明的保佑，一旦平安到達目的地就會感謝神明顯靈，所以設置在港口附近的媽祖廟不外乎就是信徒想要感謝媽祖保佑航行平安。船隻有來就有往，回去中國的船隻也是需要祈求媽祖的保佑回途平安，媽祖廟為往來的華人提供旅途上的心靈慰藉。甚至有人隨身帶著媽祖神像上船，或是有船家會把媽祖安座在船上，都是為了希望媽祖保佑的需求，正是因為這些需要，讓媽祖信仰飄洋過海傳播到任何有華人聚居的地方。在中國，媽祖是跨地域與方言群的信仰，祂不單屬於任何一群人，來到新加坡以後也是呈現這種現象，不少方言群都設立自己的廟宇祭拜媽祖，[27] 例如本文討論的天福宮、潮幫的粵海清廟和瓊幫的瓊州天后宮等。

　　十九世紀裡，天福宮除了提供華人的心理需求外，祂還具有清朝政府的象徵。除了清朝政府數次褒封媽祖以外，天福宮內現存的兩塊匾額顯示清朝政府和天福宮的聯繫，一是中國派駐新加坡的領事左秉隆於1881年所贈的「顯徹幽明」，二是1907年光緒皇帝御賜匾額「波靖南溟」。清朝政府尚未被推翻時，新加坡華人認同自己是大清帝國的子民，天福宮裡有強而有力的國家象徵，自然可以吸引更多華人信徒。因此，不分方言群的新加坡華人普遍接受媽祖信仰，事實上媽祖常被視為較大範圍的區域裡具有整合不同性質的人群的作用，[28] 加上十九世紀末期和二十世紀之初，天福宮獲得清政府贈賜匾額，具有國家的象徵代表性，有助於穩固閩幫在華族社會的領導地位。

---

27 有關新加坡和馬來西亞地區媽祖信仰的討論，參見蘇慶華，〈從媽祖崇祀到媽祖文化研究——以馬、新兩國為例〉，收錄於蘇慶華著，《馬新華人研究——蘇慶華論文選集》，吉隆坡：馬來西亞創價學會，2004，頁81-102。

28 林美容，《祭祀圈與地方社會》，台北縣：博揚文化，2008，頁9。

2. 大伯公

　　大伯公信仰與媽祖信仰相同的一點是，不同方言群的新加坡華人也都有設立自己的大伯公廟祭祀，例如有客幫主持的望海大伯公廟，主要由閩幫建立的梧槽大伯公，聯合嘉應五屬、豐永大和廣惠肇方言群的海唇大伯公廟和各幫群的墳山也都建有大伯公廟或祠。如此看來，大伯公信仰是跨族群的一種崇拜現象，而大伯公是一種什麼信仰？到底拜的是什麼神呢？有學者認為大伯公信仰其實是混合了地祇和人鬼崇拜活動的產物，以人格化的稱呼來傳達對地祇和人鬼的尊敬，所以大伯公信仰不是單純只是土地神的崇拜。上面曾經提到有一個老乞丐在樹下歸化，所以客幫人士就在那裡建起望海大伯公廟，這則傳說正是人鬼崇拜的一種證明。

> 東南亞的大伯公崇拜，不是單純福德正神的土地公，而是晉位於神境的土地神或地頭神，具有著「祇」與「神」的雙重身分，同時也包含著「鬼」與「神」的雙重身分，比其他神明更能被東南亞華人所接納而普遍流傳，成為華人社區主要的崇祀神明。大伯公廟成為超越族群的信仰象徵，不再是客家人的專屬信仰，扮演著地區公廟的角色，是多種方言族群共同管理與奉祀的廟，如此的轉變也反映出東南亞華人族群的複雜性與交融性。[29]

　　既然大伯公信仰不是只限於客家人崇拜，那麼應和會館和豐永大公會選擇大伯公信仰來結合，只是因為偶然性嗎？在客家話裡，對他人的稱謂「伯公」有遠近的兩層涵義，近一點的是指家中輩分與自己

---

29 鄭志明，〈客家社會大伯公信仰在東南亞的發展〉，《華僑大學學報（哲學社會科學版）》1(2004): 68。

爺爺同輩，並且年紀比爺爺長的男性長輩，遠一點的則是指離自己輩分很遠的祖先總稱或是和自己沒有親屬關係的老年男性長輩尊稱。另外，指涉得更遠一點，伯公也可以當作是對地祇和人鬼的神明稱呼，例如有河壩伯公、榕樹伯公、橋頭伯公、石頭伯公、水圳伯公和開庄伯公等。研究者陳波生和利亮時曾經著文研究新馬兩地其中三座由客家人創建的大伯公廟[30]，他們也整理了研究東南亞大伯公信仰的文章，發現雖然沒有學者可以肯定「伯公」這個稱呼到底是哪個籍貫的人先使用，但是至少可以推斷廣東地區「伯公」稱呼的產生，可能是客家人和潮州人在此地區相互交流的產物。[31] 東南亞的「大伯公信仰」，普遍被認為與土地信仰「土地公」有著某種密切關係，追溯客家人在原鄉的居住環境和謀生方式就不難看出這種關係的形成。[32] 在閩粵一帶的客家人多居於丘陵或山區地帶，並且倚靠農耕維生，與土地的關係十分密切，因此對土地信仰的崇拜是非常崇敬，所以當客家人南來時，自然會把根深蒂固的信仰習慣也帶來。從「伯公」稱呼和客家人在原鄉的生活來理解大伯公信仰對新加坡客家人的重要性，也可以解釋為什麼他們會選擇大伯公信仰來凝聚認同。

五、廟宇策略之具體實踐

當閩幫和客幫分別確定自己的族群發展目標，廟宇變成一種達到目標的發展策略機構，賦予具體實踐發展策略的使命。實踐策略的過程是透過廟宇在社會服務、教育和信仰文化等方面來顯現。

---

30 此三間廟宇分別是新加坡望海大伯公廟、檳城海珠嶼大伯公廟和怡保大伯公廟。見陳波生、利亮時，〈客家人與大伯公的關係：以新馬為例〉，收錄於林緯毅主編，《民間文化與華人社會》，頁64-66。

31 陳波生、利亮時，〈客家人與大伯公的關係：以新馬為例〉，頁66。

32 近期有關東南亞等地區大伯公信仰的多篇研究論文，收錄於徐雨村主編，《族群遷移與宗教轉化：福德正神與大伯公的跨國研究》，新竹：國立清華大學人文社會學院，2012。

（一）天福宮

在社會服務方面，早期一些主要廟宇或會館被殖民地政府授權指定證婚處，華人結婚也多會到其所屬廟宇或會館舉行證婚儀式。西元1860年左右，陳金鐘接替其父陳篤生的天福宮的領導地位已經有一段時間。根據記載，當時閩人結婚會到天福宮去註冊登記，因為天福宮還是閩幫的最高領導機構，其結婚證書裡會蓋上陳金鐘的印章，作為證婚的證明。[33] 到了二戰後，福建會館已經成立許久，進入陳六使領導福建會館的時代，閩幫的華社事務辦事處從天福宮轉移到福建會館已久，天福宮長久以來建立跨族群幫群的影響力也轉移到福建會館，包括替閩人證婚的業務也移動到福建會館辦理。從西元1956年至1960年，福建會館一共主辦了17屆的集團結婚，這個集團結婚的特色就是新人來自各行各業，也來自不同的方言群。[34] 以西元1959年舉行的第12屆集團結婚來看，新人的籍貫有福建、潮州、客家、海南、廣東和廣西。[35] 天福宮曾經肩負起見證婚姻儀式的功能，有一部分是因為英人對華社是採取分而治之和間接統治的態度，幫群組織就必須擔負起更多的社會性功能，這也間接強化天福宮在閩人心目中的地位，天福宮在獲得閩幫認同後就往擴展閩幫勢力努力，獲得的成果轉移到後來的福建會館，福建會館的公信力也得到跨幫群的認同。

在興辦教育方面，天福宮也有許多貢獻。西元1852年，天福宮旁由閩幫領袖陳金聲設置了崇文閣，創立時就擁有跨方言群的支持，捐款人有客幫、潮幫以及義安公司的領袖。[36] 崇文閣被學者認為是新加坡第一間私塾性質的華校，或最早講習教化的華人文化場所。[37] 崇文

---

33 吳華，《新加坡華族會館志》，新加坡：南洋學會，1975，頁57-58。
34 新加坡福建會館，《波靖南溟：天福宮與福建會館》，新加坡：新加坡福建會館，2005，頁98。
35 新加坡福建會館，《波靖南溟：天福宮與福建會館》，頁98-101。
36 杜南發主編，《南海明珠：天福宮》，新加坡：新加坡福建會館，2010，頁31。
37 柯木林，〈崇文閣與萃英書院〉，收錄於林孝勝等人著，《石叻古蹟》，頁217。莊欽永則認為崇文閣的主要功能是奉行道教的敬惜字紙的信仰。但也不否認它是教化華人的場所。見莊氏，《新甲華人史史料考釋》，新加坡：青年書局，2007，頁201-212。

閣在天福宮之右側，顯示出早年華族廟宇和文教事業的密切關係。崇文閣的文教事業一直受到跨幫群的支持，在〈重建崇文閣碑記〉中被發現到潮幫領導人物余有進捐金二百元。余有進熱心於閩幫人士的教育事業，反映了藉由教育可以突破幫群的界線。[38] 天福宮藉由興學的方式成功吸收了其他幫群的幫助，顯示天福宮在當時華社有一定程度的號召力。

　　從十九世紀初期開始，閩幫除了運用天福宮開拓閩幫的勢力，也企圖讓天福宮成為一個跨幫群的宗教信仰中心，其實這兩者是相輔相成的。到了二十一世紀，我們可以從天福宮的出版物來看看，天福宮是如何看待自己在新加坡社會的定位。新加坡福建會館近年出版的天福宮歷史專輯，《南海明珠：天福宮》（2010年），從當屆福建會館會長寫的獻詞可以看出現在的天福宮被定位在保存民間信仰和傳承中華文化的古老廟宇。[39] 雖然這本書裡強調天福宮和福建會館的關係，但是寫作角度是針對整體華人社會讀者。天福宮在西元1973年被列為「新加坡國家歷史文化古蹟」，在西元2001年獲得「聯合國教科文組織亞太文化遺產建築優異獎」，再加上西元2009年媽祖信仰被認定為「聯合國人類非物質文化遺產」，此廟宇成為新加坡社會的重要文化遺產已經無庸置疑，事實上這座獅城名勝現在也變成外國遊客的旅遊景點之一。學者徐李穎認為從西元1840年到現代天福宮的功能性變遷是從注重政治－教育性到凸顯宗教－文化性。[40] 雖然現代新加坡由於推行講華語運動，方言幫群的觀念相對淡薄，嚴格說甚至已經不存在幫群社會，但是如果將這個變遷方向置於幫群發展的歷史脈絡下，這個變化趨勢也是使天福宮成為一個跨幫群的宗教信仰中心。

---

38 柯木林，〈崇文閣與萃英書院〉，頁218。
39 黃祖耀，〈獻詞〉，收錄於杜南發主編，《南海明珠：天福宮》，頁4。
40 徐李穎，〈在國家與社群之間：新加坡華人廟宇社會功能的轉換——以天福宮為例〉，收錄於林緯毅主編，《民間文化與華人社會》，頁34。

（二）望海大伯公廟

望海大伯公廟的一個重要作用是凝聚客幫的團結力量。由於望海大伯公廟的規模不大，並沒有像天福宮一樣，被授權舉辦證婚儀式，因此也無法藉此服務項目，擴大自己幫群對其他幫群的影響力。教育方面，客幫雖然也熱衷推動教育事業，但客幫興辦教育的方式是由各個客家機構自行成立私塾或學堂，如應和會館創辦應新學堂，茶陽會館創辦啟發學校，各自為政。客幫的團結是實踐在廟宇活動中，望海大伯公廟的活動主要是提供應和會館與豐永大公會交流的平台，共同管理此廟和一起進行祭拜儀式。

在出版物部分，新加坡茶陽（大埔）會館出版一本關於望海大伯公廟的歷史專書，《百年公德被南邦：望海大伯公廟紀事》（2006年），書中收錄許多建築調查報告，這些報告都是為了保留望海大伯公廟成為國家古蹟而執行的。除了建築報告外，還有一些廟宇歷史以及大伯公信仰與客家人有關的文章，重點是每一篇報告和文章都有英文摘要或翻譯，看來此書針對的讀者不只是客家人士和一般的華族民眾，還期待讓慣用英語的政府官員容易閱讀，無非是希望讓政府官員可以更了解此廟的歷史與文化的重要性，從而希望政府能改變其對該廟所作的徵收和搬遷令。望海大伯公廟一直都是為了團結客家人而存在，所以書中轉載兩篇學術文章，都是討論客家人與大伯公信仰的關係，藉由學術的深入討論來提醒現代的客家人不要忘記望海大伯公廟的歷史任務。[41]

六、結論

廟宇是早期華人移民社會生活中心，領導人多為幫群領袖，形成

---

41 此兩篇文章分別是鄭志明，〈客家社會大伯公信仰在東南亞的發展〉，原刊載於《華僑大學學報（哲學社會科學版）》1(2004): 64-74；陳波生、利亮時，〈客家人與大伯公的關係：以新馬為例〉，原收錄於林緯毅主編，《民間文化與華人社會》，頁59-68。

「神權」與「幫權」結合為一的幫群管理組織。閩幫領導人利用神權穩固內部幫權，再藉由神權和幫權的結合來統領整個華社，乍看之下像是兩個階段的目標，但是回顧天福宮的歷史可以發現其實是重疊並行的，只是第二個目標更為清楚外顯。另外一方面，客幫領導人以神權為基礎，凝聚幫權內部的向心力及認同，因為對於客幫來說，他們是華社中少數的少數，團結才是在幫群結構社會裡不被欺負的唯一辦法。早期閩客幫群的組織大小和財力，正是影響天福宮和望海大伯公廟功能性意義不同的原因，廟宇被當作一種策略來服務閩、客幫群的發展。這種策略的形成也與新加坡的時代背景息息相關，早期英國統治新加坡是以分而治之與間接管理的方式，就如研究者陳育崧所說：

> 在政府未將社會事業與公眾福利，納入政治範圍之前，所有民間一切公眾生活，多通過廟宇替大家安排、處理和執行。
> 廟宇是滿足人民的宗教生活，對神祇的崇拜，除了原有的機能外，它的副產物或副作用，往往超過主作用。[42]

天福宮和望海大伯公廟不但具有信仰神聖性，對於幫群發展來說，更是具備組織功能性，分別成為閩幫擴展勢力和客幫集結凝聚力策略的有效機構。

---

42 陳育崧，〈序〉，收錄於林孝勝等人著，《石叻古蹟》，頁i。

參考書目

一、專書

Cheng Lim Keak, 1985, *Social Change and the Chinese in Singapore: A Socio-Economic Geography: With Special Reference to Bang Structure.* Singapore: Singapore University Press.

Liu, Hong & Sin-Kiong Wong, 2004, *Singapore Chinese Society in Transition: Business, Politics & Socio-Economic Change, 1945-1965.* New York: Peter Lang Publishing, Inc.

何炳彪主編，2006，《百年公德被南邦：望海大伯公廟紀事》。新加坡：新加坡茶陽大埔會館。

吳華，1975，《新加坡華族會館志》。新加坡：南洋學會。

吳龍雲，2007，《遭遇幫群：檳城華人社會的跨幫組織研究》。新加坡：新加坡國立大學中文系、八方文化創作室，2009。

李天錫，2001，《華僑華人民間信仰研究》。北京：中國文聯出版社。

李亦園、郭振羽編，1985，《東南亞華人社會研究（上冊）》。台北：正中書局。

李恩涵，2003，《東南亞華人史》。台北：五南圖書出版有限公司。

杜南發主編，2010，《南海明珠：天福宮》。新加坡：新加坡福建會館。

林孝勝，1995，《新加坡華社與華商》。新加坡：新加坡亞洲研究學會。

林孝勝等著，1975，《石叨古蹟》。新加坡：南洋學會。

林美容，2008，《祭祀圈與地方社會》。台北縣：博揚文化。

林緯毅主編，2006，《民間文化與華人社會》。新加坡：新加坡亞洲研究學會。

柯木林、林孝勝著，1986，《新華歷史與人物研究》。新加坡：南洋學會。

徐雨村主編，2012，《族群遷移與宗教轉化：福德正神與大伯公的跨國研究》。新竹：國立清華大學人文社會學院。

莊欽永，2007，《新甲華人史史料考釋》。新加坡：青年書局。

陳育崧、陳荊編，1970，《新加坡華人碑銘集錄》。香港：香港中文大學。

陳衍德、卞鳳奎編，2007，《閩南海外移民與華僑華人》。福州：福建人民出版社。

崔貴強，1994，《新加坡華人——從開埠到建國》。新加坡：新加坡宗鄉會館聯合總會、教育出版有限公司。

麥留芳，1985，《方言群認同：早期星馬華人的分類法則》。台北：中研院民族學研究所。

黃賢強主編，2007，《新加坡客家》。桂林：廣西師範大學出版社。

新加坡中華總商會，1964，《新加坡中華總商會大廈落成紀念刊》。新加坡：新加坡中華總商會。

新加坡福建會館，2005，《波靖南溟：天福宮與福建會館》。新加坡：新加坡福建會館。

鄭麗航、蔣維錟主編，2004，《媽祖研究資料目錄索引》。福州：海風出版社。

二、專書文章

文崇一，1985，〈新加坡華人社會變遷〉，收錄於李亦園、郭振羽編，《東南亞華人社會研究（上冊）》。台北：正中書局。

甘永川，2007，〈新加坡客家人的經濟生活〉，收錄於黃賢強主編，《新加坡客家》。桂林：廣西師範大學出版社。

利亮時，2007，〈新加坡客家信仰習俗——以望海大伯公廟和客家墳山為例〉，收錄於黃賢強主編，《新加坡客家》。桂林：廣西師範大學出版社。

林孝勝，1975，〈十九世紀星華社會的幫權政治〉，收錄於林孝勝等著，《石叻古蹟》。新加坡：南洋學會。

林孝勝，1986，〈開埠初期的新華社會〉，收錄於柯木林、林孝勝著，《新華歷史與人物研究》。新加坡：南洋學會。

柯木林，1975，〈古色古香的天福宮〉，收錄於林孝勝等著，《石叻古

蹟》。新加坡：南洋學會。

柯木林，1975，〈崇文閣與萃英書院〉，收錄於林孝勝等著，《石叻古
蹟》。新加坡：南洋學會。

高華昌，2006，〈丹戎巴葛客屬八邑福德祠〉，收錄於何炳彪主編，《百年
公德被南邦：望海大伯公廟紀事》。新加坡：新加坡茶陽大埔會館。

陳波生、利亮時，2006，〈客家人與大伯公的關係：以新馬為例〉，收錄於
林緯毅主編，《民間文化與華人社會》。新加坡：新加坡亞洲研究學會。

蘇慶華，2004，〈從媽祖崇祀到媽祖文化研究──以馬、新兩國為例〉。收
錄於蘇慶華著，《馬新華人研究──蘇慶華論文選集》。吉隆坡：馬來西
亞創價學會。

三、期刊文章

鄭志明，2004，〈客家社會大伯公信仰在東南亞的發展〉，《華僑大學學報
（哲學社會科學版）》1: 64-74。

蕭新煌、張維安、范振乾、林開忠、李美賢、張翰璧，2005，〈東南亞的客
家會館：歷史與功能的探討〉，《亞太研究論壇》28: 185-219。

四、網路資料

"Census of Population 2010 Statistical Release 1: Demographic Characteristics,
Education, Language and Religion", http://www.singstat.gov.sg/pubn/popn/
c2010sr1.html，2010年10月9日瀏覽。

馬來西亞檳城海珠嶼大伯公的族群性格：
客家與福建人之間[*]

張維安[†]

摘要

本文以關於大伯公的相關文獻，田野觀察，知識份子的訪談為基礎，處理馬來西亞檳城海珠嶼大伯公廟的身分與族群問題。相傳，大伯公是東南亞華人普遍的信仰，但大伯公的意義相當多元，他可能是一個幫會的主神，可能是許多人的財神，也可能是土地神，福德正神。和台灣和中國潮州相比，雖然這兩地的人也稱土地公為伯公，但是稱為大伯公者相當少見，本文的討論：（1）將針對一般所謂大伯公的神性加以分析，以安煥然的論文為根據，說明東南亞大伯公作為土地神的論點；（2）其次是討論大伯公是怎樣的土地神，特別是這種土地神可能背後都有一個真正人為基礎，由陰神轉變為陽神可能是大伯公本身的一個重要屬性；（3）大伯公是誰的神：分析福建人與客家人對大伯公的爭奪，並解析客家領事對官司結果的影響；（4）海珠嶼大伯公作為客家神的論述，說明張理的故事與當地民間社會的神話傳說的意義，無論張理的故事所牽涉到的事物之真假，故事的完成對於大伯公的論述與神性之開展是重要的。

關鍵字：海珠嶼、建德堂、大伯公、大伯公會

＊本論文進行期間，得到吳龍雲、陳劍虹、陳耀威、李永球、黃賢強、陳波生、王琛發等多位先生以及檳城多家華人會館理事們的協助，謹此致謝。初稿曾發表在2007年台灣社會學年會及2012年台灣的東南亞區域研究年度研討會，本文在國科會計畫協助下補充新的訪談與書面資料修訂（99-2410-H-007-079-MY2）。
† 國立交通大學人文社會學系教授、國立中央大學客家社會文化研究所合聘教授。

一、前言

在我們的社會中宗教信仰是自由的，可以選擇信仰媽祖、觀音或信仰基督，一個宗教聚會裡往往有許多不同族群的人。不過，有時候宗教信仰也可能成為某些人群的識別，例如早期媽祖屬於海邊的人群，原住民則有自己的崇拜，又如，在台灣有一些人把三山國王的信仰，視為客家族群的信仰，有時候會說「哪裡有三山國王，哪裡就有客家人」，雖然不一定如此，但在某時某地也有一些可靠性。以三山國王信仰為例，在其發源地方三山國王並非客家的「族群神」。相同的，台灣的義民信仰也有相似的情形，接受過清政府頒授義民的族群，並非只有客家族群，[1] 後來有些族群有意無意的放棄了義民信仰，或者因不在意而忽略之。於是，台灣的義民信仰漸漸的和客家族群的信仰劃上了等號，雖然義民信仰也非客家的「族群神」。此外，在潮州附近的韓江流域山間，據說有座廟，當客家人主持的時候稱為寒婆廟，河洛人主持的時候稱為寒媽廟，廟的命名和族群語言發生了關聯。

有時宗教可以作為族群的識別，有時不同的族群對宗教的詮釋權會有爭議，更常見的是對於廟產的爭奪。本文要處理的對象，「馬來西亞檳城海珠嶼大伯公」，有當地福建人與客家人爭奪的歷史，如今他是客家人的大伯公，雖然開放各族群祭拜，廟內掛滿了客家五屬的燈籠，宣示著對大伯公廟的所有權，但是每年農曆正月十四晚上開始三天，仍然保留給福建公會的寶福社大伯公進行請火及相關的儀式。

「大伯公信仰」在東南亞的華人信仰中，具有重要的地位，是一個相當特殊的信仰，近年來以詩巫永安亭大伯公廟為中心的大伯公節，更是集結了東西馬與印尼的大伯公團體，進一步發揚了大伯公信

---

1 事實上那個時候，台灣的客家族群作為一個身分認同的對象，也還沒有真正的形成，當時被稱為來自「粵東」義民。

仰在東南亞華人社會中的特質（張維安、張翰璧，2012）。馬來西亞檳城當地的張少寬（2003: 155）指出「以華裔社會民間信仰的地方神，作為道路的命名，是檳城的其中一個特色。我們翻查本嶼的華譯街名，以『大伯公』命名的道路，竟有二條之多及一個村落。即大伯公街，本頭公巷，與丹絨道光的本頭公嶼漁村」。大伯公街，位於前殖民地政府設置於舊關仔角的行政廳附近。在1803年的地圖上已誌明其所在的地理位置。本頭公巷，則因該地前為閩幫祕密會社建德堂（一個供奉大伯公的會社）的創立而命名。本頭公嶼漁村，據知該村因建有「海珠嶼大伯公廟」而著名。廟內的「乾隆壬子」（1792年）古香爐，是檳城的古物之一。有人因此據以推測該廟在檳城開埠（1786年）六年後就已建立（張少寬，2003: 155）。這個「海珠嶼大伯公廟」，就是本文的分析對象。

關於大伯公街，「在二百年前已是集工商業經濟活動的地帶，為華人宗祠、廟宇、會館的聚集之地。這條街的建築物計有嘉應會館（1809年），增龍會館（約成立於1795年），臺山寧陽會館（1833年），伍氏家廟，武帝廟及福德祠等」（張少寬，2003: 157），當然最重要的還是，這條街有一座「福德祠」。從1865年的「大伯公街福德祠碑記」可知該廟年代久遠，張少寬（2003: 157）認為：「福德祠的成立時間，與海珠嶼大伯公廟相當接近」。這個福德祠與一般奉祀大伯公的祠宇有所不同，它分前廳及後廳二部分，前廳供奉大伯公，後廳則奉祀關公（張少寬，2003: 158）。這座福德祠與海珠嶼大伯公廟有密切的關係，安煥然（2003: 9-10）指出1810年，「客家人在檳城市中心的大伯公街建立了『福德祠』：它成為客家五屬人的活動中心。每年二月十五日，客家人都恭送這裡的福德正神駕往海珠嶼正廟，隔天便在那裡慶祝大伯公誕辰，[2] 到二月十七日上午再迎接福德尊神駕返市區的分祠」。張少寬（2003: 155-6）認為本頭公是大伯公

---

2 這裡的大伯公誕辰在二月十六日，與台灣的二月二日不同，值得再比對其意義。

的另稱，同是南洋華裔社會獨有的地方神。不過，值得進一步釐清的是本頭公與大伯公之稱呼可能有地區性與族群性的關聯性，雖然福建人也稱福德正神為大伯公，但以檳城的大伯公街與本頭公街來看，可能是不同地區的移民使用不同的看法。大伯公街可能與客家族群有比較密切的關係，本頭公街則可能與福建人或潮州人較有關聯。本文所分析的大伯公廟址所在地「海珠嶼」又名「本頭公嶼」，正好說明了不同族群對同一地點命名的差異。

關於東南亞大伯公的信仰，過去曾經有過系列的學術討論，特別是在《南洋學報》上面針對大伯公究竟是怎樣的神？廟中文物的詮釋、名稱的來源、碑刻的解讀，[3] 幾乎涵蓋了各層面的議題。吳詩興（2009）在〈馬來西亞的福德正神信仰探析——以砂拉越的大伯公廟為主要探討〉、安煥然（2003; 1991）在〈淺談新馬的大伯公信仰〉都曾對這些爭議做過系統的回顧。[4] 不過南洋學報所爭論的議題與本文所關心「宗教與族群」的問題，雖有許多重疊，但基本上並不相同。例如，大伯公何以稱「大」？伯公的稱謂和「族群」身分有沒有關係？以及大伯公是一般的土地公，還是有一個生前為人所認識的重要人物，死後被奉為大伯公？以下的討論將分成四部分，（1）大伯公是怎樣的神：以安煥然的論文為基礎，說明東南亞大伯公作為土地神的論點；（2）大伯公是怎樣的土地神：討論大伯公是一種特殊的土地神；（3）大伯公是誰的神：分析福建人與客家人對大伯公的爭奪；（4）結論：海珠嶼大伯公作為客家神的論述，討論張理的故事與地方社會神話傳說的意義。

---

3 有時候有碑刻文字，也不能據以做為證據，因為有些已經被移動過，因此需要更細緻的專家訪談與說明。

4 安煥然（2003），〈淺談新馬的大伯公信仰〉，《本土與中國：學術論文集》（南方學院學術叢書第五種）。馬來西亞：南方學院出版社。這篇論文登載於《道教學探索》第伍號，出版處是中華民國道教會台灣省台南市支會，成功大學歷史系道教研究室。推測安煥然可能還在成功大學攻讀歷史研究碩士學位。

二、大伯公是怎樣的神？

安煥然（2003: 2）在〈淺談新馬的大伯公信仰〉提到：「大伯公是東南亞，尤其是新馬華人社會中特有的神祇，流傳甚古，被普遍的奉祀。但其來歷如何，卻頗不清楚」。正因為來歷不清楚，所以大伯公信仰的意義因此有許多爭議，在40、50年代初期，南洋學人韓槐準準、酈國祥、衛聚賢以及許雲樵等都參加了討論，1991年安煥然自己也加入了這個問題的討論。

大伯公究竟是什麼神？陳達主張「大伯公與土地神祭祀的起源有關，認為大伯公其實就是當年夏禹命令去開闢土地，使民有居的『伯益』」（安煥然，2003: 2-3）。「許雲樵認為，大伯公就是中國的土地公」（安煥然，2003: 5），「廣東客家人稱土地公為『伯公』，『大』字只是尊稱。故大伯公就是中國的土地公」（安煥然，2003: 6）。另外，韓槐準認為「大伯公即由水神演變而來」，並「認為大伯公名稱之由來，或因前人視舶主督綱，或都公，或孥公，或托公，其性質實質等於番土地神。因土地神之廟多名為福德祠之故，後因大伯公已蛻變為土地神，故星嘉坡 [按：即新加坡] 凡有華人公共墳塋之場所，必設一大伯公廟，可謂一變而再變」（安煥然，2003: 3-4）。基本上，他們同意一個基調，就是大伯公也是福德正神，我們所見檳城大伯公街的大伯公廟稱為「福德祠」，大伯公廟裡面被香火燻得黝黑的匾，所寫的是「福德正神」，大伯公與福德正神的關係應有一定程度的關連。不過進一步來看土地公與大伯公的關係，我們將發現土地公的崇拜，是因地因時因人而異的。有些地方土地廟稱為福德祠，土地神稱為土地公；有些地方福德正神稱為伯公，特別是在客家及潮州地區，同樣的對象，不同人群給予不同的稱呼。[5]

關於大伯公的來源，「許雲樵認為大伯公最初應是由客家的土地

---

5 福建惠安亦有稱趙玄壇為大伯公，而大伯公並不是指某一人。

神演變而來的，此乃由於客家人最先在礦區奉祀土地神，稱為伯公，後來和馬來語Dato一詞連稱，而作Topekong，才變成大伯公。而後才又逐漸演變成又像姜太公，又似趙玄壇，才和中國的土地公有些不同」（安煥然，2003: 6）。安煥然認為「雖然，對大伯公的來歷，眾說紛紜，然而大伯公卻是新馬一帶相當普遍崇拜的神祇」。就整個馬來西亞來說，「大伯公並非專指一人，大伯公的人選往往因地而異。在檳城私會黨，大伯公是被奉為開山祖師的張理。韓槐準說大伯公是舶主督綱，而在婆羅洲的坤甸，大伯公被認為是羅芳伯。……而在印尼椰加達的大伯公廟，卻還有個大伯婆伴隨。該廟的大伯公據說是鄭和下西洋的一個士兵，死後顯靈為神。大伯婆則是該士兵流落在爪哇時所討的番婦。新加坡的龜嶼的大伯公廟，供奉的也是一對老夫婦」（安煥然，2003: 6）。

如同許雲樵所說，「大伯公是祈求平安和發財的神祇們的混合象徵。因此他所具備的神能性質，似乎又比一般的土地公多，而且也已經本土化了。大伯公托廊（Topekong Tolong）成了信仰大伯公的新馬華人的口頭禪。Tolong其實是馬來話『保佑』的意思。因此呼 "Topekong Tolong" 可發財，可愈病，可風平浪靜，可轉危為安」（安煥然，2003: 7-8）。從這些資料可以理解，並非各處的大伯公都是同源的，背後所指稱的對象也不一定相同，大伯公可能是早期華人先驅者精神的象徵之崇拜，[6] 有些則是移民社會將原鄉信仰在地化的展現。

---

6 關於大伯公並非專指某一人的主張，安煥然進一步指出「凡居多猛虎之逼的，乃呼猛虎為伯公，凡居多鱷魚之處，乃呼鱷魚為伯公，而且甚至有把身有五點黑色標記的竹莢魚（Chor inemus，馬來話為Ikan Talang）亦俗呼為伯公，不敢當膳之禁忌。而其他各地所拜的大伯公，也大都不知道是誰，故大伯公籠統的認為，應是早期華人先驅者精神的象徵之崇拜。如茲說，或許較為貼切，是新馬或東南亞一帶華人所特有的神祇之一，但並不像崇拜三寶公鄭和一樣，專指某一人」（安煥然，2003: 7）。安煥然也不同意其他地區的伯公與珠海嶼大伯公分享張理的故事與祕密會社的背景。

三、大伯公是怎樣的土地神？

　　關於大伯公的身分，據說「最早提出此一問題的是1879年，英國官員J. D. Vanghan在其書中說大伯公廟是祠天地會之魁傑，逋逃南洋者張理。關楚公在《星洲日報》半月刊二期〈談談大伯公〉一文，引用了J. D. Vanghan的話，並論斷大伯公可能原是洪門會黨內的一種最高職位，而拜大伯公」（安煥然，2003: 2）。[7] 陳達在《南洋華僑與閩粵社會》一書似引用了上說，並根據檳城海珠嶼大伯公廟的碑文一節及某華僑的口述，認為大伯公是嘉應五屬人所特別崇拜的神祇。其來源乃是咸豐年間，有一年疫癘流行病盛行死了很多人，唯獨嘉應五屬出身的馬某（燒炭工人）、張某（塾師）、丘某（鐵匠）不死，而被尊稱為「開山大伯」，後人追其功德而立廟奉祀（安煥然，2003: 2-3）。鄺國祥也指出大伯公的三位主角乃是客籍人士，[8] 他認為「大伯公是由潮東的土地神演變而來，而海珠嶼大伯公廟其神即客籍人，而且斷定張理是『開山地主』，最先被祀為神者的（安煥然，2003: 3）。這個敘事架構後來成為了解珠海嶼大伯公的重要方式。

　　雖然前述有許多學者把大伯公和土地神的信仰，特別是在中國本地稱土地為伯公的信仰都拉在一起，但是這裡的大伯公還是擁有許多特殊之處，「與中國或台灣的土地公所不同的是，在中國的土地公是不能進入家宅，有壇無屋。但是新馬所奉的大伯公（或土地公）卻是進入民屋，供奉在家裡，且安放在香案底下，猶如宅神，這種情形極為普遍」（安煥然，2003: 8）。在中國本地，土地神也不會供奉在桌面上，特別是不會供奉在家裡。在台灣，口頭上客家人稱土地公為伯公，但是在台灣「伯公」的稱呼只是口頭語，名稱多半還是寫成福德正神，土地公廟稱為福德祠，即使在客家莊，也相當少看到一個土

7　安文原注：韓槐準，〈大伯公考〉，《南洋學報》一卷二輯，民國29年12月，頁20。

8　鄺國祥撰，〈檳榔的海珠嶼大伯公廟重修碑記〉，認為該廟建於嘉慶四年（1799）（安煥然，2003: 3）。

地公廟被刻上伯公廟，「大伯公」這樣的名稱更是少見。故事既然是從來自中國的客籍人士張理開始，紀念張理三人的廟何以稱為大伯公廟呢？伯公之稱與客家人（或潮汕地區人士）稱土地公為伯公是否相關？檳城海珠嶼「大伯公廟」內，仍寫著「福德正神祠」，表面上這裡的大伯公就是福德正神。不過當地人似乎並不是把這個大伯公當作像台灣的土地神，大伯公廟除了大伯公之外另有土地神。大伯公究竟是什麼神？針對這些說法，安煥然的看法是，這幾則關於大伯公的起源之說，似乎不能解答整個新馬地區華人信仰大伯公的普遍現象。安煥然認為（2003: 3）鄺國祥的說法只是傳說，缺乏有力證據支持，而以張理說為大伯公者，似乎僅適用於檳城海珠嶼大伯公廟這個特例，且參雜祕密幫會私會黨的神祕附會色彩，在新馬其他地區的大伯公廟除了分香於此廟的怡保霸羅古廟[9] 和馬六甲三多廟的「海珠嶼大伯公」[10] 之外並無此說，故其他大伯公廟的大伯公並不一定是指張理。

大伯公會是檳城當地的祕密會社，大伯公是大伯公會的主神，「1844年漳泉人在檳城創立『建德堂』，是以膜拜大伯公為紐帶的一個從事械鬥的祕密會社，而被一般人稱為『大伯公會』。會內設有爐主，負責埋葬及祭祀無親無故的黨員。當時漳泉豪族藉著『大伯公』的威靈號令福建人，以便和以關帝爺為守護神的廣東人的義興公司對抗」（安煥然，2003: 10）。「建德堂在1890年英殖民政府取締之後，組織了『寶福社』來照顧建德堂所奉祀的『大伯公』，每年農曆正月十五日（按：十四晚），亦送大伯公去海珠嶼大伯公廟請香火，當時常常是萬人空巷，盛況非凡」（安煥然，2003: 10-11）。由此可知，海珠嶼大伯公和福建人有關，同時也和祕密會社有關，這樣的大

---

9 1872年前由嘉應州僑領梁輝從檳榔嶼（檳城）的大伯公原廟請來的香火。

10 網路上曾有〈大伯公顯靈傳乩諭〉一文指出，這座從馬六甲鳥貝島迎回並安奉於三多廟的海珠嶼大伯公之墓石碑安放在大殿神桌旁，但石碑前有一片屏風阻擋，造成石碑處於「面壁」角度，不容易被外來善信察覺。後來，馬來西亞沙巴及砂拉越福德祠之西馬古廟訪問團於2012年2月13日參觀甲州古剎三多廟時，座主大伯公突然借成員之身「顯靈」傳乩諭，希望三多廟屏風後的大伯公石碑能「重見天日」。

伯公也是在中國或台灣所沒有發現過的現象。事實上，除了檳城的這個大伯公和族群、幫會有關以外，「在吉隆坡，以惠陽人葉亞來（1837-1885）為首的海山公司，亦稱為大伯公會，其成員多為惠州人（有部分閩南人），大本營在吉隆坡。與當時義興公司進行械鬥，相互爭奪錫礦場權」（安煥然，2003: 11）。建德堂以福建人為主，海山公司的葉亞來則是客家人，事實上在當時「大伯公亦不只是惠州客家人的信仰神祇。閩南漳泉，甚至說廣府話的廣州人亦同祭之，也是一個超方言群的信仰神祇」（安煥然，2003: 11）。可見大伯公信仰可以超越族群的範圍，並非客家族群所專有。

天官賜在〈對於韓槐準、許雲樵兩氏意見之批判——大伯公是何方神聖？〉[11] 所說的大伯公是南洋華人社會中所塑造出來的偶像崇拜，可分為狹、廣義。狹義即福德正神（土地公）；廣義則是包括了象徵地方性的高級私會黨的「大哥」，死後奉祀為地方神者；家族上遠古的祖先神，宗族上的始祖，各會館各墳山創辦人等等，總之，可以Victor Purcell所說的，大伯公即是「早期華人先驅者精神的象徵」（安煥然，2003: 12）。

在我們觀察的大伯公廟，似乎過去曾是真有其人，王琛發（2006: 1-52）在《馬來西亞客家人的宗教信仰實踐》一書中，把馬來西亞客家人的宗教信仰分成幾類，一是「從原鄉移植到本地的鄉土信仰」，例如三山國王、譚公廟、何仙姑等等，王琛發共列出15種之多，但是比較特別的是另外一類，「馬來西亞客家人的本土神明」，王琛發共列出了：張、丘、馬大伯公、東馬的劉善邦、鍾萬仙師、中馬仙四師爺、打金業的胡靖祖師爺、拿督公與唐番地主（吳德芳，2006: 76）。其中，關於客屬人在本土神化開拓的人物，他們稱這種信仰為「人鬼」信仰。這也是華人世界中關於人神演變關係的一種普遍的模式。這和張少寬（2003: 159）的說法相近：「伯公為檳海開山之初

---

11 安文原註：《南洋文摘》合訂第4卷第1期，頁25-28。

祖，生以為英，沒以為神。因此，一般以為他是張理，即海珠嶼大伯公廟的開山鼻祖」。

新加坡應和會館的陳波生有這樣的觀察：大伯公是來南洋開拓的華人先人，他們死了以後被封為神。也就是一個對社會人群有貢獻的人，死了以後被封為神，從人變成神，是一種轉變。大唐總長羅芳伯去世以後便被尊稱為大伯公（「伯」字可能是其名字也可能只是一種尊稱），這個大伯公背後有一位具體的人物。新加坡海唇大伯公就是有一個具體的人，而且還知道是一位陳姓長者：新加坡海唇的「福德祠的建立，有一段神話，據前輩流傳下來：在清嘉慶年間，約為新加坡開埠後之第三年即1822年，有一位陳姓長者的屍體，為洶湧波濤沖到直落亞逸海唇。居民即將之撈起安葬；後來往祭者日眾。廣客兩幫人士，於道光甲申年（1824），在該地建福德祠，供奉大伯公」（茶陽會館，1999）。

這幾個大伯公看起來並不是無名的土地神，他是一個開山地主，特別是在移民社會初期的知名人士。在台灣，伯公、土地、福德是一樣的，雖然也有傳說某某伯公（土地公）是某人死後被派去當土地公，這和東南亞的大伯公還是有些不同。在中國我們看到人們相信，死者身後被封為土地，也有人死後被封為城隍。他們在諸神中的地位不同於昔日所見的土地神，新加坡海唇大伯公廟像是一座小型的四合院，大伯公這個主神在中間，觀音菩薩和關公分列於兩旁成為陪祀神。「新加坡恆山亭是福建人進行喪葬祭奠的祠廟。廟裡供奉的主神是福德正神（俗稱大伯公），其左側是城隍爺公，右側是注生娘娘」（安煥然，2003: 10）。這幾座大伯公廟中大伯公在眾神的排行中，和台灣、潮汕的伯公地位有了根本的差異。

大伯公的性質多樣，來源眾說紛紜，功能也很多元，不僅有土地公的性質，而且還是祈求平安、求財等各神祇的混合象徵。在田野現場，我們看到大伯公作為財神的功能，大伯公信仰與當地樂透彩的開獎活動有密切的關係。陳劍虹（R2007）說：「在檳城華人的財神，

除了文武財神之外還加上一個大伯公」。大伯公身後化成大家的守護神，是一個土地神也是財神。

王琛發指出：「早期大伯公的神像是從潮州進口為多。有一個特點，就是拿著黃金，而檳城的開拓者也是來這裡找黃金，開拓神也是，神就是我的大伯公」。這種情形與大伯公先作為陰神的存在可能有關係，一般說來陽神沒有求明牌的。王琛發指出：「檳城的海珠嶼大伯公，就是這類由陰轉陽的神，人們認為張理帶領著大家來開拓，對大家有功，華人以他的形象來和英國人爭論開拓主權，華人以大伯公來證明比英國人來得更早，而且他們來到檳城的時候，當時還沒有發達，他作為開拓者，協助地方的發展」。據了解繼承建德堂（大伯公會）的寶福社在請火的儀式中有一段是挨家挨戶的跟伯公請安、拜香的儀式，王琛發（R2007）的解釋是，這個儀式等於是向所有先烈請安，先烈的總領導人就是大伯公，等於是一個陰神與土地神的神像附和成一體，同時又變成開拓主權的象徵。因為他是帶大家來開拓，來賺錢的，所以死後就一直保護大家來賺錢，變成大家心目中的財神。這樣大伯公已經脫離中國的土地神的神像，也脫離了陰神的形象。

大伯公做為財神的現象，除了可以從樂透彩觀察到之外，寶福社正月十四晚上的請火儀式內容，則是另外一個相關的觀察對象：陳耀威（2008）指出：「海珠嶼的請火儀式是由市區本頭公巷的寶福社遊行請神到此廟。晚上待子時海水漲潮過一礁石，理事們就拉上鐵門謝絕信徒們進入，跟著全場熄滅燈火，用五令旗掩護香擔，在鐘鼓齊鳴下力煽擔爐發出火焰，每年，理事就以三次的火焰的高低強度，做出對新的一年上、中、下三季的經濟盛衰預測」。以2008年為例，我們在報紙上可以看到其所預測的一整年經濟情勢，1至4月是下，5至8月是平，9至12月也是平。

「原本請火也許是『再充電』的動作，不知何故竟變成經濟預測單位。據知，自1946年第二次世界大戰後重新舉行以來就如此，檳城

商家頭家尤重視年度請火的『火勢』對市場好壞的影響。一位老社員說，早年用他來預測橡膠和錫米等原產品股市的起落。看來，後來在林蒼佑當首長時代，他對大伯公請火的關心變成火焰代表檳城的經濟運程。漸漸的，這請火的『威力』又擴大了，從檳城涵蓋到北馬，近年已被『說造』成是代表馬來西亞（尤其是檳城）的經濟了」（陳耀威，2008）。

　　王琛發（R2007）也說：「對大伯公會來說，這個大伯公是他們的主神，每年還是要來這裡預測檳城的經濟，檳城經濟怎麼會由福建人來預測呢？但是偏偏大家都接受了」。「借點香著火的火勢強弱預測檳城一年的經濟走勢。這也成為檳城華社共同關心的習俗」（王琛發，2006: 31）。[12] 檳城海珠嶼大伯公是藉著原鄉許多不同的神格，[13]來形成的一個新的神格。土地神，先民崇拜，開拓主權的象徵，同時也是財神，這可以說是移民社會才有的，在故鄉並沒有。

四、檳城海珠嶼大伯公是誰的神？

　　福建私會黨認為大伯公是他們的主神，但對客家而言大伯公是客家的祖先，是開闢檳城對社區有貢獻的先賢。尤其是大伯公也是財神爺，大伯公廟的主權，牽涉到幫會利益的爭奪，關於神廟主權的爭奪，也牽涉到社會上具體的權力的較勁，也就是說，神權的後面也牽涉到具體的「社會秩序」（張翰璧、張維安，2011）。大伯公廟主權的官司，起於不同族群的祕密會社，官司的進行也牽涉到檳城華人官員的介入。

　　關於大伯公信仰與族群的關係，在訪談中可以清楚知道，大伯公

---

12 檳城有兩處著名的廟宇舉行常年的「請火」儀式，一是在東北岸的丹絨道光海珠嶼大伯公廟，一是西南區的萬腳蘭蛇廟裡（陳耀威，2008）。前者比較為人所知，後者是擁有160多年歷史的峇六拜萬腳蘭蛇廟（http://www.sinchew-i.com/node/72134?tid=267，2013.1.17。

13 有些地方的大伯公並不是張理，張理的名字可換成其他的先民，其他的開拓者。

信仰並不限於客家人。幾乎所有華人都拜大伯公，馬來當地的土著、外來人都會來祭拜大伯公。更特殊的是前面提過的「建德堂」祕密會社他們也拜大伯公，事實上建德堂的英文名字就叫Topekong，他們的敵對黨是義興公司，拜關公。陳劍虹（R2007）指出：文獻上最早提到義興是指「義興館」，不像中國的同鄉組織，已經是公司的名字，公司這個名詞，其含意很廣，與我們一般所了解的意義很不相同，需要做慎重的考察，可以是行會，可以是作為經濟單位的商辦組織，可以是一個宗鄉組織，也可以是一個祕密會社。[14] 大伯公會，即是建德堂，因為其信仰以大伯公為主，所以殖民地官員便稱之為大伯公會，這個「會」字應該是「會社」的組織。在英文他們並沒有把「會」字用音譯的方式講出來，例如用society來翻譯「會」這個字。事實上檔案上的文字，除了廣東省籍的祕密會社以外，我們看到福建人有兩大幫派，其中一個稱為大伯公會，這是殖民地官員對他們的稱呼，另一個稱為義興公司，或義興館，而不稱為會。事實上，那時候公司也好，館也好，會也好，就是祕密會社。

　　兩個祕密會社究竟和海珠嶼大伯公的爭奪有何關係？陳耀威（R2007）提到：建德堂在1890年已經解散（法令通過解散時間為1889年），後來有一個社團叫做寶福社，他們自稱是承繼了建德堂，傳承了建德堂的組織。根據我們的田野觀察，寶福社的使用海珠嶼大伯公廟的方式是，正月初十四將金身送入海珠嶼大伯公，初十五晨請火，清晨往市區送香火給會員，初十六在寶福社犒軍（十六實際上沒在海珠嶼伯公廟進行活動），初十七送回五德宮的大伯公金身。初十五（事實上是初十四晚）子時以後福建人就關在裡面，其儀式也相當神祕，不是寶福社的成員不能參加，而且他們會用黑令旗蓋起來，[15]

---

14 南洋華人社會中有許多著名的「公司」，海山公司、義興公司之外，婆羅洲的「大港公司」、「蘭芳公司」都是歷史上有名的「公司」，蘭芳公司部分可參考張維安、張容嘉（2009）。

15 黑令旗是道教的旗幟，不屬於哪一個族群，在台灣的黑令旗，是由義民起義所使用的旗幟，太平天國也是用黑令旗，和法國人打仗的劉永福部隊，也稱為黑旗軍。

有一些祕密會社的性質，他們認為是傳承了建德堂，因為這個請火本來就是建德堂的一個儀式。[16] 陳劍虹（R2007）則補充：「檔案上，並沒有請火的字眼，如果根據十九世紀40年代最早的一份關於海珠嶼大伯公的檔，這方面的官方說明文書，並沒有提到請火」。這個福建人的祕密會社到客屬的大伯公廟來請火儀式的現象，應該是兩個族群對大伯公廟之爭奪結果的一項協定。根據陳劍虹（R2007）的了解，客家人拜海珠嶼大伯公，可能是在辛亥革命前後，客家人的「嘉德社」來朝拜大伯公，[17] 客家人對海珠嶼大伯公廟主權的主張，應該在十九、二十世紀之交。這個 [與主權有關的] 官司應該是在這個時候打的。惠州客家在檳城的政治影響，具有非常重要的意義。在十九、二十世紀之交，當時客籍的楊輝（楊廷芳）擔任滿清駐檳城的第四任副領事，相關的官司資料在發文抄稿應該可以找到證據。[18] 另外，從大伯公廟所持有的地契也可以知道這件事情發生於何時，但是大伯公廟的管理者不肯出示。這兩個可能的資料目前都還沒有證實，當地知識份子陳劍虹推測應是在1900年前後，所謂族群對大伯公廟的爭奪，已經開始。

　　因此，在1900年前後，兩個族群對海珠嶼大伯公的爭奪之前，那個時候還是閩粵兩省人士共同擁有的公廟，主權問題可能還沒有發生。這項推測在所留下的物件上可以看到有關福建人的記載。

　　客家人與福建人爭奪海珠嶼大伯公廟的導火線為何？似乎無法得

---

16 為何在這時來請火？傳說當時建德是在正月十四的時候，獲知義興與首領將出現，在他出現的時候他們把他「幹掉了」，請火的意義是表示他們勝利。陳耀威表示不太贊成這個說法，但目前還是有人這樣講。

17 「嘉德社」是嘉應會館專門祭拜大伯公的組織。各會館都有以祭拜大伯公為宗旨的組織，例如大安社（大埔會館）、永安社（永定會館）、惠福社（惠州會館）與增龍社（增龍會館）（利亮時、張維安、張翰璧，2011）。

18 關於這方面的歷史資料，如發文抄稿，可能在台灣的國史館可以找到。發文抄稿是當時領事館每個月向清廷提出的報告，事事無大小都會報告（進出口、人口調查、民生、經濟都有），關於這件事，可能會有相關的報告（駐檳榔嶼副領事相關的資料，商務月報、學部月報都是實印本，這份資料可能是手抄的），檳榔嶼這邊保留的是手稿，一份保留，一份寄到中國去，可以從這裡去了解這場官司究竟怎麼打的，情況如何，甚至究竟發生於何時？

知，目前沒有可靠的資料可以證實爭奪大伯公廟的導火線。但是陳劍虹（R2007）指出從一些作品的論述，如傳記等所發現的蛛絲馬跡，可以推測有這樣的一場爭奪。傳說這場爭奪曾經告到英國樞密院去，官司的判決、協調結果，才演變成主權屬於客家族群，但正月十四日晚（元宵節前夕）保留給福建人可以使用，讓福建人請火。也就說，這樣的現象可能也是官司的判決或協議，客家人最後取得主權，福建人仍保留請火的「權利」。在這場產權爭奪過程中，當時中國駐檳城的領事館可能扮演重要的角色。陳劍虹（R2007）的推測是那個時候還是楊廷芳擔任副領事一職。誰擁有政治資源，誰便能有所影響力，這是一條重要的線索，反之，如果是福建人擔任領事的話，結果可能不同。

陳劍虹（R2007）認為在這官司之前，海珠嶼大伯公本來是福建人和廣東人共有的公廟。直到今天，還可以找到海珠嶼大伯公廟該地本屬於福建人的「證據」，例如周邊的居民都是福建人以及若干歷史遺跡乃為閩人所有。雖然陳劍虹也提到，觀察今天居民的族群身分來回答歷史上的問題也不一定可靠，需要細心對待這些證據。林西祥（音）的捐獻則提供了另外一個說明，林是一位擁有大片土地的閩籍富商的太太，她捐出一筆錢來修整當地的自來水供應等，從這裡可以推測這座公廟原來並非客家人所獨有。因為如果是純粹客家的信仰廟宇，似乎可能不會有一個福建人來捐贈這筆經費做公益。建築師陳耀威則指出該廟「前後有五次修復紀錄，最後一次修復，在宣統元年修建，大伯公廟，是閩南式建築，並不是客家人的建築，屋面、頂脊、曲度等因素，受當地的影響，採取當地的建築。前面的獅子是廣東獅，很難確定是客家的。1878年還是公廟。廟裡沒有大伯公的神像」。另外，在海珠嶼大伯公廟大門入口的右邊，目前還有一間平時可以使用的「寶福社涼亭」，請火時除了寶福社大伯公金身外，還邀請附近五德宮（金門人為主的廟宇）的大伯公金身參與。再舉前述提過的地名為例，海珠嶼又名「本頭公嶼」，是否也意味著福建人參與

其中的歷史痕跡？

陳劍虹（R2007）另外引述一位看過地契的鄺國祥的說法，一開始的時候這個海珠嶼大伯公本來就不是客家人的。具體的解讀捐款人的英文名字，可以發現裡面廣東的勢力非常的大，但是不能證明海珠嶼大伯公是「客家人的」。現在，可以清楚看得出來，客家五屬已經擁有這座海珠嶼大伯公，陳劍虹（R2007）認為是客家族群對政治資源的掌握影響到主權的判決。雖然官司把主權判給了客家，但還是不得不對福建人的需求做出一定的安排，這個安排，是誰做的？是真的到了樞密院後的協調判決？並未有證據可考，但咸信當時的客籍副領事（第四任）楊廷芳發揮了作用。

目前海珠嶼大伯公這邊，幾乎看不到關於客家五屬以外的其他的證物，例如碑文或一些其他的遺跡，也就是說，從當地現有的物證來看，都是和客家人有關的物證。據說是當海珠嶼大伯公的產權被判給客家人之後，一些不利於說明本廟為客屬的碑文遂被移走。接受訪問的陳劍虹認為客家人把這些石碑給移走了，這些碑刻在市區大伯公街上的「福德祠」內還可以找得到。

這場官司的輸贏，和張理的傳說之進一步完整性有一些關係。張、丘、馬三個人事實上也都難證明為客家人。雖然2012年檳城鄭永美找到永定馬福春的家族的後代馬先富，甚至從族譜說明台灣馬英九總統是其遠親，間接的說明馬英九的客家身分，但是廣東大埔的丘兆進與張理都還沒有得到客籍身分的證實。當時可能就是以這幾塊碑做為證據，加上張弼士的協助，傳言張弼士是慈禧太后前面的紅頂商人，據說鄺國祥說過「張弼士曾經去向光緒皇帝請封他的伯父做為大伯公」。果真如此，這個大伯公在從陰神轉為陽神的過程中，是根據了中國傳統的方式，由皇帝加封的，雖然這個奏摺並沒有人看過。但是張弼士在檳城做了不少這些事，例如檳城的廟宇極樂寺等，英國人不讓他發公民權給馬來西亞華人，他就利用這些廟宇、學校、大伯公來做。因此，楊廷芳等合作打贏這場官司，和張弼士等客家籍人士長

期擔任檳城的領事有所關連。

關於張理的身分，特別是其族群背景，學者有一些爭議，張理是不是客家，事實上並無事證，[19]「1851年任檳城員警總監的Vaughan記載，地方上曾傳說張理是永定人，而另有來自嘉應人的說法則傳說大伯公叫『李妹記』」（王琛發，2006: 28; 2010）。陳劍虹（R2007）則說，目前墓碑只能看到張公兩字並無「張理」之名，因此張「理」之名是根據何處，也不得而知。張理的理根據何在？張理是永定人？還是大埔人？這些問題在海珠嶼大伯公廟1958年立的重修碑記定了論，碑記上建構了張理的身世歷史，撰重修碑記的鄺國祥因為是張弼士的人，他的記載在潮州人的觀點中有許多意見，張弼士、鄺國祥、楊廷芳連在一起，張理這位張公開始有了名字，從被懷疑的永定人，確定成為與張弼士相同的大埔客，甚至成為張弼士的伯父，其中有許多被質疑的地方，這也是陳劍虹所說即使有碑刻也不能直接作為可信的資料。陳劍虹進一步說「最先到檳城的客家人是從西婆羅州來的人，張理，如果他是客家人的話，可能是這群客家人當中的一位。姓丘的那一位，可以從丘氏族譜裡面看得出來，他是第一個來這裡的姓丘的人士，有人推論他比張理還先到檳城。張理的故事，相當程度應該被視為是為了加強客家人所需要的一些論述」。

五、結論

整個東南亞來說，羅芳伯是一個大伯公，主要是聞名於西婆羅洲（印尼西加里曼丹），在檳城，有人認為張理是第一個大伯公。各地大伯公各有自己的源頭，自己的背景和故事，有從海珠嶼分香出去的，就像台灣的義民廟有從新埔枋寮分香出去一樣，但是有更多的是平凡的土地神，光是在馬來西亞的砂拉越就目前所知就有接近70座的

---

[19] 如果傳說可靠，應該考證張弼士的族譜是否有關於張理的記載。

大伯公廟。因此，東南亞的大伯公信仰不能等同對待，張維安、張翰璧（2012）認為與華人社會網絡的重建有密切的關係。

有些大伯公有真人真事的背景與歷史故事，特別是對早期移民社會來說，一位對移民社會有貢獻的人，去世之後被奉祀為大伯公，這便和一般我們所說的土地神，一個人生前行事公正，常會主持正義，照顧社區，去世以後，從「鬼」升格為「神」的情形相似，「福而有德千家敬，正則為神萬世尊」所講的可能就是這個現象。海珠嶼張理的故事，有名、有姓、有廟、有紀念碑、有墓碑，看起來歷史真相十足，能將整體故事講得感人，故事的完整性對信徒便有一定的影響力。

一個社會的信仰，可以從兩方面來討論他的意義，一是從歷史證據的考證比對，來看社會上所流傳的這些說法是否「真實」，這可以從許多地方來看，甚至要從國史館的檔案中來挖掘資料以證明其真假。但是，在民間信仰的這一層，不能說實證這一層不重要，但是故事本身也能塑造許多「真實」，通過合於邏輯的故事情節，假以一些實際的證物，甚至是因為某些人群在特別時空之下的需要，建構的（或虛構的）故事也能發揮一定程度的效用。張理是不是客家，到目前並無事證，甚至張理的「理」是根據何處，也不得而知，但鄺國祥加以闡釋分析，並說張弼士提出張公是為其伯祖，並向清朝皇帝請封為大伯公，從這裡可知，大伯公相當程度是一種人格神的性質。從張理的請封傳說，可知在檳城海珠嶼大伯公的神話建構中，有個重要的人士張弼士曾經扮演一個角色，特別是張弼士、楊廷芳與鄺國祥合作所創作的各種正當性的事證。王琛發（2009）提供了這個說法的佐證：「這個廟本來是廣商的廟，但是1900年代以後客家人把它拿過來了。他們有一個很特別的做法，這種做法是神道設教，就是把大伯公講成是張弼士的伯父，伯父是你們的保護神，他是整個華人開拓當地的先驅，我是你們的領事」。「領導華社的南洋首富兼清廷總領事張弼士證諸於族譜，指張理為他本人的嗣伯公，便進一步加強了張弼士

領導華社的聲望與神話淵源」（王琛發，2006: 28）。「大伯公開闢檳城的神話已隨1909年大伯公街大伯公廟重修時，出現一系列講述他在海外開天闢地的對聯，進一步鞏固了神話化的開拓英雄。客人的光榮地位就在於張理三結義兄弟『亟為殖民謀福利』」（王琛發，2006: 28），鄺國祥撰寫1958年立的重修碑記更加清楚，加上陳劍虹（R2007）所推測的楊廷芳對官司結果的影響，從這裡可以了解大伯公與客家人之間的關係。

　　在解答大伯公的身分之謎以及歸屬問題上，故事的敘說扮演著關鍵的地位，故事中的三個人，正是一個開墾之初非常需要的三種頭班，王琛發（2006: 28）說，「雖然也有人懷疑過開埠之初，何來教書先生？何來鐵匠及炭工？但從神話學的觀點來看，客家夫子教書傳播文化，客家鐵匠製造生產工具，客家炭工提供家家戶戶的爐具能源，正是藉傳說去強調這是一個完整地區，以及強調其主權屬於客人」。海珠嶼大伯公廟之側有幾座墳墓：張、丘、馬三公之墓、守廟僧人的「順寂沙彌西濱禪師」墓（葬於1854年），使傳說中的人物有所根據。這些促使一個故事的完成，也回答了誰是大伯公與誰的大伯公的問題：「相傳在乾隆年間，張理和同鄉人丘兆進及另一福建永定客人馬福春，一道乘帆船到海珠嶼，成為比英殖民者更早到檳城的華人。碑記依傳說的說法，記載說：三人之中，張為塾師、丘為鐵匠、馬為燒炭工人，情誼很深，並結拜為兄弟；張理一直住在海珠嶼，丘、馬二人在鄰近找生活，但他們常常歡聚；一日，丘、馬二人到海珠嶼探望張理，見他已在石岩之中坐化了。丘、馬二人把他安葬和祭祀他。丘、馬二人去世後，人們把他們安葬在張理墳左右，並奉祀三人和祈求他們的保護。據說在他們踏上海珠嶼的土地一角，就成了大伯公廟的建廟處，也即大伯公神靈的發源地」（王琛發，2006: 25-27）。

參考書目

王琛發，1998，〈檳榔嶼客屬的大伯公信仰〉，《檳榔嶼客家兩百年》。馬來西亞：檳城客屬公會出版。

王琛發，2006，《馬來西亞客家人的宗教信仰實踐》，馬來西亞：馬來西亞客家公會聯合會。

王琛發，2009，〈嘉應學院客家研究院演講錄音整理〉，http://www.xiao-en.org/cultural/magazine.asp（2012.4.14）。

王琛發，2010，〈大伯公節話福德〉（房翠瑩採訪報導），《孝恩雜誌》www.xiao-en.org/cultural/magazine.asp（2012.4.14）。

安煥然，2003，〈淺談新馬的大伯公信仰〉，《本土與中國：學術論文集》（南方學院學術叢書第五種）。馬來西亞：南方學院出版社。又見於1991年出版的《道教學探索》第伍號，中華民國道教會台灣省台南市支會，成功大學歷史系道教研究室。

利亮時、張維安、張翰璧，2011，〈海珠嶼大伯公廟與客家五屬祭祀團體〉，「2011年族群、歷史與文化亞洲聯合論壇」論文。中壢：中央大學客家學院，2011.10.29-30。

吳詩興，2009，〈馬來西亞的福德正神信仰探析——以砂拉越的大伯公廟為主要探討〉，《成大宗教與文化學報》，13: 97-138。

吳德芳，2006，《馬來西亞客家文物館落成紀念特刊》。馬來西亞：馬來西亞客家公會聯合會。

茶陽會館，1999，〈簡介「新加坡海唇福德祠暨綠野亭公所」〉，《南洋客屬總會七十週年紀念特刊》。新加坡：新加坡南洋客屬總會。

張少寬，2003，〈大伯公街話伯公〉，《檳榔嶼華人史話》。檳榔城：南洋田野研究室。

張維安、張容嘉，2009，〈客家人的大伯公：蘭芳共和國的羅芳伯及其事業〉，《客家研究》，3(1): 57-89。

張維安、張翰璧，2012，〈馬來西亞砂拉越大伯公節意義初探〉，徐雨村

編，《族群遷移與宗教轉化：福德正神與大伯公研究論文集》。新竹：清
華大學人文社會學院。

張翰璧、張維安，2011，〈神的信仰、人的關係與社會的組織：檳城海珠嶼
大伯公及其祭祀組織〉，「福德正神研究國際研討會」論文。詩巫：永安
亭大伯公廟，2011.9.17。

陳仲敏，1976，〈檳城特寫：海珠嶼大伯公廟〉，《馬來西亞嘉聯會銀禧紀
念特刊》。馬來西亞：馬來西亞嘉聯會銀禧紀念特刊出版委員會。

陳耀威，2008，〈請火〉，《星洲日報》，2008.03.02。

鄧國先，2004，〈客家人的信仰與廟宇〉，《客家情流水緣》。馬來西亞：
東風出版社。

訪談資料

陳耀威，R2007，2007年8月23日於檳城訪問。

陳劍虹，R2007，2007年8月23日於檳城訪問。

王琛發等，R2007，王琛發及四位檳城知識份子，2007年8月23日於檳城訪
問。

陳亞才，R2009，2009年1月13日於檳城訪問。

李永球，R2009，2009年1月13日於檳城訪問。

新加坡中藥業的族群分工與族群意象

張翰璧[†]

經濟移民在抵達另一個社會時，通常因為語言與文化的障礙，無法進入當地勞動市場找到工作，因而傾向於自雇型態的移民創業（immigrant entrepreneurs），這便是一個相當普遍的選擇。經濟移民當中，學者只發現不同的族群團體有相當不同的自雇比例的現象，但是並未看到族群內部的差異性。而Turnbull (1989) 指出，在十九世紀新加坡的產業，的確有族群獨占與分工的現象，例如福建人多為開設銀行、保險業主要在廣府人手中、金銀業中則是潮州人和廣府人分庭抗禮、典當業多以客家人為主要經營者等。

因此，本文強調族群團體的差異性以及族群文化的「互動性」，從族群比較的觀點出發，以新加坡的中藥產業為例，分析產業中的族群分工，以及業者與顧客間的族群印象，進而建構「客家」的族群特質與文化，並從客家的內部觀點分析族群互動，深究新加坡中藥產業內族群分工的形成，及經由市場所產生的族群意象。

關鍵字：族群經濟、族群分工、新加坡、中藥業、族群意象

---

† 張翰璧，國立中央大學客家文化研究所副教授，國立清華大學人社中心訪問學者。

一、新馬的客家族群產業

　　典當與中藥產業是新加坡與馬來西亞地區客家族群主要從事的傳統行業。新加坡中藥店的創業早在1819至1829年間，即有數間中藥店在經營，例如同善堂、福和堂、開源堂和成德記藥行。戰前新加坡中藥店的經營者已是客家人為最多，在319家中藥店中，客家人所經營的有256家，占80.5%以上。根據2006年新加坡當商公會的紀錄，92位會員中，約有80位是客家人，占87%。同樣的情形也出現在馬來西亞，根據馬來西亞當商總會與馬來西亞華人醫藥總會的資料，全馬來西亞共有210間當鋪以及42個與中藥產業相關的公會團體組織。在客家移民普遍「不善經商」的趨勢中，新加坡、馬來西亞典當業與中藥產業的經營者主要為客家族群，幾乎形成壟斷的現象（張翰璧，2007, 2011）。

　　中藥產業是馬來西亞與新加坡華人主要的傳統行業，其中客家人扮演重要的角色。根據馬來西亞華人醫藥總會的資料，全馬來西亞共有42個與中藥產業相關的公會團體組織[1]。根據作者於2007至2010年間，在馬六甲、檳城與新加坡針對中藥產業的田野調查資料顯示，中藥產業的業者都以客家人居多，尤其是有中醫師把脈問診的中藥材店。本文希望在上述研究的基礎上，進一步探究新加坡中藥產業中的族群分工現象，以及在買賣行為中所產生的族群意象。

二、移民網絡與族群經濟

　　族群經濟運用於移民與少數族群團體的研究是相當多的，最早這個概念追溯至Weber比較經濟史發展所衍生出來的「異地人的交易」（alien trader），以在先前歷史經驗影響下，某些團體專門在某些交

1　馬來西亞華人醫藥總會50周年特刊，2005年。

易與商業活動上，而這些歷史經驗包含某些特定專業與經營方式。不論是Weber與Sombart，他們都談到現在資本主義的浮現，源自一群主要的族群作為一種先驅者的角色。以猶太人為例，從他們商業活動傳統面貌為範本（Light, 1994）。Weber認為從傳統主義過渡到理性中產階級資本主義，需要一個決定性的中斷，而猶太人本身並未完成，因為他們只是作為一個外來者，不需講求情面、短暫地停留的商人。但到了新教徒，其所成立的企業強調的普遍性（univeralism）使得理性的中產階級資本主義漸漸優於傳統的資本主義（如猶太人）。像是普遍性允許法律的契約與關係，而減輕社會層面的信任與文化面向的理解；同時，允許科層組織出現等現象。Weber融合馬克思主義觀點，兩者都區別前資本主義到資本主義過程，但兩者也間接地忽略以某族群作觀察切入角度的資本主義，而為後來相關的研究所關注。但與大規模的現代企業有所不同，「族群資本主義企業」被認為無法擴大規模、以科層組織方式經營、無法採用簿記制度等種種不利因素，使得現代的、普遍性、以獲利極大化企業被預期有取代傳統企業之姿，最終傳統企業的重要性會逐漸下降。

Bonacich與Modell是最早對族群經濟（Ethnic Economy）進行操作型定義，同前所述，族群經濟是指任何族群或移民團體的自雇對象，包含了雇主、其同族群的員工，以及他們未支付薪資的家人。而社會科學最早對族群經濟開始產生興趣，始於1972年由Ivan Light所寫的 *Ethnic Enterprise in America* 一書。Light在書中比較1880年到1940年的華裔、日裔、非裔美人在美國自雇情形，把族群經濟視為由社會信任支持的企業，其組成包含了社會與文化資本交織運用，以及借貸給少數族群的貸款信用組織。因為其嚴格定義，似乎可從以上數據比例上來衡量該族群經濟的規模大小（Light and Karageoris, 1994, 2005; Light and Gold, 2000）。

這也遇到一個問題，研究者該如何定義族群團體，例如許多研究族群經濟的學者採取的是從他們來自哪個國家，但國籍不是區別族群

的一項完美指標，在華人的國家或社會，像新加坡、香港本身有不同的方言。但族群經濟是立基於他們的族群性而不是國家來區別他們的界線，國家只是一項便利的族群指標。實際上，一個族群經濟的形成，源於某個族群他們的流動管道是同族群的。

Light和Karageoris (2005) 認為族群經濟應包含了同族群自雇者（self-employed）或稱雇主（employer），以及相對前者的受雇者（employee）。亦即這是研究移民與族群少數團體的最狹義的定義（Light and Gold 2000）。在此定義下，族群經濟被認為移民或少數團體能創造自己的就業機會，這種型態並不同於一般勞動市場的就業情形。族群經濟是基於族群性（ethnicity）而不是理性。Light與Gold (2000) 族群經濟這個名詞的定義可追溯三個主要研究的傳統，第一來自歐洲歷史社會學的創始；第二來自起源於前者，有關中間人少數團體的研究；第三來自非裔美國經濟思想家，三個傳統研究途徑形成族群經濟的研究。

無論是古典經濟學者與社會學者對於在經濟與社會的研究上，對於其族群性（ethnicity）其實都沒有太大的興趣。無論是Weber與Sombart都認為現代資本主義會取代先前原初的、族群的經濟起源。Sombart認為現代資本主義企業的特色就是去個人化。即決策者把獲利視為優先考量，並超越個人的關係，亦包含同族群的關係。相較之下，傳統廠商的決策者反而是受到如兄弟般與互助的情誼所影響。傳統廠商營運的每個階段包含某些特徵，像是偏袒主義（favoritism）、傾向重用親戚（nepotism）、社區主義（communalism）以及特殊主義（exceptionalism）。從Weber的觀點，前資本主義是以價格—道德雙元的運作方式，反映了對族群宗教團體完全的忠誠而不是追求自身極大化利益。

而中間人少數團體的研究源自Weber在談到賤民資本主義（pariaih capitalism）的概念，即以同族群為主的少數團體在前資本主義市場交易專業化所形成的結果。Light (2005) 指出中間人少數團體產

生了一個三角衝突的關係。不同於資本主義所談論的外商公司，而是較為傳統的當地貿易商。這三角指有三種行動者，其一為當地居民；其次為殖民地統治者或稱為殖民地掌權者；最後為少數族群，移民者，屬於殖民地最下層。例如在印尼的華人就是屬於少數中間人團體，華人通常擁有一定的經濟實力，卻沒有政治實權。而當統治者試圖要合法化其政治權力時，其透過操弄此種衝突與仇恨，如宣揚印尼國家經濟百分之七十都掌控在華人身上，但是華人只占印尼人口百分之三，這些華人享受大部分經濟成果。但實際上沒有證據顯示，華人就變成是一個代罪羔羊的角色。中間人少數團體過去比較放在族群的商業媒介的中間角色，而現在把文化意涵放進來，從經濟社會關係轉變為族群關係的討論。

　　以往的族群經濟已經注意到不同國家或區域（台灣、新加坡和香港）的華人，在自雇的比例上有所差異，並未關注華人內部的族群差異性，例如台灣閩客族群的差異，或是香港、新加坡社會中族群的不同。本文以新加坡的中藥業為例，分析產業內部的族群分工，以及對不同族群性的意象。

三、移民網絡與族群差異性

　　研究東南亞的族群經濟發展，都需要先了解移民的過程與網絡關係，顏清湟（2005: 159-160）指出，從十八世紀末至二十世紀初，華人移民的模式基本上可以區分成港口、礦區和農村社區型三種城市。

（一）港口型城市

　　港口型的城市在時間上是最早的移民模式，約在十五世紀，主要的移民是閩南到馬六甲王朝的商人階級，人數或許不是很多，多是進行貿易的商人階級。爾後於1786年的海峽殖民地開啟英國時期的自由貿易階段，檳城和新加坡的相繼開發，吸引許多東南亞鄰近國家的二

次移民，以及閩粵華人前來尋找新的經濟發展空間。

（二）礦區型城市

此類型的城市最早是砂拉越河流域的石隆門（Bau），因為金礦開採的需要，十八世紀中葉，許多華人金礦工人從加里曼丹西部湧至石隆門礦區。之後為了因應十九世紀海峽殖民地的錫礦開採，大陸的客家地區礦工大量的湧入馬來西亞。他們在森美蘭州（Sembilan）的蘆骨（Lukut）與雙溪芙蓉（Sungei Seremban），吡叻州（Perak）的拉律（Larut）及雪蘭莪州（Selangor）的吉隆坡（Kuala Lumpur）開採錫礦。與港口城市移民比較，礦區移民較少流動，也不易轉換工作。

（三）農村社區型城市

受到殖民經濟發展的影響，以華人為主而建立的農村社區，較前兩種類型的城市出現的晚。隨著十九世紀中葉，胡椒和甘蜜的商品化趨勢，以及之後橡膠需求量的大增，許多的中國移民開始聚集形成農村社區型的城市。新加坡與馬來半島的移民主要是透過契約勞工來到新馬，並經由英國政策與港主制度組織起來，進行大規模的農地種植。東馬的移民許多則是透過教會的規劃，提供土地以吸引閩粵移民，例如1883年沙巴（Sabah）古達（Kudat）的客家農業移民。以及二十世紀初砂拉越（Sarawak）福州籍農業移民。

由於不同地區的中國移民會從不同港口出發，加上移民網絡與地區方言的差異性，以及移入國的地域性差異，移民會因應不同的社會條件與生產方式，產生不同的華人社會結構。一般而言，福建人的宗親組織主要是建立在血緣性基礎上，而客家人則較強調方言性的會館組織。因為客家在大陸分布於閩、粵、贛地理範圍，無法完全適用「閩」或「粵」的分類，再加上客家的移民大多在契約華工興起時移入新馬地區，職業又多屬於礦工或工匠。因此，會館的性質多屬方言

會館（顏清湟，2005: 41-42）。

　　與客家人相比，福建人的宗親關係主要是地方的血緣性。造成差異的原因大致上有幾個，諸如福建人早期已在海峽殖民地經商以及海外的自然環境所造成。早期的福建人在海峽經商提供了一個良好的基礎，使福建移民人口迅速的成長。因在海外不斷地擴展商業，致使福建商人不得不從中國招募人手，愈來愈多人獲得親戚的支助前來馬來西亞當店員和商業貿易的助手。因此，新移民在經濟和情感上不得不更需要依賴親戚們的支持。當有強烈的感覺需要宗親們的支助時，而以地方血緣性為主的宗親會便被建立起來（顏清湟，2005: 161-162）。福建人非常活躍地設立他們的宗親組織。他們不僅建立馬來西亞最早的華人宗親會，即是1820年的謝公司，同時也在檳城和新加坡成立許多強大的宗親組織。檳城的邱公司、楊公司、林公司和陳公司，至今在馬來西亞還是非常富有與著名。換言之，移民的時間早晚、移民的人數、職業的類別、中國和英殖民地的政策，都影響著不同族群在移入國的人群組成方式。

　　職業與族群間的關係又如何呢？萊佛士（Raffles）是對華人社會方言集團和行業之間關係的第一位觀察者。1822年，在規劃新加坡市區發展藍圖時，他希望市政規劃局為來自廈門的華人畫出一塊特別區域，這群華人指的是作買賣的閩南籍商人。[2] 他並沒有提到廣府人、客家人、潮州人或海南人，只特別突出閩南商人的位置，對萊佛士而言，當時的華人只被分成商人與非商人，非商人包括工匠、工人與農夫，有可能是其他的四種方言團體在商業經營上並不特別引人注意，也或許多屬於農工階層。

　　進一步指出職業與族群差異性的是潮州商人佘有進，他的觀察彌補了萊佛士忽視上述四個方言集團的不足。佘有進是當時華人社區的

---

2 見〈T. S. 萊佛士致C. E. 戴維斯上校，1822年11月4日〉，載「新加坡紀要」《印度群島與東南亞學報》（J. I. A.），第1卷，第8期，1854，頁105。

領袖，對於新加坡華人社區有內部與深刻的了解，對方言集團與行業之間的關係了解比萊佛士更為詳細和準確。按照他的說法，1848年時潮州人是新加坡最大的方言群，成員約19,000人，多數是棕兒茶（亦譯為「甘蜜」，gambier）和胡椒經紀商，店主和種植園主。第二大的才是福建人，人數約在10,000（包括閩籍移民後裔的馬六甲華人），他們之中約40%是買賣人、商人和店主，20%是種植園主，其餘的則為苦力、船工、漁民和搬運工人。在6,000名廣府（澳門）人中，75%以上是工匠和工人，分別為木匠、裁縫、製鞋業、理髮師、伐木工及泥瓦匠等。客家人（總數約為4,000人）也像廣府人一樣，大多數為工匠和工人：他們中有鐵匠、製鞋匠、金飾匠和理髮師、建築工和伐木工。海南人是最小的集團，僅有700人，他們多半是從農村僱來的店員或夥計（佘有進，1848: 290）。

除了新加坡，在同一時期檳榔嶼的華人中，也可以找到同樣的行業模式。J. D. 沃恩在1854年寫到，他觀察到所有的木匠、鐵匠、鞋匠和做其他費力氣工作的工人都是廣東人，而福建人和漳州人（閩人）都是店主、商人和香料種植園主。[3] 顯然，沃恩的「廣東人」一詞包括了廣府人和客家人（顏清湟，1991: 109）。這些客家人來自六邑（包括新會、台山、恩平、開平、鶴山和赤溪），同屬於叫「古岡州」的地區性集團，職業幾乎清一色是工匠，承攬了早期檳榔嶼的公共建築的營造（梅玉灿，1964: 73-74）。

麥留芳（1981: 43-46）曾針對方言群與行業間的關聯性提出以下的問題：為什麼某一特定的方言群會壟斷某一特定行業？這種行業壟斷的經濟模式其持續性又如何？麥留芳提出諸如自然環境、移民的先後次序、行業職業化的延續以及祕密會社的干預等，都是造成某一方言群獨占產業的因素。針對麥留芳的分析，顏清湟（1991: 110）認為

---

3 見J. D. 沃恩，〈簡論檳榔嶼的華人〉，載《印度群島與東南亞學報》（J. I. A.），第8卷，1854，頁3；轉引自顏清湟，1991: 124，註58。

麥留芳忽略了不同方言群間所長期保持的行業劃分中，宗親和方言組織的影響力。宗族或方言組織作為社會基本組織性，發揮了疑似初級連帶的功能，不但凝聚類似擴大家庭的「我群」情感連帶，更發揮經濟與其他的社會功能，不但幫忙介紹職業，也會照顧移民的福利，形成小型的「社會」。在殖民社會結構尚未分化的階段，「我群」的基礎就是宗族與方言組織，許多宗教、祭祀、經濟行為都在此分類基礎上進行，形成社會秩序的基礎。

也就是在宗親與方言組織的基礎上，華人開始移動並尋找新的經濟機會，經由社會網絡的牽引，進入不同的產業與職業中。華人移民的社會與語言背景、移民過程的特性，決定了早期華人社會的組織與結構。不同的語言與祖籍除了各自成立代表其方言與地區的會館外，也形成重要的職業網絡。開店除了資金的籌措外，在移民之初的方言群不同的社會，找一位可以溝通和信賴的員工是個挑戰，在這種情況下，對一個經商的人來說，親屬關係就顯得很重要了。「由於方言不同以及移民社會性質的差異，他也許很難找到可信賴的職員協助他經營店鋪。這些成功的小商人如果需要勞動力的話，一些人便再次返回中國，招募親屬或親戚。於是，一條親屬移民的鏈環建立了起來，從而推動了中國人往這一地區的移民」（顏清湟，1991: 4）。

據訪談資料顯示，如此的職業與產業發展模式，一直保留到現在，但會因為不同產業文化而有些微的差異。例如典當業，因為典當的物品多在店內，且為大量現金流動的行業，加上餉碼制對擴店的限制，雇主與職員間需要相當穩固的信任基礎，所雇用的員工多為親友與同鄉。甚至許多行話與術語多是客語發音，不是相同方言群的人，和雇主沒有社會網絡作為信任基礎的人，很難進入典當業工作（張翰璧，2007）。若以新加坡的中藥材店而言，中藥材店都是華人開的。其中客家占80%，接下來是潮州人占7、8%，廣東、海南約占10%左右。客家人中，大埔的比例又多於永定人。儘管現代教育會降低方言集團之間的差異，但是不同的方言集團仍控制了某些特殊的行業和經

濟領域，許多典當業和中藥材店的老闆和頭手都是客家人，客家人仍控制著新馬地區的典當業與中藥業。

四、新加坡的中藥產業與族群分工

當某一個產業的族群多元性漸漸出現，在經營文化上便會出現差異性，以下本文將以新加坡的中藥產業為例，分析客家與中藥產業的關聯性。

客家人在中藥經營可以分成兩個部分，第一是生產，第二是出口跟批發，出口批發分成成藥跟草藥，還有用料，那麼最後是零售這一塊，以往客家族群壟斷的是在零售部門，在零售部門中，客家人占的比例是最大的，尤其是有中醫師駐診的店鋪。在草藥進口批發，客家人占的比例不大。1960年代以來，最有名的進口中草藥的是廣東人，生草藥的進口主要是廣東幫。在中成藥的進口，客家人經營的也不多，主要原因是貨源多從香港進口。

雖然，草藥進口批發的客家商人不多，但是中成藥的生產領域中就有許多客家人，尤其是永定的客家人，最有名的就是胡文虎的虎標，以及三角標驅風油。傳統而言，中成藥生產這部分是客家人多，而且是客家裡面的永定人多「做出名的，什麼中央啦，有聯化學製藥廠，有聯耀……都是永定人，可是慢慢就有其他人進來了……80年代就開始有其他人進來了。」（SICHM1_2010）

在貴重藥材的部分，則是以潮州人為主要經營的族群。客家人經營的規模不大，主要是江西的客家人。新加坡中藥的貴重用料一定要找潮州人，例如泡蔘、高麗蔘、鹿茸，「這些昂貴的中藥材百分之百是潮州人的天下，其他族群的人連邊都碰不上……那個財力要很大才可以，都是他們在幹的。」（SICHM2_2010）

客家族群為何選擇了學藥材呢？如何進入中藥生產與零售的領域？因為語言的使用會影響方言群的形成，使得不同方言群的人傾向

進入相同的產業。例如過去新加坡的雜貨店，不是潮州人就是福建人在經營，那你進去潮州人、福建人開的雜貨店，就要使用他們的方言，即使去潮州人的店，你跟他講印度話或馬來話，他還是跟你講潮州話。方言的使用初步將不同人群區隔在不同的職業與商業領域中。客家人喜歡學藥材，似乎與重視文化或教育有關，也或許是因為客家族群不是新加坡華人中的優勢團體，學會許多不同的方言，可以和不同的方言群溝通、抓藥。

> 「以前的人為什麼想學藥材，因為很多人受的教育不高嘛，那你去學生鐵啊，白鐵啊那些，你接觸文化的機會很少……所以以前的人覺得做藥材是一個很……高尚的行業，為什麼呢？做藥是人命關天的行業，你一定要懂那個人的話你才能夠了解他要買什麼，你才能夠清楚跟他講，所以以前做藥材店的人，他們不管是福建人抓藥，海南人抓藥什麼人抓藥，他對文字的那個了解的能力比人家是多……所以文化的修養要比人家好，他對語言的掌握要比人家好，所以為什麼很多客家人喜歡學藥。」（中藥公會訪談2010/05/07）

基本上，藥材店會傳承到現在有兩個原因，一是虎標永安堂胡文虎的影響，當時永定會館會照顧南來的鄉親，來的人不是經由會館找工作，就是到永安堂的藥店工作，等到找到其他工作之後才離開，有些也自立門戶開店。胡文虎是在緬甸出生的永定人，父親在緬甸即創設永安堂國藥行，1927年胡文虎將成藥廠的總廠設於新加坡，成為萬金油、八卦丹和頭痛粉的東南亞銷售中心。

雖然，中藥零售業其中一半以上是永定人，但是與原鄉的維生方式鮮少有直接的關係。

> 答：其實我們永定人喔，來這邊都是做手工藝比較多……打鐵

的嘛，以前做白鐵匠啊，白鐵匠就是做那些水桶啊，那些
都是客家人。

問：所以做農作物的不多？

答：農作物不多。……打鐵的，永定的打鐵，白鐵，剛剛開始
怡保那邊做錫礦要用的桶。因為你錫礦的工具都是鋤頭這
些啊，都要打的啊，桶啊這些鐵桶啊……就是說我們客家
人比較勤奮，社會上需要什麼我們就生產什麼嘛，不過拿
木桶來講，不是我們的專長，做木桶是廣西的（柳中）那
邊的，他們就做木桶……賣印尼也很多，剛才他講的因為
印尼的船載運物的船啊，載那些木材的船啊都停泊在那
邊，所以他們就把這些船丁啊，要製造船的東西都帶上
去，印尼船嘛，買了很多客家人打鐵，就在那一帶嘛！

（中藥公會訪談2010/05/07）

顏清湟（2010: 40）指出，客家人的職業大致分為兩種類型，一
是數量較多的礦工，其他是相對少數的工匠。在當時，一個自立門戶
的手工業者和一個熟練工人的收入，與店主、外國公司職員或政府低
階官吏的薪資所差無幾（顏清湟，2010: 134）。

如果客家人的職業以「工」為主，又是如何進入「商」的領域
呢？中醫師的競爭以及客家人對中醫師的尊重，或許可以解釋發展的
原因。

「我猜想一百多年前新加坡馬來西亞醫藥比較少啊，那如果你
同時競爭的那幾個人呢，福建幫的海南幫的潮州幫的，五個醫
師出來，十個醫師裡面可能有三個是客家人啊，這三個醫師要
是他的療效比別人好，口碑就很快傳出來了，那很快就會把其
他人比下去，那麼我們同鄉的人來嘛，一定投靠自己人嘛，那
麼我們這一村的人在這一行發展，我們自然會順著他走嘛，我

想這樣的可能性會比較高，你說本來就在那邊很了不起來這邊做有什麼用啊，如果那邊做得很好就不出來了。」

（中藥公會訪談2010/05/07）

「人命關天」也使得客家和中藥業產生密切的關聯性。顏清湟（2005: 114）研究會館時，指出客家方言社團的重要性，除了負擔起社會福利的種種照顧功能外，最獨特的是創辦了復康中心（回春社）。創辦此福利兼醫藥的機構，是因為客家人的職業結構多為礦工與工匠，當時又缺乏住院設備與免費醫療設施。因此，在檳城、吉隆坡與新加坡陸續成立回春社，照顧鄉人健康。

直到現在，新加坡中藥材的門市一半以上還是客家人在經營，但是產業的上游，例如二盤或頭盤就非客家人天下，而且越上游、越需要大量資金的部分，客家人越少。

答：目前來講囉！藥材店還是客家人多啦！

問：藥材是哪一個？門市嗎？

答：門市……。

問：那二盤就不見得？

答：二盤就不見得。

問：然後頭盤也不見得。

答：頭盤就更少……我們客家人還占比較優勢的，是生產這一塊。

問：可是比較少啊！

答：以前啦！傳統來講，藥品品牌是客家人的天下，以前喔！6、70年代，80年代之前，新加坡做品牌的你想得到的都是客家人做的。

問：所以，你剛說有出品的東西就是在頭盤那邊對不對？

答：對！在頭盤……以前，傳統是我們客家人的天下，這一塊

是我們客家人的天下。

問：那二盤呢？

答：二盤就不一定啦！二盤就一下來是什麼人都有，你看以前
　　做比較大的，做二盤比較大的有客家、福建、廣東。

問：所以到現在大概門市裡頭還是客家人比較多？

答：門市大概客家人占一半以上。

問：但是頭盤就沒有了？

答：頭盤你要看賣什麼啦！賣草藥的話還有啦！

（中藥公會訪談2010/05/07）

　　基本上，中藥產業從批發、中盤到零售都有客家族群在經營、而
以往也多為客家族群所壟斷。自1970年代以來，其他族群慢慢進入此
產業，客家的獨占性也漸漸消失。根據田野觀察，客家人對於進貨較
保守，也不會經營昂貴食補藥材的買賣，經營上偏向「守成」。

五、客家族群的中藥產業經營

　　十位受訪者的創業過程幾乎都是繼承家業，當初的創業過程80%
都是因為在藥材店打過工，接觸過中藥產業而開店。

問：您叔公在大埔有開過藥材店嗎？

答：我看應該不是，應該沒有。叔公是到這邊一個萬泰和那邊
　　打工。其實萬泰和在那個時候也是很出名的啦，跟那個
　　……他們都是。所以父親也到了這邊打工。然後累積資金
　　就開店。其實資金不用很多，因為認識嘛，都可以遲還錢
　　的嘛。

（SICHM3_2010）

就這樣客家人逐漸進入中藥產業，網絡提供他們創業的資源，可以先叫貨，後付款。社會網絡提供客家人產業的基礎，也在後續經營上發揮「信任」的功能，可以相互調貨或延遲付款。與其他族群間的交易也會在以往的交易經驗上，建立信任關係。

問：所以萬安和的資金從哪裡來？爸爸怎麼有錢開店？

答：那很簡單，那時他們不是……，錢是不多可是……存了一點錢。剛好那時有相熟的那些……好像那個萬全喔，萬全他們先做（批發）。

問：所以萬全是大埔人還是永定人？

答：一樣我們那邊的我們那邊……

問：您剛說他們有資助你們嘛！

答：不是大筆資助啦，他可能就是一些……以前的人沒有集資的啦，就是他們一個信用，他們就給貨給你賣啊！給貨給你賣，你賣了錢再給我，所以給你們賒那個原料。

問：都是客家人嗎？

答：應該是吧，除了一些潮州的永泰隆這些囉，早期是永泰隆，可是變永大隆了，永泰隆我記得。

問：所以基本上會賒帳給你們的都是客家人？

答：會，會。

問：那別人福建人會賒帳給你們嗎？

答：應該會啊，因為我父親在那邊信譽蠻好的。

問：而且在那邊打工打很久。

答：對對對。

（SICHM3_2010）

　　在藥店打工，不只建立網絡與信任關係，也可以學習將來開店的製藥知識，當然這個過程是很辛苦的。平均的訓練過程需要三年左

右，且必須靠學徒自己細心的觀察。

答：先這個研藥，用腳啦，搭那個船啊，用水船一樣的，這樣
用手這樣拉住，腳⋯⋯磨那個研那個藥。我們說以前那個
研藥是吧，現在用磨的，機器來磨。研藥，先開始學⋯⋯
打雜的先開始學這個研藥。研藥之後了就用剪。我們打雜
的剪，剪那個藥啊，剪藥材啊一枝枝的藥啊，什麼要剪的
嘛，都做！

問：然後咧？

答：剪藥之後就學切，刨啊⋯⋯切⋯⋯切⋯⋯切⋯⋯切藥。我
還記清楚了。回來再刨，刨藥刨一片片，剪藥是剪⋯⋯

問：剪一段段？

答：剪一段段，不只是段段，有的要薄薄的，也是白杓啊那些
要薄薄的，以前很認真的，做藥不是像現在很簡單的什
麼。這個還要泡製啊，什麼剪藥這個人還要泡製那個，打
火啊，硫磺打火啊！打火之後藥材比較耐，是不是？耐，
藥材比較不會蟲去蛀。

問：還要學泡藥啊做藥丸啊，是不是？

答：不是，這個最後了，這個是研藥粉的責任了，研藥粉啊做
藥丸啊中藥丸啊，所以這個是他的責任了。但做藥丸呢全
部大家一起做。

問：一起做？

答：不是，頭手沒有做。頭手不會做的。

問：您說打雜完對不對就研藥。

答：就研藥，研藥後就剪藥，然後切藥刨藥。刨藥也是大功夫
咧⋯⋯這個可以刨藥、切藥就可以當第三個頭手了。幫抓
藥啊，秤藥啊！

問：所以喔，這樣子訓練完要多久？

答：我看要三幾年吧！

（SICHM6_2010）

　　頭手是藥店經營的知識中心，因此需要信任的人，通常藥店中的
僱工不會挑選特定的族群，只有頭手需要是自己信任的人，一般多是
自己的親戚。

　　在以社會網絡建立起來的族群經濟中，經營者對其他族群顧客的
「族群性」有不同於客家的特色與印象描述，可以看出客家族群與其
他族群文化上的些微差異。

> 答：客家人就是我要一分錢買兩分的貨。……一定要物超所
> 值。客家人是不願把錢花在不實的包裝上面，不實在的
> 那種虛榮上面，所以他不會去買最漂亮的伏苓，最漂亮的
> 人蔘，對不對，我要買價錢便宜但是……它具有一定的功
> 效，同樣藥效。……那我為什麼要花大錢去買便宜……貴
> 的東西？沒有道理嘛，所以像我們自家吃的高麗蔘都是蔘
> 節嘛。賣給別人都是大條的，自家吃就吃蔘節嘛，但是廣
> 東人不一樣，廣東人我要漂亮的，漂亮的，我就是要大片
> 的啊，要新鮮的嘛。
>
> 問：那潮州人呢？
>
> 答：潮州人，潮州人最精，潮州人對吃蔘最精，所以你在潮州
> 人在的地方賣的蔘都必須是好的蔘，如果你在潮州人聚集
> 的地方，你去買便宜的陽蔘去混，去冒充是好的蔘，你招
> 牌一定爛。因為什麼人都好矇，你就不要去矇老潮州，他
> 們比我們還要精。
>
> 問：那海南人呢？
>
> 答：海南人就比較難摸啦。因為我本身對海南人的習慣不熟
> 嘛。但是海南人就……你要說嘛，對我們中藥我們藥材界

來講，海南人生意是比較少做的。

問：那馬來人呢？

答：馬來人好做，馬來人是他只要相信你，你講什麼都對的。你可以講的好像當你朋友一樣，那就好辦了。所以馬來人講難聽一點，好騙。你可以這樣子講啦，但是馬來人就是你要讓他覺得你跟他真的是朋友。……他就跟你這樣，而且你做他一個人生意，等於做他一條村生意，他會呼朋喚友來跟你買。……很可愛，但是我們藥材店傳統就不喜歡印度人，印度人錢很難賺耶。……印度人他不捨得花錢，什麼東西都要講價，然後那個專買那些沒有錢賺的東西，就是廣告天天打得很響喔，西藥那些很出名的藥啊，那些完全沒有利潤啊，所以印度人的錢很難賺。

（SICHM6_2010）

　　在中藥銷售上，每個方言群或族群都有其些微的差異性。而且這些差異性會受到中成藥的規格化生產的影響，讓顧客看不到藥材的好壞，也消弭社區中藥材店的獨家特色。現在藥材店特色的流失，在於大部分的中藥飲片是不需要自己泡製以及貨源都相同，逐漸消失的差異性也就無法凸顯個別藥店的特色。

六、小結

　　一般來講，中成藥生產到目前為止還是客家人多，而且還是永定人多，貴重藥材的進口，客家人做的不多，其中有一家是江西的客家人，加上另一位客家人共兩家，這兩家就是客家幫做用料批發裡面最早期的，但是規模做得不大。新加坡做用料一定要找潮州人。這些名貴的藥材的批發不是客家人的專長，主要都是潮州人與福建人。而目前最大的草藥批發，做得最大的可能是潮州人經營的「永發隆」，他

們是新加坡做藥的潮州幫，由「永太隆」發展出來的。雖然，零售店面多是客家族群的天下，但是做用料的批發就百分之百是潮州人的天下，其他族群的人連邊都碰不上，因所需的財力要非常大。

　　許多傳統的藥材店現在都面臨同樣的問題，就是後繼無人。其原因除可從文化與學習的面向來看，與過去以來新加坡政策發展較著重英文教育，而輕華語教育的情形有關，但華語文與中醫習得兩者間息息相關，例如中藥材的名稱皆是中文，以及中醫的知識體系相較西方醫學，其根本必須出自於華人傳統文化的醫學觀；另在市場結構與社會流動面向上，我們從族群經濟理論的觀點來看，當移民的第二代如果可以進入主流社會，來找到更好的職業，將會放棄族群經濟的經營，正因族群經濟來自於與主流社會的區隔，與無法適應當地的社會等現象有關。而逐步與當地社會融合等因素都使得新加坡的中藥產業（尤其是傳統的藥材店）面臨未來經營上的困境。

參考書目

Bonacich, Edna, and Modell, John, 1980, *The Economic Basis of Ethnic Solidarity*. Berkeley and Los Angeles: University of California Press.

D. 沃恩，1854，〈簡論檳榔嶼的華人〉，《印度群島與東南亞學報》（*J. I. A.*），第8卷。

Light, Ivan and Karageoris, Stavros, 1994, "The Ethnic Economy", Neil J. Smelser and Richard Swedberg eds., *The Handbook of Economic Sociology*, pp. 647-671. Princeton, N. J.: Princeton University Press.

Light, Ivan and Karageoris, Stavros 2005, "The Ethnic Economy", Neil J. Smelser and Richard Swedberg eds., *The Handbook of Economic Sociology*, pp. 650-677. Princeton, N. J.: Princeton University Press.

Light, Ivan and Gold, Steven J., 2000, *Ethnic Economies*. New York: Academic Press.

Sombart, Werner, 1969, *The Jews and modern capitalism*, translated with notes, by M. Epstein. New York: B. Franklinc.

Turnbull, C. Mary, 1989, *A History of Singapore, 1819-1988*. Singapore: Oxford University Press.

Weber, Max, 2004, *The Protestant Ethic and the Spirit of Capitalism*. London: Routledge.

佘有進，1848，〈新加坡華人人數，幫派職業概覽〉，《印度群島與東南亞學報》（*J. I. A.*），第2卷。

馬來西亞華人醫藥總會，2005，《馬來西亞華人醫藥總會50周年特刊》。

張翰璧，2007，〈新加坡當鋪與客家族群〉，黃賢強主編，《新加坡客家》，頁89-111。江西大學出版社。

張翰璧，2011，〈客家族群產業的制度性脈絡與網絡特性：以馬來西亞檳城中藥業為例〉，江明修主編，《客家企業家》，頁267-284。台北：智勝文化公司。

梅玉灿，1964，〈古岡州六邑先僑在馬活動史〉，檳城台山寧陽會館編，

《馬來亞古岡州六邑總會特刊》。馬來西亞怡保：檳城台山寧陽會館。

麥留芳，1981，《祕密會社的社會學：新加坡和半島馬來西亞華人祕密會社研究》。吉隆坡：牛津大學出版社。

顏清湟，1991，《新馬華人社會史》。北京：中國華僑出版公司。

＿＿＿＿，2005，《海外華人的社會變革與商業成長》。廈門：廈門大學。

＿＿＿＿，2010，〈海外華人民族主義——在傳統與現代化之間〉，《海外華人的傳統與現代化》。新加坡：八方文化創作室。

附錄：新加坡中藥受訪者資料對照表

性別	出生年份	籍貫	是否接受華文教育	移民世代（以受訪者名來說）	親明牽引的移民過程	家族成員最早從事相關中藥業	經營方式與主要市場	代號
男	1956	永定	南洋大學與蒲博高中（華校）	第三代	姑婆→祖父與父親依親	太姑丈開藥店。	自己做藥、自己門市賣藥，亦有批發。	SICHM1_2010
男	1943	永定	未提及	第一代（大陸出生）	祖父→父親→受訪者	有提及父親剛來時曾替藥店打工，兩者父親自己獨立開業。	自己做藥、自己門市賣藥，無批發。藥膏、藥水、涼茶、感冒茶、肉骨茶、風濕油，亦有替人看病。	SICHM2_2010
男	1957	大埔	南大肄業，亦是念華校。	第二代（新加坡出生）	叔公→父親→哥哥	父親在叔公的店【萬泰和】打工。	過去父親與母親曾做過中藥店兼理雜稻型生意。自己目前是走調理路線，保健食補、自己就是走診堂醫師。	SICHM3_2010
男	1951	大埔	未提及	第一代（大陸出生）	同鄉→大伯→父親	伯父在同鄉大埔的中藥店發和（同春）】打工，後來父親才去哥哥的店。	三間泰興堂、泰安堂、泰和堂，沒有醫師駐診，賣藥材為主的店面（零售業）、產品有中成藥、草藥等。	SICHM4_2010
男	1936	大埔	未提及	第二代	父親在馬來西亞與新加坡任返	舅舅做藥店頭手工作也在藥材行工作，自己第一份是受訪者。做最久是【櫻安堂】。	賣藥為主的製造、批發、貿易。製藥配方是由同業一位劉先生提供，自己負責賣藥，有中藥也有西藥。	SICHM5_2010
男	1933	大埔	念華校、中正中學林學校後直接在藥店工作	第二代	父親自己前來	父親自己開藥店。	店裡賣藥，亦有駐診醫師。	SICHM6_2010
男	1933	永定	中正中學	第三代	祖父堂兄弟先來、祖父之過來依親	祖父在堂兄弟開的藥店【萬春和】當中醫師。父親後來也是中醫師，並未成為受訪者自己與他人合開過【百年藥行】，自己駐診。自己現在藥店看診有到其他藥店看診。	出品的三角標的中藥、西藥、真真涼茶（原屬廣東人開）、被受訪者收購。永健藥業的產品主要銷售到馬來西亞比較多、新加坡的市場小。	SICHM7_2010

性別、族群與宗教之交織：
印尼亞齊客家女性改信伊斯蘭教的經驗與過程之初探[*]

蔡芬芳[†]

一、前言

目前東南亞客家研究中與宗教相關研究多以民間或俗民信仰為主，如福德正神與大伯公（徐雨村編，2012），或有少數探討客家與世界性宗教之關係，如馬來西亞客家與基督教關係（黃子堅，2007）。然而，至今尚未將研究觸角延伸至信仰伊斯蘭的客家人身上。有鑑於部分東南亞國家，除了新加坡、馬來西亞之外，例如本研究所要探討的印尼，在伊斯蘭教占絕大優勢的情形之下，生活在其中已有數代以上的華人，包括客家人在內，可能因為通婚、政府政策、受穆斯林幫助等諸多不同的原因改而信仰伊斯蘭教。改信不僅意味著華人與當地社會的互動，更可從中一窺與原生族裔文化之關係，其中他們的家庭、教育、人際互動與原來宗教信仰皆扮演重要角色，因為改信經驗牽涉改宗者如何調和與信仰相關的新舊意義體系。在此過程中，性別、族群與宗教之交織串起了亞齊（Aceh）客家女性改信伊斯蘭之經驗，以及呈現出在印尼脈絡下因為改宗而涉及的多樣面貌。亦因如此，本研究的意義在於以研究客家改信伊斯蘭作為勾勒東南亞客家人在地生活之探針，並且期能增補現有的東南亞客家之宗教研究。

* 由衷感謝李靜教授、蔡源林教授以及匿名審查委員給予研究者的寶貴意見，使本文內容臻於完善。此外，相當感謝中央大學客家學院補助研究者赴印尼田野調查費用，讓本文得以順利完成。最後，向梁炳順與陳慧珍夫婦、梁春霞小姐致上最誠摯謝意，熱心協助研究者順利完成田野調查工作。

† 蔡芬芳，中央大學客家社會文化研究所助理教授。

而研究目的係為未來相關研究建立與累積資料，以利與其他地區的客家穆斯林進行比較研究，以探掘客家族群與文化內部的異質性。

本文包括以下三個部分，首先介紹亞齊的歷史背景、族群組成，以及客家人在當地的發展，包括其信仰特質、族群與會館組織、客家最新發展現況，以呈研究對象所處的宏觀脈絡。其次，將從性別、族群與宗教之相互交錯面向作為觀察女性的改宗經驗之切入點。同時並運用「相互交錯性」（intersectionality）概念作為分析女性改宗者改信伊斯蘭教的過程之理論架構。最後，則以改宗經驗為討論主題，重點涵括改宗者的背景、改信伊斯蘭教的原因、伊斯蘭教如何吸引亞齊客家女性以及改信之後的轉變。本研究以半結構式之深度訪談與參與觀察為研究方法，主要針對四位改信伊斯蘭教的客家女性之改宗經驗與過程進行研究，地點皆為受訪者家中。此外，為求了解當地客家與信仰特質，因此訪談對象包括靈宵宮（Vihara Dharma Bhakti）、海神廟（Vihara Dewi Samodera）與大亞齊佛學社（Vihara Buddha Sakyamuni Banda Aceh）的管理人員，共計三人，以及印尼亞齊客屬聯誼會總主席一人，地點分別為上述兩間廟宇、大亞齊佛學社與印尼亞齊客屬聯誼會。同時，為增進筆者伊斯蘭知識，前台北清真大寺伊斯哈格・馬孝棋教長亦為本研究訪談對象，地點為台北清真大寺。

二、亞齊的客家

2004年12月26日發生的南亞大海嘯造成印尼超過23萬人死亡，其中尤以位於印尼蘇門答臘島西北端的亞齊地區為受創最嚴重地區，卻也因此成為國際關注的焦點，同時自1976年以來以武裝抗爭方式爭取亞齊獨立的「自由亞齊運動」（Gerakan Aceh Merdeka，簡稱為GAM）亦因海嘯與印尼政府在2005年簽下和平協議而劃下休止符。亞齊地區的特殊性除了顯現在因歷史背景所造成的長期以來對獨立的渴望，更在於建立一個有別於由爪哇人領導的伊斯蘭國家。這與亞齊

地區作為伊斯蘭傳入馬來世界[1] 的門戶有關，伊斯蘭曾在此地有過相當輝煌發展的歷史，伊斯蘭的信仰也由此地區向外傳播（林長寬，2009: 6-7）。因為伊斯蘭教傳入印尼信史之始為1112年，由阿拉伯、波斯與南亞商人帶入亞齊、然後才繼續傳至馬六甲（Malacca），十四世紀時擴及爪哇（Java）（Mak, 2002: 225）。在伊斯蘭教未傳到內陸與鄉村地區之前，皆以沿海城市為發展傳播據點，例如亞齊、馬六甲與其他伊斯蘭王國皆是如此（Taylor, 2005: 153-154）。由於亞齊在七到十二世紀時，已因為許多阿拉伯與西印度商人而帶來大量的阿拉伯文化，亞齊人改信伊斯蘭教，為東南亞地區接受阿拉伯文化圈之先驅，因此有「麥加前院」之稱（續培德，2004: 7）。更因為該地區伍拉瑪（Ulama，宗教學者）致力於將伊斯蘭教深植於亞齊人的日常生活之中，因此可以說，在某種程度上，亞齊人的世界觀是在伊斯蘭的信仰架構下醞釀而生的（同上引：4）。

亞齊自十六世紀以來為阿拉伯、波斯、印度商人與葡萄牙人聚集之處，因此顯現出不同文化彼此激盪現象。亞齊的族群主要由亞齊人（Aceh）、阿拉斯人（Alas）、巴達克人（Batak）、嘎寓人（Gayu）、賈莫人（Jamee）、卡羅人（Karo）、克魯特人（Kluet）、馬來人（Melayu）、西莫魯人（Simelu）、塔米昂人（Tamiang）、烏魯興基特人（Ulusingkit）組成（梁敏和、孔遠志，2002: 26-40）。華人移民到達當地的時間主要集中在十九世紀中期之後至二十世紀前半期間（陳欣慧，2007: 38），與十八世紀中期後開始從廣東東部的嘉應州、潮州、惠州移民至婆羅洲西加里曼丹（Kalimantan）開採金礦的客家人相較之下，目前在班達亞齊（Banda Aceh）的客家人到達當地的時間是較晚的。華人當中以客家人、福建人、海南人居多，其他還有潮州人、廣府人。然而，值得注意的是，

---

1 馬來世界並非現代的馬來西亞地區，而是馬來文（Bahasa Melayu）通行地區，即今日東南亞穆斯林國家或區域，西起泰國南部的北大年（Patani），東至菲律賓南部的民答那峨島（Mindanao）（林長寬，2009: 4）。

在亞齊首府班達亞齊當地所有的華人在如唐人街（Peunayong）、市場等公開場合或一般互動皆以客家話做為溝通語言[2]。這點和張翰璧與張維安（2005）所觀察到的在東南亞公共領域中，客家語言與文化無法彰顯的狀況相當不同，因為一般來說，東南亞客家認同因為同時受到當地民族的民族主義與華人作為一個整體華人性所形成的雙重壓抑之影響而隱形。此外，班達亞齊顯著的客語現象也可增補目前東南亞客家研究中對客語為優勢語言分布的認知，如在蕭新煌等人（2007）的調查中，提到沙巴的古達、砂拉越的石隆門、加里曼丹的山口洋（Singkawang）為以客語為華人間通用語言的少數東南亞城市，然卻未將班達亞齊列入。

班達亞齊總人口數近22萬人，根據印尼亞齊華人慈善基金會統計（2005），該市華人共計3,055人，占全城總人口約0.014%。華人多以信仰佛教為主，佛教徒2,467人，占所有華人（3,055人）之80.8%，少數信仰基督教、天主教、伊斯蘭教、印度教。在基督教徒部分，計254人，占8.3%；天主教徒199人，占6.5%；穆斯林127人，占4.2%；印度教1人，占0.032%；伯公信仰3人，占0.1%；未填寫3人，占0.1%；填問號 1人，占0.032%（轉引自陳欣慧，2007: 44-45）。在佛教信仰部分，相關的廟宇計有靈宵宮、海神廟、觀音寺（Vihara Maitri）。與筆者於2011年7月底至8月初在印尼雅加達與山口洋所參觀的廟宇的相同之處在於這些廟裡除了主祀神之外，亦有許多陪祀神，例如靈宵宮內以伯公為主神，下方為鄭和。陪祀神則有觀音、釋迦牟尼、彌勒佛、關公、土地龍神，廟宇外面則有四面佛與虎神。然而，相異之處在於班達亞齊廟宇的外觀色彩並不如前面兩個城市的廟宇鮮豔，形式也較為簡樸。除了上述廟宇之外，以較有組織的方式在運作的則為大亞齊佛學社，當地華人簡稱佛堂。該佛堂不似其他廟宇有多位陪祀神，僅單純祭拜釋迦牟尼佛。佛堂在週日辦有學經

---

2 筆者在當地與福建人或海南人交談時皆以客語為溝通語言。

活動，以印尼文與華文隔週交叉教學。在印尼禁華文階段，佛堂仍繼續教授華文。遇有特殊節日或活動時，佛堂則成為班達亞齊華人匯集之所，例如過年、母親節、或如筆者在田野調查期間所參與的供養師父的活動，參加成員以小朋友為主，大約200人左右（2011年11月13日田野筆記）。

值得注意的是，當地華人組織亦與廟宇結合，例如福建人的天益社與靈宵宮結合、海南人的瓊州會館則與海神廟結合。目前這兩間廟宇的信徒雖無明顯族群特色，甚至信仰佛教的印度人也會前往海神廟祭拜，但在爐主與管理人部分依然保有族群色彩，亦即靈宵宮爐主是福建人，海神廟管理者與爐主皆為海南人。客家人方面，在過去則有惠東安會館，但現在已不復存在。[3] 在大海嘯過後，有跨宗教組織出現，以便進行救援與物資分配工作，例如印華總會、印尼亞齊華人慈善基金會（陳欣慧，2007: 52），然極為短暫，而且由於牽涉到華人不同群體之間的利益問題，因此約於2006年已解散（與印尼亞齊客屬聯誼會總主席古啟祥先生於2011年11月15日在班達亞齊進行的訪談；大亞齊佛學社管理人於2011年11月17日在班達亞齊進行的訪談）[4]。班達亞齊已於2011年6月成立印尼亞齊客屬聯誼會，該會並非以傳統的個人為會員單位，而以家庭為會員單位，目前會員有371個家庭，90%來自班達亞齊，10%則為大亞齊縣，多數成員的祖籍皆為廣東梅縣[5]（與印尼亞齊客屬聯誼會總主席古啟祥先生於2011年11月15日在班達亞齊進行的訪談）。該會雖掛有客家之名，但會員不限客家，而以全部的華人為主，除此之外，也希望能與當地其他族群，例如亞齊人、巴達克人建立關係，該會主要以慈善活動為主，例如捐贈書籍、

---

3 筆者根據陳欣慧的研究（2007: 52），在2011年11月進行田野調查時，向靈宵宮、海神廟與大亞齊佛學社的管理人員與印尼亞齊客屬聯誼會總主席詢問是否知道惠東安會館，但皆表示這個會館已不存在。

4 梁校長在與筆者閒談間也提到這樣的情況（2011年11月15日田野筆記）。

5 感謝古啟祥先生提供筆者翻閱會員資料表格，除了多數以中文或印尼文填寫廣東梅縣、還看到僅有一個會員填寫福建、另位一個則填寫山東梅縣，此暫時推論為填寫者筆誤，或中文程度不足，抑或對「祖籍地」毫無概念。

文具給窮困家庭的孩童。由於該會成立時間短暫,但可以視為當地客家發展的最新狀況,同時可做為我們觀察亞齊客家發展以及客家認同建構的切入點。

三、性別、族群與宗教之相互交錯

在2011年11月10日前往印尼亞齊首府班達亞齊進行田野調查之前,請求在當地曾經擔任過衛理學校的校長梁炳順夫婦幫忙找尋十位改信伊斯蘭教的客家女性,以便進行訪談。結果他們告知僅有三位給予正面回覆,另外一位需待丈夫的同意[6],因為當地已成為穆斯林的客家女性「害羞」,所以要找到十位受訪者,恐非易事。筆者當時認為,屆時到達田野地點之後可以用滾雪球方式在當地再找到其他受訪者,以解決受訪者人數不足的問題。雖然如此,這樣的情形,在筆者心中留下了一個疑問,並思考他們會「害羞」的原因為何。到達班達亞齊之後,開始進行調查與訪問的頭幾天,梁校長夫婦繼續幫忙詢問是否有客家女性願意接受訪問,也親自帶筆者到一位經營男性服裝店的女性家中詢問,結果在她的店裡等了一個多鐘頭,中間二度請她的小孩轉達來意,但遲遲不見蹤影。第二天,梁校長夫人陳慧珍女士再度致電詢問該位女士的意願,仍無回音,因此作罷(2011年11月14日田野筆記)。雖然之前已被梁校長夫婦告知尋找研究對象的困難,但是此一經驗更加深了筆者原來的疑問,同時愈加意欲探索造成如此現象的原因究竟為何。與此形成對比的個人研究經驗則是在2011年8月前往西加里曼丹[7]研究印尼客家人口居多的山口洋之客家人改信伊斯蘭教的情形與過程[8],在與當地的客家人接觸過程則無此問題。當時

---

6 這位女士最後同意接受訪談。

7 印尼西加里曼丹位處婆羅洲(Borneo)南部,另外婆羅洲北部為馬來西亞領土,中間在馬來西亞沙巴(Sabah)與砂拉越(Sarawak)之間則屬汶萊(Burnei)。

8 山口洋為西加里曼丹島的第二大城,閩粵華人移民到當地開發採礦的時間約為十八世紀中期之後。根據

是由印尼華人穆斯林組織DEWAN PIMPINAN DAERAH, PEMBINA IMAN TAUHID ISLAM（以下簡稱PITI）[9] 山口洋分部負責人在當天（2011年8月3日）除了本身接受訪問之外，還安排三位男性受訪者，與此同時，也替筆者找到一對改信伊斯蘭教的夫妻並在第二天進行訪談。兩相對照之下，在尋找研究對象的過程方面，山口洋與班達亞齊代表著不同的研究經驗，也因為之前的山口洋經驗，值得深入思考的是，班達亞齊客家女性改宗者難尋的背後所隱藏的意涵究竟為何？

　　此外，與研究對象難尋相關的問題則是訪談對象人數過少，此亦引發筆者對本研究是否能夠繼續進行的疑慮，然而以Mak Lau-Fong的觀點來說，這是一個普遍遭遇到的困難（Mak, 2002: 252）。在他有關探究新加坡華人改宗者與馬來人穆斯林之間的族群關係研究中提到受訪者的資料與背景時，他指出研究對象的資料與數量不足是導致一些探究具種族間通婚或收養經驗的華人穆斯林研究（The, 1993; Hitchcock, 1996: 68; Ma, 2000）無法建構出細緻架構的原因；此外，由於華人穆斯林不願意視自己為華人，因此面臨一個如何定義華人穆斯林的問題（Amran, 1985: 72; Suryadinata, 1997: 189-194）。除非是由相關官方或準官方組織進行的調查，否則研究對象的人數是很難令人滿意的。更具體言之，Mak以Winzeler (1983) 與Tan Husim (1988) 的研究為例，他們的研究對象分別為五個與九個，而Mak本身的研究則有十

2007年統計資料，山口洋市人口約有197,079人，比例上占62%的華人，又稱唐人，構成該市主要人口，其次為馬來人與達雅人，該地係為東南亞中少有以客家話為華人通行語言的地區。由於在2007年12月19日就職的市長黃少凡為該市首位華裔市長，因此該市較過去多增添了華人文化氣氛，例如舉行全市元宵燈節遊行，此外，該市又於2010年與台灣桃園縣楊梅市結為姊妹市，由此可見山口洋市因為行政首長的族裔背景，而使得客家文化得以更加發揚光大。在有「千廟之城」稱號的山口洋，除了如大伯公、關帝、媽祖及觀音等傳統民間信仰之外，尚有基督教、天主教信仰以及伊斯蘭教。穆斯林人數則約計千人，其中華人約占400人。當地規模最大的清真寺於1813年興建。至於伊斯蘭教何時傳入山口洋，則可暫時從西加里曼丹所在的婆羅洲地區的伊斯蘭化時間粗估。該地區約於十六世紀初開始伊斯蘭化，且到了1600年左右，婆羅州海岸地區大致已伊斯蘭化（林長寬，2009: 15）。由於山口洋位居西加里曼丹的西北海岸，若從上述資料，可間接推算山口洋應於十七世紀初開始接受伊斯蘭化，但是為求謹慎，伊斯蘭教傳入山口洋的確切時間仍待考證。

9 總部設於印尼爪哇島東北部的泗水（Surabaya）。

一位。

　　初步推斷研究對象之所以難尋的主要原因在於東南亞國家華人對伊斯蘭普遍存有的刻板印象，施堅雅（William Skinner）（1960）也曾提到在爪哇的華人鮮少有受到伊斯蘭教的吸引，其中一個原因則是華人認為伊斯蘭教是低下的（Mak, 2002: 226）[10]。當然這樣的情況不單單只發生在東南亞國家，2001年 911事件更是加深一般非穆斯林對伊斯蘭原本就已存在的負面觀感，進而在穆斯林與恐怖份子之間畫上等號。伊斯蘭教亦常因其針對女性的行為與衣著有所嚴格規定，而讓其保守、壓制與迫害女性的形象深刻地留在世人腦海之中。此外，再加上西方媒體一再地複製並向全世界放送「恐怖份子」、「暴力」、「有違婦女人權」、「製造問題者」等印象，因此，長此以往，伊斯蘭已被同質化為單一形象。[11] 然深究其因則是西方文明自啟蒙時期所建構出的現代性之中所隱含的西方與非西方二元對立觀點，以及淪為西方殖民地的歷史經驗，因而致使穆斯林被本質化為「他者」（蔡源林，2011: iii）。不過，值得注意的是，在西方將伊斯蘭建構為「他者」的過程中，學術研究扮演著不可或缺的角色，以薩依德（Edward Said）（1979）觀點來看，伊斯蘭世界自拿破崙入侵埃及（1798）之後所極力促成的「東方學」研究是使伊斯蘭世界與文化陷入「東方主義」的建構當中之主因。[12] 鑑於上述因素，大部分改信伊斯蘭教者不易獲得原來所處的家庭、社會網絡正面回應，即使被接受，亦須經過一段較長的時間之後甫獲認可。不論是如馬來西亞、新加坡、印尼等東南亞國家的華人（例如Mak, 2002；陳欣慧，2007；邱炫元，2011），或是西方社會中的西方女性，如德國（Hofmann 1997）、

---

10 另一原因為伊斯蘭教的排他性格。因為對華人而言，信仰伊斯蘭教意味著要嚴格遵守教義規定，獨尊真神阿拉，造成斷絕與原來華人文化關係。此外，由於如馬來西亞或印尼華人長期以來受到穆斯林主政優勢之壓迫，因此若信仰伊斯蘭教則被視為背叛華人之舉。

11 阿克巴‧阿赫美德（Akbar S. Ahmed）在其《今日的伊斯蘭：穆斯林世界導論》（2003）中明確指出穆斯林敗於西方媒體所大量傳遞的負面形象（Ahmed, 2003: 278-290）。

12 詳細討論請參閱蔡源林（2011: 4-14）。

美國（McGinty 2006, Haddad 2006）、瑞典（McGinty, 2006）等，在改信伊斯蘭教的過程中總是遭受反對。雖然本研究在初次田野調查中遭遇到尋找改信伊斯蘭教女性的困難，然而這反而因此更加強研究的動機，因為除了上述因對伊斯蘭教的負面刻板印象使然之外，筆者認為，若從性別、宗教、族群的交織將有助於釐清並更進一步深入思考造成這個現象的背後原因究竟為何，同時得以描繪出本研究客家女性改宗者的生命面貌與生活圖像。

Karin van Nieuwkerk在其所主編的 *Women Embracing Islam: Gender and Conversion in the West* (2006) 的導論中即明言：「西方的女性改信伊斯蘭可能會引發敏感的議題。跨越宗教與族群界線通常會破壞傳統規範且可能導致敵意的產生。女性改宗可能甚至挑起更強烈的反應，因為傳統常常將女性建構為族群與宗教界線的象徵。改信伊斯蘭教的女性特別會引起激烈的爭戰，因為性別議題在『伊斯蘭』與『西方』之間的他者性（Otherness）建構是具有重要性的」（2006: 1）。女性改宗者因此特別會受到他人帶有敵意的對待，如同一位荷蘭女性改宗者所言，「人們會瞪著你看，因為他們看到的是一個白人。也許這是他們為何會用帶有侵略性的眼光看你的原因，因為你是種族的背叛者」。在這段導言中所提到的內容正與本研究所欲探討的問題相關，van Nieuwkerk以跨越宗教與族群界線來定位改宗的意涵，同時原本傳統規範亦因此遭受破壞。更甚者，由於女性常被建構為維繫族群與宗教界線的象徵，因此當她們改信其他宗教時，即意味著原來涇渭分明的族群與宗教界線產生鬆動。

在性別與族群的交織關係中，女性因其兼具生物孕育與文化再製能力而被建構為維繫族群命脈的象徵地位，並且標示出自身族群與他群之差異，負有固守族群邊界的任務與責任（Yuval-Davis and Anthias, 1989: 7; Yuval-Davis, 1997: 47）。由於女性具有「生物」上孕育子女的本能，同時被賦予傳遞文化的重責大任，故女性可說是兼具生物上延續生命的再製者，亦為文化的再製者，以此區分我族與他者。然

而，Yuval-Davis 提醒我們，在族群建構過程之中，女性卻處於一個在集體內矛盾的位置，一方面，女人被納入國族主義計畫而且被賦予維繫國族命脈、固守族群邊界的任務與責任；另一方面，卻又被排除在組成國家的人群之外，女性不屬於「我們」，而是被置於客體位置的「他者」（Yuval-Davis, 1997: 47）。在國族計劃中，性別是一個靜態的二分概念，亦即女人是待在家中的家務勞動者並且負有教育未來忠心於國家的公民之責任，而男人則為公民與護衛國家的軍人；如此男女之間的區分呈現的是公私領域間的固定劃分。值得注意的是，有關女性的特定意象是由建立國族的父祖所發明的概念，其意象的建構揭示了帶有民族價值與集體的女性呈現。依南斯拉夫哲學家 Rada Iveković 之見，如此的概念安置了性別秩序及顯露性或性別是相當強而有力且具**規範性**（normative）的概念（Iveković, 2005: 29，強調為 Iveković所加）。性別秩序被置入女性特定意象，同時是一個循環過程——「關於性別的敘事與刻板印象直接被使用來建構社群、國族與國家的意象，反之，社群、國族與國家又將此用以描繪性別」（同上引）。在國族主義論述中，男人是主要的國族行為者，而女人卻被建構為具有象徵性的國族承載者及政治工具，但不被視為國家公民，亦被切斷了與國族行動的直接關聯性（McClintock, 1995: 354）。同樣地，在性別與宗教交錯層面上，女性亦被視為象徵，且被賦予特定價值，以符合宗教論述中的「理想」的女性形象。Vanaja Dhruvarajan (2002) 以女性主義的角度探討女性面對宗教中的父權與不平等所採取的策略中指出，不論男女都需要從宗教所提供的許多滿足社會生活的重要功能之中找到生命意義與生活的目標，宗教也為他們在生命歷程中碰到困難無解的問題與不確定提供解答（Dhruvarajan, 2002: 273-274）。然而，男女卻獲得不同的答案，因為這些宗教是父權制的（同上引：274）。再者，宗教正當化人們在社會階層（social hierarchy）中的位置，並且以自然的規則來解釋並定位（naturalize）人與人之間的社會關係，因之，在以男性為主導的性別階層之下，女

性被放在從屬地位，她們被認為不如男人，身體因為月經與生產而不潔，容易衝動而且在道德上是有問題的，尤其有著無法控制的性衝動，也因為這些女性特質正當化女人在父權家庭與宗教社群內的附屬地位，女人也因而接受自己的低等地位（同上引）。Dhruvarajan認為，如此的不平等不僅經由不斷地複製而一代傳一代，而具有父權特質的宗教之儀式與象徵更有助於養成堅定的信念，認為性別階層（gender hierarchy）是自然且正常的（同上引）。

在諸多與伊斯蘭女性與性別相關研究中，可以看到男性在身體與道德規範方面施加權力控制與壓迫女性（如Accad, 2005; Saadawi, 2005; Imam, 2005; El Guindi, 2005; Odeh, 2005），但也同時觀察到女性並非僅僅是被動的客體而有其能動性（如Safa-Isfahani, 2005; Murray, 2005），這呼應了Susan Starr Sered的觀點，她認為當我們在分析宗教體系中的性別時，了解兩個在本體論上不同的議題是相當重要的，亦即，作為行動主體的女人（women as agents）與作為象徵的女人（Woman as symbol）（Sered, 1999: 194）。首先，women[13]意謂著真實存在的人，在特定社會情況內有不同程度的能動性。作為行動主體的女人可以要求權利、與他人協商並且抗議不公平的對待。若以宗教來說，則表示女性能夠自由地表達自己的宗教需求，以開放的心態和其他心靈相通的人一起舉行儀式，而且可以自由地選擇（不）參加儀式：其次，Woman是融合了性別、性及性慾特質之象徵構造物（a symbolic construct），並包含寓意、意識形態、隱喻、幻想以及（至少在由男性主導的宗教）男性心理投射。雖然Woman可能在women的真實經驗中少有基礎，但在宗教的互動上，這兩個在本體論上不同的概念趨於融合。作為象徵的女人常常與宗教傳統中一些最深沉、最具強迫性的、最牢不可破的神學與神話結構有關，而這些結構在那些

---

13 因作者分別以women表示作為行動主體的女人（women as agents），用Woman表示作為象徵的女人（Woman as symbol），並具有特定意涵，因此以大寫單數形式表示，但在中文中較難簡短明確的表達作者原意，因此以原文表示。

傳統中的女人的生活留下印記（同上引）。Sered進一步指出，常常在象徵與能動性（即Woman與women）模糊不清的交會點上，我們會看到對女性最密切的控制，以及因控制而產生的衝突，從父權制度的觀點來看，women 是有問題的象徵，因為她們總是會因為變成行動者而產生威脅性（同上引：195）。她以許多中東社會將貞潔（virginity）視為家庭榮耀的重要象徵為例，說明這個象徵會因女性的行動而遭受破壞，因為女性知道自己是行動者，而許多文化皆透過宗教意識形態與儀式來控制女性的身體，以鼓勵或強迫她們將對自己作為象徵的理解內化於心（同上引）。

在分別探討性別與族群、性別與宗教之間的關係及相關案例分析之後，可以看到這兩組關係中的共同之處在於性別的階層化，亦即女性在由男性主導的國族、族群或宗教的建構過程中，往往被標示為代表群體完整性的象徵以及維繫傳遞群體價值的承載者，女性因之被「他者化」為客體。然而，從上述部分分析與研究可知，女性並非全然處於被動狀態，而有其能動性與主體性。因此，若要較完整了解本研究中的研究對象如何面對與詮釋成為穆斯林的過程中所經歷的性別、族群與宗教的相互交錯，則必須觀察她們既為Woman又為women的身分，如此方能掘深改信過程中所牽涉的複雜面向。更甚者，筆者認為「相互交錯性」概念能夠結合性別、族群與宗教這三個不同形式的差異，因此可以提供本研究進一步深化探究印尼亞齊客家女性在改信伊斯蘭教的經驗的概念架構與理論依據。

「相互交錯性」有助於我們了解各種不同的社會類別——如性別、種族、階級、族群、國籍、殘障、性慾特質等如何交織。「相互交錯性」被運用在各種不同的情境與脈絡，但大部分是在女性權利與平權範疇當中[14]（Bradley, 2007: 190）。這個概念係由美國法學家Kim-

---

14 一般說來，性別研究者與女性主義者將相互交錯性運用在分析受壓迫且位居社會邊緣的女性的社會位置，但在2009年1月22-23日於法蘭克福大學所舉辦的國際研討會Celebrating Intersectionality? Debates on a Multi-faceted Concept in Gender Studies的發表論文中，可看到相互交錯性已開始將焦點放置在男性及陽剛

berlé Crenshaw於1989年的"Demarginalizing the Intersection of Race and Sex: A Black Feminist Critique of Antidiscrimination Doctrine, Feminist Theory and Antiracist Politics"[15] 中提出，探討美國有色人種種族與性別交錯的方式，在其後續的"Mapping the Margins: Intersectionality, Identity Politics, and Violence against Women of Color" (1995) 持續探討相同的主題，然重點特別放置在看待有色人種女性所遭受到的暴力對待時的種族與性別面向。此概念主要有助於解決僅從單一角度看性別與種族所引發的問題，因為在性別研究當中，性別被視為具有多樣性的內涵，亦即男女為不同的類別，同時同一性別分類之中亦有內部差異，然而當性別與種族交錯之時，僅察覺到性別的異質面向但卻將種族視為同質單一分類。

聯合國女性與人權工作小組在2001年所舉行的第45屆女性地位委員會會議（The Commission on the Status of Women, CSW）[16] 中將「相互交錯性」概念作以下定義：

> 分析被邊緣化的女性之相互交錯途徑嘗試捕捉兩種或多種以上壓迫形式交錯的影響。它所處理的是種族主義、父權制度、階級壓迫及其他歧視體系創造出結構化女性的相對位置、種族、族群、階級等之不平等的方式……因其種族身分而受到壓迫的女性常常處於種族主義或仇外情緒、階級與性別相交之處。她們因此容易遭受到所有不平等形式所匯集而成的傷害。

Crenshaw將相互交錯歧視喻為「十字路口」（2003），這個比喻相當

氣質，例如Dubravka Zarkov之 "Exposures, invisibilities, vulnerabilities: Master narratives of war and masculinities in an intersectional perspective"，Jeff Hearn之 "Neglected intersectionalities in studying men: age/ing, virtuality, transnationality"以及Mechthild Bereswill之"Theorizing masculinity in the perspective of intersectionality"。

15 本篇文章原刊載於University of Chicago Legal Forum，但本研究中所參考的版本則取自於1993年出版的Feminist Legal Theory: Foundations。

16 舉行時間為2001年3月6-16日以及 2001年5月9-11日。

貼切地呈現出上述定義所蘊藏的涵意，亦即各種形式的歧視同時交錯在一個少數弱勢的個人或群體之上。從以上定義觀之，「相互交錯性」所處理的是因各種不同制度、體系、主義而起的歧視，這導致壓迫、邊緣化與無權力的多重形式。需要注意的是，相互交錯的歧視並非將各種歧視分開看待，而是一個人或一個團體所遭逢的各式不同並特定的歧視經驗。例如英國社會學者Harriet Bradley與Geraldine Healy在其合著的*Ethnicity and Gender at Work. Inequalities, Careers and Employment Relations* 中針對黑人與少數族群女性在英國勞動市場的工作經驗之探究即為一例（2008）。Bradley在其*Gender* (2007) 中表示相互交錯之概念因此相當於她所稱的「多重位置」及「多重劣勢」（Bradley, 2007: 190）。她接著提出，「相互交錯性」概念有三點需注意的：一、只觀看劣勢的單一面向，可能會扭曲並且遮掩其他形式的壓迫；二、在任何一個已知的脈絡下，不同的社會變化應同樣有其效用；三、各種不同形式的交錯可能會產生最極端的剝削及歧視（Bradley, 2007: 190f.; Bradley and Healy, 2008: 45）。相互交錯之概念主要是運用在探究個人或團體在社會關係中所經驗的多重不平等、壓迫及劣勢。不同形式的差異在各種不同的情況被賦予不同的比重。例如，女性的認同在性別過程中建構，而這個過程在某種程度上變化，由種族或族群背景、性別導向、殘障或宗教來決定（參閱Bradley and Healy, 2008: 46）。

「相互交錯性」概念強調的是複雜性，然而並非所有的類別，如性別、種族、族群性、性慾特質、階級、殘障、國籍都需要提及，但是哪些類別是重要的，且對誰來說是重要的，都是學者持續討論的問題（Knudsen, 2005: 63）。大部分學者都注意到性別、種族及／或族群的交錯，或是著重於性別、階級與族群。但德國學者Helma Lutz與Norbert Wenning在其合編的*Unterschiedlich verschieden. Differenz in der Erziehungswissenschaft*（不同的差異——教育學中的差異）（2001）的導論中列出多達十三項二元對立的差異，計有性別（男—女）、性慾

特質（異性—同性）、「種族」／膚色（白—黑）、族群（優勢主導群體—少數群體）、民族／國家（成員—非成員）、階級（上—下）、文化（文明—非文明）、健康（非殘障—殘障）、年齡（成年人—小孩、年長—年輕）、居住／出身（定居—移居、原生—移民）、財富（富有—貧窮）、南北／東西差異（西方—世界其他地區）、社會發展狀況（現代—傳統、進步—落後）（Lutz and Wenning, 2001: 20）。上述如此多種的類別所呈現的是無止盡的差異，然而現在大多以「等等」（etc.）加在幾個類別之後，但Judith Butler卻嘲弄如此的「等等」表達方式正顯現出「耗盡的標示以及意義本身無邊際的過程」（Butler, 1990: 143）。

那麼我們到底該如何來決定選擇哪些類別以及認定哪些類別是與研究相關的，而哪些又將被省略掉而以「等等」取代之？德國學者 Katharina Walgenbach認為這些會受到以下因素影響（Walgenbach, 2007: 42-44）：首先，歷史、地理、政治與文化因素需考量在內。例如，在非洲，由於年齡是獲得聲譽與能夠發揮影響力的資源，因此受到重視。其次，研究興趣亦是決定類別比重的因素之一。另外，類別順序亦是另一個需考量的問題，這可能會受到分析目的的影響，或因個人生命經驗而對不同的類別有不同的感受度。「相互交錯性」概念所關注的焦點會隨著不同的社會脈絡而有所差異，這也是學者始終關注的問題（例如Brah and Phoenix, 2004；Yuval-Davis, 2006）。大部分都關注在性別、種族與階級之交錯（Yuval-Davis, 2006: 193），但若細究，將會發現因國家與歷史發展而有所不同，例如在美國脈絡之下，美籍非裔女性主義者強調的是種族與性別，藉以強調在美國社會的性別主義與種族主義，而因研究的對象為貧窮與邊緣的有色人種，因此階級的類別已經隱含在理論的運用與分析當中（Crenshaw, 1995）；在北歐國家之中，所著重的類別為性別、族群與性慾特質（Knudsen, 2005: 63）。除此之外，觀察的角度亦不同。在荷蘭荷洛琳恩大學（University of Groningen）任教的Baukje Prins在其"Narrative Accounts of

Origins. A Blind Spot in the Intersectional Approach?" (2006) 中指出，美國研究者的關注焦點在於支配體系系統性地忽略邊緣團體（例如美國黑人女性）的經驗，認為認同的形塑受到體系或結構的影響，是為體系之「相互交錯性」概念（systemic intersectionality），在此觀點下的主體因此在認同上較無選擇的餘地；然而英國學者所著重的是從動態與關係取向來分析被壓迫群體的社會位置與認同，其被稱之為建構主義式之「相互交錯性」概念（constructionist intersectionality），並聚焦於一個特定的認同如何受到其他認同的影響，例如性別受到族群性與階級的影響（Prins, 2006）。雖然英美皆反對以本質主義的觀點來看待認同的形成，但是上述分類顯得過於絕對，且遭受北歐國家的性別研究與女性主義學者的批評，認為這樣的分類未將正逐漸興起的北歐研究包括在內（Phoenix and Pattynama, 2006: 188）。

　　前述英美與北歐的「相互交錯性」概念的觀察角度與放置重點因社會脈絡而不同，讓我們注意到這個概念背後所根植的特殊歷史、意識形態、制度、社會、文化與國家脈絡，同時也顯現出其為跨越國界與社會文化之「傳播中的概念」（a travelling concept）之特質（參閱Lewis, 2009）。以本文中的改信伊斯蘭教的客家女性為例，若要分析在此脈絡之下的由性別、族群與宗教構成的「相互交錯性」概念，我們則必須將研究對象所處的歷史、政治、社會環境結構納入考慮，整體來說，這個問題和華人在印尼的地位密切相關。華人（ethnic Chinese）算是印尼最大的非原住民族群，占總人口2億3,000萬的3%（Leinbach and Ulack, 2009: 22），約合690萬人。印尼華人大多來自於中國廣東、福建與海南省，主要集中於爪哇、蘇門答臘、加里曼丹、蘇拉威西、巴厘島，較多華人的城市計有雅加達、萬隆、泗水、茂物、棉蘭、巴東、巨港、坤甸、馬辰、巴理巴板、萬鴉老、登巴薩與安汶（梁敏和、孔遠志，2002: 35）。早在歐洲人抵達印尼之前，華人足跡已踏遍印尼沿海城市與貿易據點，在荷蘭統治時期，大力支持華人到印尼從事種植與開礦，因此人口數從1860年的8,908人增至

1930年的115,535人（Leinbach and Ulack, 2009: 22）。華人雖然在印尼已有久遠的居住歷史，但由於僅是印尼境內超過三百個族群的其中之一，而且也始終被視為「外國人」，因此可說華人在印尼是身處邊緣的（參考Coppel, 2005: 1）。這也是為何長期研究印尼的澳洲學者Charles A. Coppel (2005) 將自己從事與印尼華人相關的研究定位為「研究邊緣」（"researching the margins"）。Coppel認為許多印尼華人被邊緣化，同時也在本身的生活經驗中受到周遭社會的排擠（同上引）。不論是在荷蘭統治時期的法律標示為「外國東方人」（"Foreign Orientals"）[17]，或在印尼法律中為「外國血統」（"of foreign descent"）以及非「當地」的（"indigenous"），即使許多華人「返回」自己所認為的母國，但依舊被視為「外國人」而受到與當地人不同的待遇（同上引）。簡言之，印尼華人從荷蘭統治時期開始在政治、社會大環境下受到歧視與排斥，最嚴重者則慘遭殺害（如1965年930事件），雖然直到2006年印尼政府頒布公民資格法律（Law on Citizenship of Indonesia, 2006）對華人受歧視問題才有真正制度上的突破（Winarta, 2008），但是長期以來的排華政策，對於本文研究對象與其他族群互動與關係上還是具有某種程度的衝擊，而這些巨觀脈絡下的壓迫與歧視亦會影響研究對象在改信過程中所遭逢的認同建構經驗。

四、成為穆斯林——改宗經驗之探究

上述以性別、族群與宗教之相互交錯現象以及「相互交錯性」概

---

17 荷蘭殖民政府時期，因隨著白人大型企業的到來與其快速發展，他們不得不用經營公司規模較小的華商作為中介商，1854年確立華人以「外國東方人」的身分做為介於歐洲白人與土著之間的中間階層。以伐木業為例，華人雖然規模不如白人大企業，但木材實際上卻由華人控制，此外，華人又勤於勞動，致使當地以農為生的土著生活惡化，在此情形下，華人成為白人與土著交相遷怒與指摘的對象（李恩涵，2003: 318）。

念作為探究印尼亞齊客家女性改信伊斯蘭教經驗與過程的概念架構與理論依據。接下來的分析將以在亞齊蒐集的田野資料作為闡描客家女性改宗經驗之基礎，期以具體與前述理論進行對話並呈現與改宗相關議題。然實有先行提供四位研究對象基本資料之必要，俾利讀者獲悉其背景（見下頁表格）。

根據筆者的田野經驗，發現難以尋找改信伊斯蘭教的客家女性，初步推論係因一般華人對伊斯蘭教與亞齊人抱有負面刻板印象。在和研究對象接觸之後，更從其親友對她們改信的反應中，確認前述原因。例如美英由於父親在她兩歲時過世，母親改嫁穆斯林，後由伯父母扶養長大，因此當她決定要改宗時，只在意伯父母與堂哥們的意見，只有伯母持反對態度，所以每當伯母看見美英時，就會一直碎念，「為什麼華人要信伊斯蘭教？」（與美英於2011年11月13日在大亞齊縣進行的訪談）。雲真因結婚改信時，亦遭其他華人非議，而且會一直在她背後說壞話，他們會問「為什麼要嫁給亞齊人？為什麼要信伊斯蘭教？」在亞齊華人心中，亞齊人很髒、養不起家庭、嫁給他們地位變低（與雲真於2011年11月13日在班達亞齊進行的訪談）。萍華在第二次婚姻嫁給穆斯林時，父母皆已不在人世，只有阿姨是較親近的長輩。因此要改信時，徵詢阿姨的意見，亦遭反對。阿姨並責罵她，「沒有想到妳的父母，如果妳父母還在，他們也會反對」。萍華認為「如果父母在，她會考慮，但是父母已經不在了，不需考慮」。她更向阿姨明白表示，「你們要考慮我的感受」（與萍華於2011年11月14日在班達亞齊進行的訪談）。改信之後的經驗更是負面，朋友鄰居看不起她，她也因此不和他們來往。與此相對的經驗則是萍華在婚後與穆斯林丈夫曾搬到一個沒有華人的島上居住長達兩年，感到快樂無比（同上引）。

由上述改信者所受到的質疑，可以看到性別、族群與宗教以不同的方式相互交錯。例如「為什麼華人要信伊斯蘭教？」「為什麼要嫁給亞齊人？」「為什麼要信伊斯蘭教？」這一連串的為什麼意味著在

華文名字[18] / 伊斯蘭名	玉芬 / 仍使用印尼名 Mariana	雲真 / Cahaya Malam	美英 / Siti Rahmah	萍華 / N.A.
族群身分	客家	客家	客家	客家
年齡[19]	34	27	42	32
改宗年齡 / 時間	25/ 2002	20/ 2004	25/ 1995	27/ 2006
所屬伊斯蘭組織	Nahdlatul Ulama[20]	Nahdlatul Ulama	Nahdlatul Ulama	Nahdlatul Ulama
原來信仰 / 參與程度	佛教 / 到寺廟拜拜	佛教 / 拜拜與學習念經、打木魚	佛教 / 到寺廟拜拜	佛教 / 到寺廟拜拜
婚姻狀態	已婚	已婚	已婚 為第二個太太	已婚
配偶	亞齊人	亞齊人	亞齊人	第一任丈夫：華人；第二任丈夫：亞齊人
小孩	兩女	一女	無	第一段婚姻有一兒一女，與現任丈夫生一兒
教育程度	高中 （天主教學校畢業）	高中 （一般國民學校）	高中 （天主教學校畢業）	高中 （華人衛理學校畢業）
職業	商店員工	家庭主婦	自營雜貨店	早上幫妹妹賣早餐、平日與丈夫經營賣蒜頭生意
目前居住區域	班達亞齊大愛村	班達亞齊伊斯蘭區	大亞齊縣伊斯蘭區	班達亞齊唐人街

---

18 名字已由筆者變更，以保護受訪者隱私。

19 以訪問時間2011年為準。

20 該組織為印尼最大的伊斯蘭組織，在印尼相當龐大，會員約有4,000萬人，該組織朝向年輕化發展，在蘇哈托（Suharto）時期扮演重要的社會與教育角色（資料來源：前台北清真大寺伊斯哈格，馬孝棋教長，2011年12月10日於台北清真大寺訪談；Bell, 2004: 36）。

改信者家人的眼中，族群（華人）與宗教（伊斯蘭教）無法相容，族群間（華人與亞齊人）之間存在一道高牆，華人將亞齊人視為「骯髒、不潔、經濟能力薄弱、地位低等」的他者，身為女性，因為與被自身所屬族群「他者化」的亞齊人通婚，跨越「原本被認為應該清楚分隔」的界線，而且受到長輩以「沒有想到妳的父母」字句的責備，「嫁給亞齊人」隱含背宗忘祖之意，有違擔負傳承族群文化責任之角色。與亞齊人通婚，並改變宗教信仰，致使這些女性遭受周遭華人的蔑視，如「看不起」、「閒話非議」等具體作為實然根植於華人對改信女性在性別、族群、宗教，甚而是階級（經濟能力差）方面的交錯歧視。這裡值得注意的是，被研究對象所指「族群」為「華人」，而非客家。由於早期的東南亞客家認同可說是如麥留芳（1985）所提出的由操相近方言社群成員心中共享意識所展現的「方言群認同」。地方語言／方言是人們與他者區辨的主要象徵（林開忠、李美賢，2006: 215-216）。而華僑／華人成為涵蓋性的認同[21]的原因在於在華人移民到東南亞的過程中，時逢1910年代中國政治與文化變動，對海外華人在語言、教育上產生的影響，以及中國民族主義的傳播（同上引：219-227）。至於本文所研究的客家女性，在此脈絡下以「華人」作為自己的認同，與「亞齊人」作一對比，此認同可說是客家認同受到在地影響而產生的認同階序、多元面貌與情境性（蕭新煌等，2007；林開忠、李美賢，2006）。

雖有上述對改宗女性的歧視，然而，值得我們探究的是，在如此將伊斯蘭教、文化及其教徒建構為「他者」的環境與情況下，為何這些女性依然決定走向伊斯蘭教，這是本文嘗試回答的一般性問題。這個問題也是目前西方學者研究改信伊斯蘭教的西方女性（如美國、歐洲與南非）所發現的現象，女性改宗者受到較不友善的對待，而信仰

---

21 如筆者在印尼觀察發現，「華人」或「唐人」為聽到最多的自稱，亦為華人集體認同，然而在面對其他方言群的華人，則以屬於次級的方言群認同客家人自稱。

伊斯蘭教的女性形象也一直被（西方）建構為負面、落後、受到壓迫的，但是女性改宗的比率卻遠超過男性，呈現4：1的比例（van Nieuwkerk, 2006: 1）。再者，我們更需要進一步去了解伊斯蘭教如何吸引改宗者，或者是該教有什麼是原來所屬社會、文化與宗教未能滿足改宗者，而使改宗者接受在原來社會環境中被負面看待的宗教。例如，Hofmann (1997)、Wohlrab-Sahr (1999a) 與Allievi (2006) 皆提到西方女性因為受到伊斯蘭教與性別議題相關的教義吸引，尤其是伊斯蘭教義提供改宗者一個如他們祖父母輩時代的穩定的性規範與兩性秩序以及家庭概念，這有助於化解他們因與原來所屬社會不同的價值觀所產生的衝突。然而，對本文的研究對象來說，是否如西方女性在性別方面深受伊斯蘭教吸引，則需要進一步探究。與上述兩個一般性問題相關的是，改宗者的背景為何？在他們的成長過程、家庭背景、學校教育、社會網絡、族群互動與原來的宗教信仰，是何種因素促使他們改變宗教信仰，並接受所有與之相關的社會與宗教實踐。

　　一般說來，大部分非穆斯林華人認為與穆斯林通婚是華人之所以改信伊斯蘭教的主要原因。例如筆者在所參加的「2011 印尼客家工作坊」[22] 與雅加達參訪活動時而有機會與雅加達當地客籍人士（大多為印尼客屬聯誼總會及印尼梅州會館成員）交談，並且針對筆者欲研究的「華人改宗伊斯蘭教」議題，與五位非穆斯林客屬人士進行非正式訪談得到的結論是他們認為通婚是改信伊斯蘭教的主要原因，只有一位提到除了通婚之外，尚有因為改宗者遭遇不幸事件而因伊斯蘭教與其教徒提供援助與安慰而改宗。然而，經由筆者在山口洋與班達亞齊所搜集的實證資料顯示，僅將通婚視為改信的單一因素不免簡化了改宗者的生命歷程、生活經驗與改信伊斯蘭教之間的關係。雖然不可否認在穆斯林占多數的國家如印尼或馬來西亞，穆斯林與非穆斯林之

---

22 該工作坊由印尼客屬聯誼總會、印尼梅州會館、台灣暨南國際大學東南亞研究中心主辦，高雄師範大學協辦，於2011年7月31日假印尼客屬聯誼總會舉行。

間的通婚受到該國法律或伊斯蘭律法的規定或有其需考量的政治層面（Jones et al. 2009），但由於本文著重的是改宗者的經歷，因此將通婚置於個人經驗層面來觀察。以山口洋為例，六位改宗者皆認為是因為他們的人生遭受困難與不幸，而是這些生命挑戰使他們走向伊斯蘭教，除此之外，其中兩位還提到係因夢境而改變了宗教信仰。[23] 雅加達與山口洋研究經驗提供在筆者探討亞齊客家女性改信動機時，會特別注意她們接受伊斯蘭教的原因是否僅與通婚有關抑或是有其他因素。

本研究中的四位研究對象，只有美英不因結婚而改信，她於1995年改信，1997年認識她先生，1998年結婚。她從小住在伊斯蘭區，因此有許多穆斯林鄰居與玩伴，她和他們一起念可蘭經、學習可蘭經而受到潛移默化的影響。雖然如此，她之所以到25歲才改信的原因係因小時候沒有改信的自由與權力，到了18歲以後雖可自己決定，但最終還是需要仔細思考才能決定改信一事（與美英於2011年11月13日在大亞齊縣進行的訪談）。玉芬與雲真雖因結婚而改信，但是在此之前，由於生活環境或在學校與穆斯林鄰居及同學的互動，對伊斯蘭教並不全然陌生，並在互動過程中，有些正面印象，例如穆斯林較樂觀或容易親近（與玉芬於2011年11月12日在班達亞齊進行的訪談；與雲真於2011年11月13日在班達亞齊進行的訪談）。此外，萍華在尚未成為穆斯林之前，曾經到過教堂與清真寺，但卻有截然不同的感覺，在教堂裡隨著讚美上帝的聖歌（halleluiah）聲音愈來愈大而感到不對勁，與之相反地，在清真寺卻因為念經而有著感動的感覺，而且當時她並非教徒，但卻能順暢地念經文，且念完後有安心的感覺（與萍華於2011年11月14日在班達亞齊進行的訪談）。

以上是研究對象改信伊斯蘭教的原因，值得注意的是，若與前述所提及的非穆斯林的看法做一對照，即可發現他們將改宗原因定格於

---

23 2011年8月3日與8月4日在山口洋進行的訪談資料。

某一個時間點——結婚，然而，從研究對象的生命經驗看來，其實改信之前已有與穆斯林的互動，因此整個與改宗原因相關的時間面向是無法單以「結婚」一個獨斷的時間點來涵括的，而必須將促使研究對象接受伊斯蘭教的原因視為由生命歷程所構築而成的過程。這個觀察也呼應著改宗在學術上分析觀點的轉變，有的學者意圖找出改信伊斯蘭教的改宗者之典型（Poston, 1992），有的則是斷定改宗者在改信伊斯蘭教之前遭受生命困境與生活危機（Köse, 1996，轉引自van Nieuwkerk, 2006: 3），或者有的將改宗區分為兩種形式，一為關係改宗（relational conversions），又可細分為工具性（通常所指為歐洲男性與穆斯林女性的婚姻關係，但不一定會發生宗教轉型）與非工具性（因與穆斯林透過婚姻、家庭、移民及旅行建立關係而產生的改宗）；另一種則為與個人人際接觸無關的理性改宗（rational conversions），是因知識追尋而發生（van Nieuwkerk, 2006: 3; Allievi, 2006）。除了上述的分類之外，改宗已逐漸被視為一個持續前進的過程來分析（van Nieuwkerk, 2006: 4），Lewis R. Rambo (1993) 結合不同的學科發展出動態且著重於過程的改宗理論。改宗發生在不同的階段，而且是日常生活的宗教、社會與文化面向發生實質上轉變的經驗，同時，改宗體現在與身體有關的實踐，如祈禱、齋戒、飲食；例如名字與衣著等與認同相關的重要標記也因信仰改變而有不同；發生變化的還包括社會與文化實踐，這通常與節慶，或者和異性的接觸有關（van Nieuwkerk, 2006: 4）。

　　本文研究對象在名字方面改變如上表所示，但是玉芬仍為原來印尼名，而美英在身分證上仍維持原來華文名字。至於衣著部分並非如一般所認知的有著立即明顯的改變，例如雲真在未信仰伊斯蘭教之前，衣著本就趨於保守，與改信之後的差別不大。改宗者也未在改信之後立即戴上頭巾，在訪問雲真時，注意到她家中擺設的照片裡，有一張是她在亞齊公園裡抱著孩子但並未戴頭巾的合影。雲真與其他受訪者皆表示，遇有正式場合才會戴頭巾，而且她認為自己心裡還沒有

準備好，並強調伊斯蘭教並沒有強迫她一定要戴，而與她比鄰而居的婆家家人都可以接受她的決定。玉芬因為老闆為華人，所以她也不會戴頭巾去上班，至於萍華早上要幫忙姐姐在市場賣麵食早餐，煮麵是相當熱的，因此也不會戴頭巾。頭巾向來是西方論述視為穆斯林女性遭受壓迫的象徵，體現宗教之性別階層現象。然而，從研究對象的穿戴頭巾決定與行為得知，原被建構為象徵的女性，因其實踐而瓦解論述所塑造的女性被動受宰制形象。就飲食而言，如美英從小家裡就很少吃豬肉，雲真在未改信之前也很少吃豬肉，因此未有如非穆斯林華人所認定的「改信就不能吃豬肉」的立即變化。宗教實踐方面，最明顯的部分是一天五次的禮拜帶給研究對象生活上顯著的改變，改宗之後不僅內心有著愈來愈安定的感覺，尤其更因為念經文有助於解決生活問題，讓他們的生活愈來愈順遂，因此更加對伊斯蘭教持以肯定態度。例如，玉芬因與失業的丈夫感情不佳，常常吵架，以前曾想過自殺，但後來藉由禮拜而讓自己情緒不受到丈夫的影響。或者如萍華與丈夫所經營的賣蒜頭生意遇到困難，也是藉著祈禱而重獲生機。內心安定的感覺與生活愈趨順利是研究對象最常提及的變化。[24] 在華人節慶方面，四位研究對象仍有參與，例如過年、元宵、清明、端午、中秋，但參與程度不一，她們的穆斯林配偶皆會陪同參加。在參與過程中，也有可能遭受其他穆斯林朋友的反對，例如玉芬的朋友認為她不應該參加華人過年活動，但玉芬告知他們過年是她的文化，她一定要參加。此一情況顯示出改宗者仍將華人文化視為本身所屬文化的一部分。相同的情況，可以在研究對象家中的擺飾看到既有華人的裝飾品，也有屬於伊斯蘭或印尼的擺飾。由此觀之，改宗者並不會因為改信伊斯蘭教而全然捨棄原生文化，此亦意謂族群（華人）與宗教（伊斯蘭）之界線並非如一般論述中所認為的無法跨越。

如上所述，本文研究對象因改宗而發生的變化可見於名字、宗教

---

24 山口洋的研究對象亦提到相同現象。

實踐、行為、服裝、飲食，除此之外，研究發現尚有一個值得注意之處在於因為改宗而引發人際關係的變化，尤其是須面對來自親友的質疑與鄰居的覬覦、如何看待亞齊華人與亞齊人之族群互動，以及比較佛教、基督教、天主教與伊斯蘭教的特質。這些都是伴隨改宗而來的發展，「成為穆斯林並不是真正抵達終點」（McGinty, 2006: 13），而是改宗者原有認知的意義體系或意義模式連結至皈依的宗教，但須特別注意的是，新宗教的意義體系或模式並非取代舊有的，而是原有的結構因改宗而進行重整（Hofmann, 1997: 27-28）。改宗者本身即是創造意義的行動者，因為特殊的改宗經驗及記憶讓他們重新思考過去的行為並賦予意義於新的實踐，在此過程中，認知、感受與情緒亦包含在內。同時，改宗者藉由帶有主體性、情緒及渴望的不同想法與知識連結到特定記憶來內化與了解伊斯蘭教，他們被連結到來自孩童時期、青少年時期或更晚的時期之特定重要的想法及情緒經驗，且被由改宗過程所獲得的穆斯林想法與新的經驗加強或修正（McGinty, 2006: 10）。此外，改宗不是只有心理層面，還涉及社會實踐與宗教實踐。在實踐與學習新的行為時，新的想法與洞見會創造出來，在改宗者不同階段的生活中，修正過的與新的論述可以產生意義。

在班達亞齊進行的田野調查中，初步發現上述因為改宗而產生的意義體系結構重整現象展現在本文研究對象對原有的行為、所屬文化、族群與宗教實踐加以批判，然以正面態度肯定現有的伊斯蘭信仰、實踐與人際互動。例如四位研究對象皆同時都指出在改宗之前所信仰的佛教或所念經文，只知盲從祭拜，但無法得知意義，然而，相形之下，伊斯蘭經文會相當清楚說明祈禱與經文意義，並解釋用途。同時從改信伊斯蘭教的過程中比較出華人與亞齊人的不同之處，他們認為華人較勢利，交朋友以對方的背景與富裕程度為考量，不會互相幫忙，而伊斯蘭教講求平等、互助合作、向需要幫助的人伸出援手。或者如雲真所提到的，華人會依對象而有不同的應對態度，例如雲真的婆家家人生病，需要吃藥，則請她到位於唐人街內的華人藥鋪去買

藥，因為老闆是不會把中藥賣給穆斯林的。研究對象對華人的負面看法又因隨著他們改信伊斯蘭教而更加深，因為一般華人對伊斯蘭教及其信徒帶有普遍的偏見與刻板印象，所以研究對象可以感受到其他華人對她們嫁給信奉伊斯蘭教的亞齊人並隨之改宗是抱持著負面觀感，以及閒言閒語。因此對研究對象而言，並非亞齊人討厭華人，而是華人本身先築起高牆排斥信奉伊斯蘭教的亞齊人，例如從與梁校長家人的相處過程以及與四位受訪女性言談中皆可獲悉華人與亞齊人的族群關係是不融洽的，同時是帶有偏見的。例如亞齊穆斯林女孩安妮[25] 和梁家去Lampuuk海邊出遊，碰到梁家的華人朋友，梁校長介紹安妮留學台灣，已經畢業回到班達亞齊教華文，但是他們的異樣眼光讓安妮感到相當不舒服。此外，根據梁校長的觀察，華人自視甚高並且高傲，覺得亞齊人又髒又懶。而這點與一般華人的看法有很大的出入，因為在一般華人論述與認知當中，亞齊人排華，對華人不友善，或甚至會以暴力對待。

　　上述的情形說明改宗並非只涉及宗教信仰的改變，還有改宗者的社會與族群認同也會重新建構，而這些新的認同又體現在新的身體實踐，如前所述的祈禱、飲食與齋戒；意義體系結構也因改變宗教信仰而重整。此外，我們也需要注意到的是，改信伊斯蘭教在表面上看來似乎是改宗者接受了伊斯蘭教的教義、規範、行為規定以及新的世界觀，然而，事實上，改宗者卻是在原來的以及新接受的宗教與文化之間來回擺盪，這可從上述本文研究對象如何與原來華人文化的連結以及家中擺飾中得到印證。Monika Wohlrab-Sahr (1999b) 在"Conversion to Islam: Between Syncretism and Symbolic Battle"提出，西方的改宗是與結構相關（structurally relevant）的，因為它有著由下列兩個要素所構成的雙重框架（double frame）：改宗者背離但仍然有關聯的宗教與文化，以及他們新選擇的世界觀，但卻無法完全認同的。作者認為這

---

25 名字已由筆者變更，以保護受訪者隱私。

雙重框架與在其中所引發的緊張對了解西方脈絡下的改宗是極具重要的，同時，它意味著改宗者在自己的社會脈絡下融入與區隔的問題。因此，新接受的宗教變成在自己的社會脈絡之內啟動與這個脈絡的距離之方法，同時與自己的社會脈絡的關係是具衝突性質的（Wohlrab-Sahr, 1999b: 52）。雖然Wohlrab-Sahr以西方為理解改宗的宏觀脈絡，但若以本文身處印尼的研究對象來說，研究對象的確是背離原有的宗教與文化，然仍有關連，亦的確如Wohlrab-Sahr所言是與自己的社會脈絡有著衝突關係，但是在初步研究中發現他們卻是極度認同所選擇的新的世界觀，這點和Wohlrab-Sahr的看法不同，筆者推論原因可能在於這四位改宗者的改信時間並不長，本文中的四位改宗女性除了美英改宗已有十七年的時間之外，其餘都未超過十年。根據Roald (2006) 針對斯堪地那維亞移民脈絡下之改信伊斯蘭教女性的研究，發現她們經過三個階段，分別是「愛」、「失望」與「成熟」：在改信初期，在情緒上相當受到新的宗教吸引並實踐伊斯蘭訓誡的每一個細節；第二個階段則因對原來就信仰伊斯蘭教的穆斯林的信念與行為感到失望，因此傾向於遠離伊斯蘭教；第三階段則根據改宗者自己的特定文化脈絡重新理解伊斯蘭教的理念。

五、結論：未完成的探索之路

本文嘗試以性別、族群與宗教相互交錯的過程中分析印尼亞齊客家女性改信伊斯蘭教的原因、經驗與認同建構。本文雖以探索印尼亞齊客家女性改信伊斯蘭教的過程為主，並著重改宗女性在改宗過程個人經驗的探索，以及她們對於選擇伊斯蘭教的觀點與行為，但這並不表示本文忽視外在結構的影響，因為同時分析個人內在的心路歷程與外在所處社會位置之間的關係，才能解決本文於前言所提出的問題以及背後隱藏的意涵。然而，由於本文屬初探性質，再加上田野停留時間短暫，因此還有一些關於改宗者的認同建構過程問題尚須釐清，因

為改宗牽涉一個持續進行的意義建構過程，亦即改宗者如何理解自己的改宗行為，又如何看待因為改宗所引發的認同與生活變化，以及他們如何被歸類（McGinty, 2006），這些可以從「自我」、族群與性別認同的變化來觀察。

首先，「自我」作為探索改宗者的認同建構之起始點，由於改宗會引發一連串與自我相關的問題，如「自己現在是誰？過去是誰？現在該走向何處？自我如何改變？」（McGinty, 2006: 6）。在本研究中的萍華曾提及自己的改變，過去的她是個安靜的人，在第一段婚姻中默默承受華人丈夫施暴，曾兩度自殺未遂，但現在的她，變得較會表達自己的意見，不再忍受別人對她說項。但是這個自我的變化，是因為信仰伊斯蘭教的關係，或是與第二任穆斯林丈夫互動之下產生的變化，抑或是有其他的原因，這都是需要繼續探究的面向。

其次，個人自我認同的建構又與外在所處世界具有密切的關係，因此改宗者所在的外在社會環境則需要密切觀照。與本文研究對象相關的社會環境則是由不同族群所組成，亦即族群互動成為日常生活的一部分，互動對象包括婆家家庭成員、繼父或繼母（例如玉芬的繼母，美英的繼父）、鄰居、同學、同事、客戶、傭人、或因購物、辦事所接觸到的非華人，發生的場域則在家庭、鄰里、學校、市場、公務機關。然在探討研究對象的族群認同時，必須要先釐清研究對象如何自稱，因為依據筆者的研究經驗，在雅加達客屬總會的成員以華人或客家人自稱，然而在山口洋與班達亞齊則多聽到以唐人自稱，當他們須與其他祖籍為福建、海南區分時，較會自稱為客家人。但是在當地客家人的認知中，僅以語言作為族群的區分，至於何為客家文化，事實上是沒有太清楚的概念與定義，例如筆者在進行訪談時，以「客家文化」為問題作為了解研究對象與原生文化的關係，然而受訪者不知何為客家文化。除了受訪者之外，一般客家人如梁校長夫人與女兒也表示她們對何謂客家文化毫無概念，而是透過台灣的客家文化形塑才慢慢知道何為客家文化的內涵，例如客家花布。當然，這並不全然

意謂客家文化不存在，而其文化實踐或許已成為日常生活的一部分，故可在後續的研究中，從日常生活實踐與慣習中描繪出印尼亞齊客家文化的內涵。因此，我們仍然必須認可他們的客家人身分，然而，至於該以何種族群身分來標示研究對象，同時還有研究對象自己在何時、何種情境下、和誰互動時如何自我認同，都需要仔細探究與討論。此外，族群認同的議題涉及到研究對象與原來文化的關係，例如是否會繼續過原屬華人的節慶、參與程度如何，而與節慶相關的問題則有他們的配偶是否會參加，參與程度如何，雖然這些問題在前面都已略提，但是研究對象是否扮演原生文化與伊斯蘭文化之間的橋樑則是本研究應該繼續深入的問題，因為這亦涉及改宗者在族群與文化上如何定位自己。

最後，在與性別有關的認同部分，本文的研究對象大多提及在伊斯蘭文化的性別分工應為女性照顧家中，男性出外工作賺錢，但是對筆者所接觸到的四位客家女性之中，只有雲真是家庭主婦，房租為其收入來源，同時可從她家中的擺設與小孩玩具數量看出生活寬裕。其他三位都需工作，其中玉芬更是一天工作十二個鐘頭，萍華更是提到伊斯蘭教徒會讓女性待在家中，而華人男性較希望妻子一同工作賺錢，另外玉芬也提到伊斯蘭教是很注重與尊重女性。這裡伊斯蘭教對待女性的方式與意涵，實可在未來的研究中與客家文化中的性別關係比較並對照，因為在實際的狀況中，須兼顧家庭與工作的被研究對象，可說是家中完全的勞動者。在與客家相關的論述、研究、大眾觀點與媒體呈現中，客家女性向來與極具正面意涵的勤儉能幹、吃苦耐勞的勞動形象相連，同時被形塑為「全能」與「神聖化」的樣貌（李文玫，2011: 39）。囊括客家女性全面性的婦工內涵之「四頭四尾」則是建構這些形象與樣貌的要素：「田頭地尾」——家庭經濟生產活動的參與、「家頭教尾」——家族人際關係的經營、「灶頭鍋尾」——家人飲食／生存的維持、以及「針頭線尾」——女工的訓練與才能（同上引：44）。至於如何比較與對照，需要在後續研究中更縝密

思考，以釐清改宗之客家女性在改宗前如何看待與經驗客家文化中的性別關係，而在改宗後，又如何受到伊斯蘭教教義與實踐的影響，則可加以深入探討。此外，研究對象尚未以更多具體的實例說明伊斯蘭教與文化中如何建構男性概念（manhood）、女性概念（womam-hood）、陽剛特質（masculinity）、陰柔特質（femininity）、父職（fatherhood）、母職（motherhood）與家庭概念。根據Hofmann (1997) 觀點，在伊斯蘭論述中，家庭、婚姻與兩性之間的關係占有重要性，同時改宗者從中獲得清楚的婚姻與母職概念，而這也是西方女性受到吸引的地方，因為相較於目前西方一方面希望女性為獨立自主的個體，但又被期待在有家庭時，能以家庭為主，然在西方普遍的社會觀念中卻又對家庭主婦的評價甚低，如此造成衝突與矛盾關係，與之相反的是，伊斯蘭教明確認可女性做為母親與照顧者的能力。此外，相較於西方對性的開放態度，伊斯蘭教有著嚴格的道德與倫理的標準，這也是能夠滿足希望回到祖父母時代的教規之西方改宗女性所欲之社會型態。不過，值得注意的是，雖然西方學者的研究可供我們去觀察印尼亞齊改宗的客家女性是如何看待與性別、性慾特質相關面向，但是研究對象原來的觀念與理解是否如西方改宗女性一般有強烈的對比，這也是本文需要謹慎探究與分析。最後，與性別相關的議題則為女性的衣著方式，其中又以戴頭巾最為人詬病，而且也被（西方）媒體與一般論述建構為壓迫女性的象徵，亦即戴頭巾再也不是單純的衣著行為，而已轉變為帶有政治意涵與意識形態，並代表著伊斯蘭女性明顯的他者性之象徵。然而，在印尼的情況是否真如西方經驗所顯示，也是需要仔細思考的。我們是否僅能從女性受壓迫的單一角度來觀察戴頭巾行為嗎？或有其他視角，得以讓我們重新檢驗並思考頭巾之於行為者的意義及其做為宗教實踐的內涵。因為，筆者認為，若以相當簡化的「受壓迫」觀點來解釋戴頭巾行為，我們不僅陷入殖民主義及歐洲中心主義之泥沼，更將穆斯林女性推入「他者」的深淵。

綜觀言之，本文雖為初探性質，亦有上述仍待深究的問題，但是經由以性別、族群與宗教作為梳理印尼亞齊客家女性改信伊斯蘭教經驗與過程的主軸，可以發現這三個分析類別以及與其相關的概念並非同質且穩定不變，而是充滿異質性與多變的，同時，研究對象的宗教實踐亦瓦解一般華人論述中所設置的界線，因為從改宗的原因與過程中看到改宗者鑲崁於各自不同的生命故事與生活經驗有助於呈現出女性、印尼客家、伊斯蘭的真實且多樣面貌。此外，由於目前與本文直接相關的研究為數甚少，因此在本文中，運用了許多西方學者研究發現與觀察，他們對於本文在思考該從何種角度與觀點切入客家女性改信過程是相當有幫助的，但是因為需要顧及改宗者所處的特殊歷史、政治、社會與文化脈絡，因之需要審慎應用西方觀點。雖然如此，本文也可藉此與西方經驗進行對話，以豐富改宗研究的學術版圖。除此之外，在目前的東南亞客家研究中，關於客家族群信仰特質的研究仍以傳統華人信仰為主，而尚未有關於伊斯蘭教的部分，因此本文可拓展目前東南亞客家研究的視野與深化客家族群信仰特質研究。

參考書目

阿克巴・阿赫美德（Akbar S. Ahmed）著，蔡百銓譯，2003，《今日的伊斯蘭：穆斯林世界導論》。台北：商周。

李文玫，2011，《離散、回鄉與重新誕生：三位客家女性的相遇與構連》。台北：私立天主教輔仁大學心理學研究所博士論文。

李恩涵，2003，《東南亞華人史》。台北：五南。

林長寬，2009，〈馬來世界與伊斯蘭探源：爪哇地區的伊斯蘭化〉，李豐楙、林長寬、陳美華、蔡宗德、蔡源林合著，《馬來西亞與印尼的宗教與認同：伊斯蘭、佛教與華人信仰》，頁3-52。台北：中央研究院人文社會科學研究中心、亞太區域研究專題中心。

林開忠、李美賢，2006，〈東南亞客家人的認同層次〉，刊於《客家研究》1: 211-238。

邱炫元，2011，〈穆斯林「公共領域」中的「反公眾」穆斯林：印尼華裔穆斯林與其他非伊斯蘭宗教的兩個遭逢〉，發表於「2011第1屆台灣境外宗教研究研討會」，南華大學宗教研究所主辦。嘉義：大林，2011年 6月10日。

徐雨村編，2012，《族群遷移與宗教轉化：福德正神與大伯公的跨國研究》。新竹：國立清華大學人文社會學院。

陳欣慧，2007，《印尼亞齊客家人之研究》。國立政治大學民族學系碩士論文。

梁敏和、孔遠志，2002，《印度尼西亞文化與社會》。北京：北京大學出版社。

黃子堅，2007，〈馬來西亞巴色基督教會與沙巴客家特質的認同〉，丘昌泰、蕭新煌主編，《客家族群與在地社會：臺灣與全球的經驗》，頁369-383。台北：中大出版中心、智勝文化。

張翰璧、張維安，2005，〈東南亞客家族群認同與族群關係：以中央大學馬來西亞客籍僑生為例〉，刊於《台灣東南亞學刊》2卷1期，頁149-182。

蔡源林，2011，《伊斯蘭、現代性與後殖民》。台北：國立台灣大學出版中心。

蕭新煌、林開忠、張維安，2007，〈東南亞客家篇〉，徐正光主編，《台灣客家研究概論》，頁563-581。台北：行政院客家委員會與台灣客家研究學會。

續培德，2004，《印尼亞齊地區穆斯林社群之研究：經院教育、伍拉瑪和信仰生活之脈動》。淡江大學東南亞研究所碩士論文。

Accad, Evelyne, 2005, "Sexuality and Sexual Politics: Conflicts and Contradictions for Contemporary Women in the Middle East", in Haideh Moghissi ed., *Women and Islam: Critical Concepts in Sociology. Vol. II Social Conditions, Obstacles and Prospects*, pp. 3-16. London & New York: Routledge.

Allievi, Stefano, 2006, "The Shifting Significance of the *Halal/Haram* Frontier: Narratives on the *Hijab* and Other Issues", in Karin van Nieuwkerk ed., *Women Embracing Islam: Gender and Conversion in the West*, pp. 120-152. Austin, TX: University of Texas Press.

Anthias, Floya and Nira Yuval-Davis eds., 1989, *Woman-Nation-State*. London: Macmillan.

Bell, Daniel A., 2004, "Is Democracy the 'Least Bad' System for Minority Groups?" in Susan J. Henders ed., *Democratization and Identity: Regimes and Ethnicity in East and Southeast Asia*, pp. 25-42. Lanbam, Boulder, New York, Totonto & Oxford: Lexington Books.

Bradley, Harriet, 2007, *Gender*. Cambridge: Polity.

Bradley, Harriet and Geraldine Healy, 2008, *Ethnicity and Gender at Work. Inequalities, Careers and Employment Relations*. New York: Palgrave Macmillan.

Brah, Avtar and Ann Phoenix, 2004, "Ain't I A Woman? Revisiting Intersectionality", in *Journal of International Women's Studies*, Vol. 5, No. 3, May 2004, pp. 75-86.

Butler, Judith, 1990, *Gender Trouble: Feminism and the Subversion of Identity*. New York/London: Routledge.

Coppel, Charles A., 2005, "Introduction: Researching the Margins", in Tim Lindsey and Helen Pausacker eds., *Chinese Indonesians: Remembering, Distorting, Forgetting*, pp. 1-10. Singapore: Institute of Southeast Asian Studies and Clayton: Monash Asia Institute.

Crenshaw, Kimberlé, 1993, "Demarginalizing the Intersection of Race and Sex: A Black Feminist Critique of Antidiscrimination Doctrine, Feminist Theory, and Antiracist Politics", in D. Kelly Weisberg ed., *Feminist Legal Theory: Foundations*, pp. 383-395. Philadelphia: Temple University Press.

Crenshaw, Kimberlé, 1995, "Mapping the Margins: Intersectionality, Identity Politics, and Violence against Women of Color", in Kimberlé Crenshaw et al. eds., *Critical Race Theory. The Key Writings That Formed the Movement*, pp. 357-383. New York: The New Press.

Crenshaw, Kimberlé, 2003, "Traffic at the Crossroads: Multiple Oppressions", in Robin Morgan ed., *Sisterhood is Over: the Women's Anthology for a New Millennium*, pp. 43-57. New York: Washington Square Press.

Dhruvarajan, Vanaja, 2002, "Religion, Spirituality, and Feminism", in Vanaja Dhruvarajan and Jill Vickers eds., *Gender, Race, and Nation: A Global Perspective*, pp. 273-294. Toronto, Buffalo & London: University of Toronto Press.

El Guindi, Fadwa, 2005, "The Veiling Becomes a Movement", in Haideh Moghissi ed., *Women and Islam: Critical Concepts in Sociology. Vol. II Social Conditions, Obstacles and Prospects*, pp. 70-91. London & New York: Routledge.

Haddad, Yazbeck Yvonne, 2006, "The Quest for Peace in Submisson: Reflections on the Journey of American Women Converts to Islam", in Karin van Nieuwkerk ed., *Women Embracing Islam: Gender and Conversion in the West*, pp. 19-47. Austin, TX: University of Texas Press.

Hofmann, Gabriele, 1997, *Musilim werden: Frauen in Deutschland kovertieren zum Islam*. Frankfurt am Main: Institut für Kulturanthropologie und Europäische Ethnologie.

Imam, Ayesha M., 2005, "The Muslim Religious Right ("Fundamentalist") and Sexuality", in Haideh Moghissi ed., *Women and Islam: Critical Concepts in Sociology. Vol. II Social Conditions, Obstacles and Prospects*, pp. 51-69. London & New York: Routledge.

Iveković, Rada, 2005, "The Fiction of Gender Constructing the Fiction of Nation: On How Fictions Are Normative, and Norms Produce Exceptions", in Kaser Karl and Elisabeth Katschnig-Fasch eds., *Gender and Nation in South Eastern Europe*, pp. 19-38. Anthropological Yearbook of European Cultures. Vol. 14. Münster & Wien: LIT.

Jones, Gavin W., Chee Heng Leng & Maznah Mohamad eds., 2009, *Muslim-non-Muslim Marriage: Political and Cultural Contestations in Southeast Asia*. Singapore: Institute of Southeast Asian Studies.

Knudsen, Susanne V., 2005, "Intersectionality – A Theoretical Inspiration in the Analysis of Minority Cultures and Identities in Textbooks", in Eighth International Conference on Educational and Learning Media, Éric Bruillard et al. eds., *Caught in the Web or Lost in the Textbooks?* pp. 61-76. International Association for Research on Textbooks and Educational Media.

Leinbach, Thomas R. & Richard Ulack，李美賢、楊昊等譯，2009，《東南亞多元與發展 part 1》。台北：財團法人亞太文化學術交流基金會。

Lutz, Helma and Norbert Wenning, 2001, "Differenzen über Differenz – Einführung in die Debatten", in Helma Lutz and Norbert Wenning eds., *Unterschiedlich verschieden. Differenz in der Erziehungswissenschaft*, pp. 11-24. Opladen: Leske+Budrich.

Mak, Lau-Fong, 2002, *Islamization in Southeast Asia*. Taipei: Asia-Pacific Research Program.

McGinty, Anna Mansson, 2006, *Becoming Muslim: Western Women's Conversions to Islam*. New York: Palgrave Macmillan.

McClintock, Anne, 1995, *Imperial Leather: Race, Gender and Sexuality in the Colonial Contest*. London & New York: Routledge.

Murray,Stephen O., 2005, "Woman-Woman Love in Islamic Societies", in Haideh Moghissi ed., *Women and Islam: Critical Concepts in Sociology. Vol. II Social Conditions, Obstacles and Prospects*, pp. 42-50. London & New York: Routledge.

Odeh, Lama Abu, 2005, "Post-Colonial Feminism and the Veil: Thinking the Difference", in Haideh Moghissi ed., *Women and Islam: Critical Concepts in Sociology. Vol. II Social Conditions, Obstacles and Prospects*, pp. 92-103. London & New York: Routledge.

Phoenix, Ann and Pamela Pattynama, 2006, "Intersectionality", in *European Journal of Women's Studies*, Vol. 13, No. 3, pp. 187-192.

Poston, Larry, 1992, *Islamic Da'wah in the West: Muslim Missionary Activity and the Dynamics of Conversion to Islam*. Oxford: Oxford University Press.

Prins, Baukje, 2006, "Narrative Accounts of Origins. A Blind Spot in the Intersectional Approach?" in *European Journal of Women's Studies*, Vol. 13, No. 3, pp. 277-290.

Rambo, Lewis R., 1993, *Understanding Religious Conversion*. New Haven & London: Yale University Press.

Roald, Anne Sofie, 2006, "The Shaping of a Sandinavian 'Islam': Converts and Gender Equal Opportunity", in Karin van Nieuwkerk ed., *Women Embracing Islam: Gender and Conversion in the West*, pp. 48-70. Austin, TX: University of Texas Press.

Saadawi, Nawal El, 2005, "Sexual Aggression Against the Female Child", in Haideh Moghissi ed., *Women and Islam: Critical Concepts in Sociology. Vol. II Social Conditions, Obstacles and Prospects*, pp. 17-20. London & New York: Routledge.

Safa-Isfahani, Kaveh, 2005, "Female-Centered World Views in Iranian Culture: Symbolic Representations of Sexuality in Dramatic Games", in Haideh Moghissi ed., *Women and Islam: Critical Concepts in Sociology. Vol. II Social Conditions, Obstacles and Prospects*, pp. 21-41. London & New York: Routledge.

Said, Edward, 1979, *Orientalism*. New York: Vintage Books.

Sered, Susan Starr, 1999, "'Woman as Symbol' and Women as Agents: Gendered Religious Discourses and Practices", in Judith Lorber, Myra Marx Ferree and Beth Hess eds., *Revisioning Gender*, pp. 193-221, London, Thousand Oaks, & New Delhi: Sage.

Taylor, Jean Gelman, 2005, "The Chinese and the Early Centuries of Conversion to Islam in Indonesia", in Tim Lindsey & Helen Pausacker eds., *Chinese Indonesians: Remerbering, Distorting, Forgetting*, pp. 148-164. Singapore: Institute of Southeast Asian Studies & Clayton: Monash Asia Institute.

van Nieuwkerk, Karin, 2006, "Introduction", in Karin van Nieuwkerk ed., *Women Embracing Islam: Gender and Conversion in the West*, pp. 1-16. Austin, TX: University of Texas Press.

Walgenbach, Katharina, 2007, "Gender als interdependente Kategorie", in Walgenbach, Katharina et al. ed., *Gender als interdependente Kategorie. Neue Perspektiven auf Intersektionalität, Diversität und Heterogenität*, pp. 23-64. Verlag Barbara Budrich, Opladen & Farmington Hills.

Winarta, Frans, H., 2008, "No More Discrimination against the Chinese", in Leo Suryadinata ed., *Ethnic Chinese in Contemporary Indonesia*, pp. 57-74. Singapore: Institute of Southeast Asian Studies.

Wohlrab-Sahr, Monika, 1999a, *Konversion zum Islam in Deutschland und den USA*. Frankfurt am Main: Campus.

Wohlrab-Sahr, Monika, 1999b, "Conversion to Islam: Between Syncretism and Symbolic Battle", in *Social Compass* 46(3): 351-362.

Yuval-Davis, Nira, 1997, *Gender and Nation*. London, Thousand Oaks and New Delhi: Sage.

Yuval-Davis, Nira, 2006, "Intersectionality and Feminist Politics", in *European Journal of Women's Studies*, Vol. 13, No. 3, pp. 193-209.

馬來西亞柔佛州古來縣新村客家社群的民間信仰考察[*]

黃文斌[†]

一、前言

本論文的研究範圍主要探討馬來半島柔佛州（附錄圖一）的其中一個縣屬，即古來再也縣（Kulaijaya District）的新村客家社群的民間信仰。古來再也（Kulaijaya），舊稱古來，是一個華人新村的名字，也被選作一個縣的名稱，原為柔佛州新山（Johor Bahru）的副縣，於2008年正式被規劃為一個獨立的縣屬，稱為古來再也縣【下簡稱古來縣】。古來縣裡有九個新村，其中包括：古來（Kulai）、士乃（Senai）、加拉巴沙威（Kelapa Sawit）、新港（Sengkang）、武吉峇都（Bukit Batu）、亞逸文滿（Ayer Bemban）、士年納（Sedenak）、沙令（Saleng）及泗隆（Seelong）[1]（附錄圖二）。基本上，這九個新村都是在馬來亞緊急時期（Emergency, 1948-1960），為了隔絕華人與馬來亞共產黨的互動而設立的，雖然一些村名在此之前已存在。英國殖民地政府於1948年6月宣布馬來亞進入緊急狀態，強制性的將所有在鄉區及附近的華人移居到一個集中地點居住，然後用鐵絲網圍起

＊本文為作者訪問台灣國立清華大學人社研究中心期間（2011年11月-2012年4月）寫成的作品。特此鳴謝國立清華大學人文社會研究中心黃一農主任及張維安院長邀請本人前來參與由國科會資助的「季風亞洲與多元文化」研究計劃。此外，本文初稿在該中心主辦的「季風亞洲與多元文化國際學術研討會」發表，分別獲得新加坡國立大學及南洋理工大學中系的黃賢強教授及李元瑾教授的指教，也在定稿時獲得陳慧倩同學協助查找資料，筆者特此一併鳴謝。
†作者現為馬來西亞拉曼大學中華研究院中文系副教授、副院長及中華研究中心馬來西亞華人及文化研究組主任。
1 林廷輝、方天養，《馬來西亞新村邁向新旅程》，吉隆坡：策略分析與政策研究所，2005，頁176。

來，嚴謹限制人民的日常作息，以斷絕村民對馬來亞共產黨武裝部隊的援助。在這個背景下產生的華人村落，現今在馬來西亞被稱為「新村」。故絕大多數的「新村」不是自然生成的，而是「被製造」出來的新村落。[2] 依據2002年的資料顯示全國共有450個新村，居住在新村的村民有1,256,067人，而華人占人了82%。此外，新村華人占全國華人人口的21%。[3] 故我們可以說「新村」是現今構成馬來西亞華人社會重要的部分。

本文所以選擇古來縣九個新村中的客家社群作為研究個案，因為這些新村絕大部分的方言籍貫族群是客家人，雖然這些客家族群還可細分為河婆、惠州、豐順及鶴山人。根據表一：1954年古來縣華人各籍貫群人口統計，古來村客家人占了華人籍貫群的61.80%、士乃村有81.64%、沙令村有67.23%、泗隆村有86.23%、士年納村有50.80%、亞逸文滿村有72.14%、新港村有54.21%、武吉峇都村占了94.31%及加拉巴沙威村有89.10%。[4]

可見古來縣新村的客家人口幾乎都超過半數。由於客家人口在這個縣區為多數社群，故我們可以肯定這些新村的開拓和發展與客家人息息相關，而此地的客家族群之研究尚有待開發。本論文只集中在探討這些客家村落的民間信仰。

華人基本上是一個多神信仰的民族（林美容，1991: 14）。我們認為馬來西亞華人的民間信仰是與其移民社會同步發展的，因為他們到一個陌生及生死未卜的環境謀生，平安及健康是他們首要的心理需求，而藉助神明的力量能讓他們心靈安穩及有生存的勇氣。另一方

---

2 潘婉明，《一個新村，一種華人？重建馬來（西）亞華人新村的集體回憶》，2004，頁26。

3 林廷輝、方天養，《馬來西亞新村邁向新旅程》，2005，頁20-21。

4 「表一」數據轉引安煥然、劉莉晶編撰，《柔佛客家人的移殖與拓墾》，士古來：南院學院出版，2007，頁184。資料來源見F. Lees (1964: 292) 的數據表。安氏在資料來源之作者注明為"F. Lee"，原著所見為"F. Lees"。根據2006年《東方日報・古來客家人的移殖》（2006年6月10日）的報導古來的華人社群裡，客家人占了70.87%，其次是海南人11.27%、廣肇府人8.38%、潮州人4.23%。福建人僅占2.8%，另有廣西人2.32%。

表一：1954年古來縣華人各籍貫群人口統計

地區	客家	所占%	廣東	所占%	福建	所占%	潮州	所占%	廣西	所占%	海南	所占%	其他華族	所占%	華族總數
古來	4,003	61.80	740	11.43	339	5.23	201	3.10	98	1.51	1,075	16.6	21	0.32	6,477
土乃	2,571	81.64	127	4.03	37	1.17	262	8.32			152	4.83			3,149
沙令	798	67.23	138	11.63	51	4.30	74	6.23	16	1.35	110	9.27			1,187
泗隆	432	86.23	17	3.39	3	0.60	4	0.80	1	0.20	41	8.18	3	0.60	501
士年納	575	50.80	208	18.37	1	0.09	40	3.35	204	18.02	104	9.19			1,132
亞逸文滿	448	72.14	64	10.31			19	3.06	29	4.67	61	9.82			621
新港	386	54.21	72	10.11	11	1.54	15	2.11	8	1.12	220	30.90			712
武吉峇都	597	94.31	19	3.00	6	0.95			11	1.74					633
加拉巴沙威	2,437	89.10	29	1.06	36	1.32	116	4.24	34	1.24	83	3.03			2,735
羅町令（沙令）	14	9.09	36	23.38							104	67.53			154
合計	12,261	70.87	1,450	8.38	484	2.80	731	4.23	401	2.32	1,950	11.27	24	0.14	17,301

資料來源：

F. Lee, "Chinese settlement in the Kulai Sub-District of Johore, Malaysia", in R. W. Steel and R. M. Prothero eds., Geographers and the Tropics: Liverpool Essays, London, 1964, p. 292.

面,在第二次世界大戰之後,或後來英殖民政府實施的緊急法令時期,村民生活困苦,為了得到心靈上的慰藉,一些人從中國原鄉或其他村落奉請了神明香火到新村來供奉;有的將家裡膜拜的神明在建立廟宇後轉變成新村的共同神明。此外,新村以農耕生活為主,辛苦不已,也缺乏娛樂,神廟自然成為了村民尋找心靈寄託的場所,也是聯誼消遣及凝聚村民的地方。再者,這些民間信仰多屬草根性,緊扣民眾的生活,無形中也保存了其家鄉的風俗。是故,考察這個客家社區的民間宗教信仰是我們了解此社區重要的議題之一。

南方學院族群與文化研究所曾經對柔佛州的客家人做過田野調查,目前編有《柔佛客家人的移殖與拓墾》,內有一些考察及口述的新聞報導、評論及一篇成果論文。此書所收錄的41篇報導與評論文章中有13篇與古來縣的客家人相關(安煥然、劉莉晶編撰,2007)。此外,目前學界尚有一些客家研究成果略提及此縣新村客家人的宗教信仰概況[5],然尚未有專門針對此地區民間信仰作討論的文章。

依據我們對古來縣新村的觀察,其民間信仰是多元化的,並且以祈求神明保佑村民出入平安、求財靈驗及心靈慰藉等為祭祀的標準,故我們推測這或許與早期移民社會及新村的生活形態有關係。目前這些新村的華人民間信仰(天主教及基督教除外),包括了三山國王、洪仙大帝、譚公、真空教、大伯公、觀音、媽祖、黃老祖師、關帝聖君、玄天上帝、城隍爺、三清玉皇、齊天大聖等等,不一而足。在這些眾多的民間信仰中,有一些是直接與客家原鄉民間信仰相關的,如河婆客家人的三山國王(粵東區)及惠州客家人的譚公,但是也有一些神明不專屬於客家人,卻成為了客家村里流行的共同信仰,如觀音信仰。此外,又有一些是在地衍生出來的信仰,如洪仙大帝及大伯公。再者,上述的民間信仰在不同的新村有不同的發展情況,而其歷

---

5 張維安、張容嘉(2011: 3-38)的〈馬來西亞客家族群信仰〉及安煥然(2011: 185-219)的〈馬來西亞柔佛古來客家聚落〉,有略提到此地區的洪仙大帝、三山國王及譚公信仰。

史地位及重要性亦各異。例如，士乃村以三山國王信仰為主、新港與加拉巴沙威及武吉峇都村以洪仙大帝信仰為主、亞逸文滿村以大伯公為主、泗隆與古來村皆祭拜譚公，而觀音信仰則在古來較為普遍。由於這一地區的民間信仰所供奉的神明太廣泛，故本論文只鎖定在一些比較普遍及在村里歷史較悠久的民間信仰，其中包括三山國王、譚公、觀音、大伯公及洪仙大帝信仰作為本文的論述。[6]

　　本文嘗試分析這些新村的民間信仰與社區村民的互動及影響。由於文獻資料的缺乏，基本上本論文採用田野調查的方法，其中包括口述及實地考察，以輔助有限及所能見到的文獻撰寫而成。

二、三山國王信仰

　　在還未討論古來縣的民間信仰前，我們先略交代客家人到古來縣發展的背景。據安煥然的考察，從十九世紀中葉至1917年，柔佛州乃以港主制度拓殖，在此時期的華人籍貫群中尚未查找到客家人之記載。然而，不表示在這個時期柔佛州沒有客家人，因位於柔佛州首府新山的「柔佛古廟」內便有由客社信眾於1874年（同治十三年）送的「極德咸沾」牌匾。至1931年，客家人已占柔佛州華人各方言群人口的20.2%，排居第二位（安煥然，2009: 88, 90）。這些客家人口的增長，應該與內陸農耕的開發相關。古來縣的客家族群就是屬於這些內陸地區的客家人。他們是沿著內陸河流及二十世紀初火車鐵路新建之周圍地區發展起來的客家聚落，而且以務農為生，多從事割橡膠、栽種黃梨、種菜及養豬為主。這些以務農為生的客家人，有別於新山大埔及嘉應州客家人，多從新加坡移入及互動而從事售賣洋貨、布疋、

6　本文只討論古來再也縣的七個新村的民間信仰考察，不涉及沙令新村，因為該村的三清玉皇大帝廟、花果宮及五顯宮華光大帝廟所祭祀的主神屬單獨的個案並在其他村少見，加上難以論述其特色，故從缺之。此外，武吉峇都村較有代表性的廟宇是玄天廟，主要祭祀玄天大帝、洪仙大帝及大伯公，由於資料上的不足，我們只能略提及而不論述。

打鐵、藥材、當鋪等傳統行業（安煥然，2009: 91）。

　　在古來縣中，歷史較悠久的客家村是士乃新村。士乃新村曾於二十世紀20年代，由兩位廣東省揭西縣的河婆客家先賢，即黃炳南（德茂）（1867-1940）和黃子松（善合）（1881-1975）的率領下，開芭墾殖，種植黃梨、蔬菜及橡膠等，故上個世紀50年代此新村超過80%是河婆客家人[7]。士乃新村是古來縣九個新村中唯一一間供奉三山國王的廟宇[8]，其香火乃於1947年由一些先賢從河婆原鄉奉請南來祭祀之神祇。該廟有六十多年的歷史，在該新村有一定的影響力，終年香客絡繹不絕，故三山國王不僅成為客家人的守護神，也是當地民眾的共同信仰。該寺廟早期並無理事會，一直到1993年理事會才正式註冊成合法組織。目前理事會每兩年改選一次，目前共有理事14位，會員有150位之多。這間寺廟值得我們注意乃因其見證了士乃的歷史發展及與村民有很好的互動關係。

　　有關士乃三山國王廟的歷史，目前在該廟有一幅由張智海在擴建廟宇時撰寫的牌匾，其文如下：

> 柔佛士乃埠三山國王廟史略。本廟倡建於民國三十五年正月初旬，首由張智海，黃順庭，黃博平發起建廟組織，召集全埠人士開會，議決特派募捐專員張智海，黃漢庭往各埠勸捐，成績頗好，緣因進行未遂，故中途停頓。後於民國三十六年九月間，由黃國政，蔡月初，黃順庭重新提倡，再行召集全埠人士會議，決定將國王廟所捐之款，撥出貳仟元贊助士乃中正公學，建築教室，培養人材。中正公學董事接收此款後，立即開

7　1970年代以後，士乃與其他城市互動頻密（安煥然，2011: 206-207），加上周邊新花園住宅的興起、小型工業及機場的建設，又加上柔南多看新加坡電視台節目而講華語日漸普遍等因素，士乃之客家人色彩逐漸變得模糊。

8　安煥然（2011）提到除了士乃之外，江加蒲萊還有一間三山國王廟。由於此地區非在古來縣九個新村範圍內，故本文不論。

會，議定將上街場前士乃學校，即係中正分校全座屋宇餘地，永遠讓與三山國王修築建立廟堂，事得大家歡喜，雙方滿意。本廟董事擇定十月初旬吉日良時興工修築，至十二月初旬，廟貌鼎新，神像莊嚴。斯時也工已告竣，廟址丑山未兼艮分金，議由黃順庭擇定十二月十一日卯時，國王陞殿。請到潮音老三順戲，連演三天。同時江夏堂金獅音樂齊來慶祝，各港敬備豬羊來廟恭祭者十有餘副，斯時天朗氣清，一來一往，人山人海，非常熱鬧，實係歷來未有之勝景，公王大顯威靈，各方人士同沾樂利，共獲安康，順將大略情形書此為記。張智海書。

　　1947年12月三山國王廟宣告建竣，首任廟祝黃順廷從中國河婆霖田都三山祖廟，用布袋盛裝祖廟裡的香灰從中國南渡至士乃把香火請至三山國王廟供村民膜拜。士乃三山國王廟供奉的主座神為三王爺，左邊為大王爺，右邊是二王爺，因該廟負責人聽老前輩說相傳三王爺才是最驍勇善戰者（安煥然、劉莉晶，2007: 149）。三山國王的信仰，起源於廣東省潮州地區。[9] 三山指的就是廣東省潮州府揭陽縣霖田都河婆墟（今揭陽市揭西縣河婆鎮）西面的三座高山——巾山、明山、獨山。相傳北宋年間，三位山神屢次顯靈，宋帝於是分別敕封為清化威德報國王、助政明肅寧國王、惠威弘應豐國王，合祀為「三山國王」。另有一說，三山國王為隋朝三位開國大將軍，因為曾經捨命救隋文帝楊堅脫難，並鼎力幫助文帝統一天下，完成帝業，因此文帝封為「開國駕前三大將軍」，但是三人並不戀棧功名利祿，毅然退

9　劉還月有不同的看法，她認為：「在一般台灣人（無論福客）的觀念中，大多把三山國王視為客家人的守護神，但在中國的客家地區，三山國王只是中國潮汕地區的角頭神，根據邱彥貴先生的研究：『十八、九世紀時，三山國王是主要分布於潮州府全境及惠州府、嘉應州部分地區的地域性信仰，信徒包括福佬和客家兩種，似乎並無方言群／族群的區隔。』（《粵東三山國王信仰的分布與信仰的族群》），此外，其他絕大多數的客家地區都不見此神，歷史文獻中，最早出現此神的記載，應是明嘉靖年間刊行的《潮州府誌》：三山：一曰獨山，在縣西南一百五十里。一曰明山，離獨山四十里。一曰巾山，離明山二十里。脈自獨山來，如巾高掛，因名。相傳有三神人出於巾山石穴，因祀焉。今廟猶存」（劉還月，1999: 214）。

隱。也有傳說唐代時，潮州匪賊問題相當嚴重，三山神顯靈幫助官軍剿匪，因此被敕封為三山國王；也有說南宋末年，由於三位山神屢次顯靈救帝昺（宋端宗）脫險，因而被封為三山國王（鄭琪玉，2004：4-7）。當然，三山國王的傳說還有許多，這裡只是引述一些而已。無論如何，這些傳說都說明三山國王善戰英勇，為正義之神，故獲得民間之崇拜。早期士乃三山國王廟裡只供奉善戰英勇的三位王爺，一直到二十世紀80年代才開始演化成在正殿的左邊供奉三位王爺的夫人金身，又稱三姐夫人。

　　士乃三山國王廟雖是河婆客家人的家鄉祖神，然而，祂在士乃紮根已久，故已逐漸打破地緣性的隔閡，各籍貫村民甚至外族都會前往該廟上香，祈求神明庇佑。50年代時期，就有印裔信眾捐金置門，在廟外立一山門，其名字還刻在山門上[10]，可見三山國王廟在當地有一定影響力。據我們實地考察所見，士乃有不少商店及住家的大門上都貼著三山國王廟的平安符。換言之，三山國王早已成為多數士乃新村華人的共同民間信仰，張貼平安符也成為本地居民的一種特色。依據廣府籍貫的韋金娣（1942-）口述，她在二十世紀70年代初期搬到士乃居住，便有老婦人在三山國王廟慶祝神誕時將平安符送到她家。一般村民拿到平安符都會捐助一點香油錢。[11]

　　除了平安符，神誕廟慶也是寺廟與村民互動的重要日子。創廟初期，三山國王廟每年都會舉辦五次平安宴並請劇團演戲酬神，分別在三位神明的寶誕，即大王爺（二月廿五）、二王爺（八月十五）及三王爺（六月初六）；農曆正月十五日的祈大眾福儀式；以及十二月上旬的答謝神恩慶典。這些慶典的日期與原鄉不一樣，或因三山國王信仰在不同地區的傳播時作出調適而產生慶典日期的差別。[12]

---

10 《東方日報》2009年9月29日報導。

11 筆者與韋金娣女士之電話訪談，日期：2012年3月10日，時間：7.50pm-8.26pm。

12 房學嘉指出：「隨著三山國王信仰的傳播，在不同時期，不同地域，其傳說不斷豐富和發展。三山國王壽誕和祀奉儀式各地不盡相同。如三山國王的壽誕，揭西是正月二十五日，大埔為五月初四、初五，梅

每次廟宇慶典的舉辦，村民們齊聚一堂，互相交流，暫時忘卻平日的繁忙，故在這些日子三山國王廟頓時成為當地村民溝通的重要場所。廟宇的正對面於1956年建有一座半磚半木的固定戲台，戲台下為戲班人員臨時的住宿和演出裝扮之處。80年代以前神誕是非常熱鬧的，由於新村尚缺乏娛樂，村民最快樂的時光是舉家到廟裡看酬神戲。三山國王廟戲台前有好幾排木製的高長凳供村民賞戲，然仍有村民需自備椅子前往。除了看酬神戲，小孩也可以在這裡買到許多零食、霜淇淋，甚至還有人賣捏麵人藝術品等，成人與孩童們皆歡樂融融。最特別的是唱酬神戲的語言並不是客語，而是潮州語戲班，也許揭西縣河婆鎮雖以客家人為主，然而，其地理位置乃隸屬於潮州府之故。這是當年村民獲得娛樂的少數管道之一。此外，在廟慶時，許多善信尤其是通過打聖杯而被三山國王選為福首者皆主動前來幫忙。韋金娣擔任了十多年的福首，她說約在二十多年前，被選為福首者在每次慶祝神誕時需要樂捐馬幣30元，後來提高至40元。根據2009年的理事福首芳名表，約有385名福首，他們可稱為廟宇的贊助人。通過他們的捐獻及標福品所籌獲經費足以維持寺廟的經常開銷。這些福首有者以個人名義，有者則以商號名義捐款。理事會選出各區募捐主任負責募款。從芳名表中，幾乎大部分士乃的華人商號（至少有70間）都成為其中一員。福首成員來自各籍貫群，然仍以客家人為主。此外，有一所名為山度士西藥房（Clinic Sandhu），乃由印裔人士所經營，也是其中一位福首，可見此廟已突破種族的界限，受到在地印度族群的認可。除了士乃外，也有一些來自士乃以外的地區，如新山、古來和烏魯地南（Ulu Tiram）等地的居民成為此廟的福首。以前慶祝神誕較多次，對福首也造成經濟的負擔。目前的神誕已經只是慶祝三王爺（六月初六）以及十二月上旬的答謝神恩慶典。

縣為九月初十等。對三山國王的祀奉，一般在農曆正月，俗民到三山國王廟進香，祈求風調雨順，人畜平安」，「揭西縣河婆鎮習慣在正月十三抬三山國王神像出遊，揭西南山鎮俗謂『迎神送煞』」（房學嘉，2008: 128）。

福首除了需要捐錢，也會在神誕時前來協助，尤其廚房是最熱鬧及最需要人手的地方，因為宴席皆由該廟自己包辦。二十世紀70年代以前，士乃新村的酒家並不多，故宴會皆要靠村民組團互助。三山國王廟慶祝神誕扮演了凝聚村民的角色，除了祭祀活動，廟慶時有吃有喝有娛樂，就像過節慶一樣。再者，該廟在早期因酒家及大眾集合的場所缺乏，而租借給村民們慶祝婚宴及壽宴等。如今這種情況已改變。自邁入90年代中期後，神誕宴席的事務也交由酒家承辦。無形中也減少了村民的互動。此外，酬神戲受歡迎的程度已大不如前。這也許與村民的生活條件已逐漸改善有關，如今家家戶戶皆擁有電視機，故酬神戲已經不是村民主要的娛樂節目了。更甚者，傳統的戲曲也逐漸被藝人唱歌台所取代。至於廟宇成為喜宴場地的功能也被現代的酒家所取代。

　　以目前該廟的發展情況觀察，該廟與村民互動比較頻密的恐怕只是剩下遊神及神誕宴會標福品籌善款活動。自1997年開始，每隔三年的十二月初九或初十舉辦眾神出遊活動，神明環繞士乃大街及新村巡遊一圈。三山國王廟理事主席蔡明酒（1943-）說：「遊行主要的目的是通過諸神出遊，祈求國泰民安風調雨順，事業興隆，此外，也促進了地區一帶客家人的團結，同時亦讓我們的子子孫孫，認識我們自家精緻的風土文化」[13]。此遊神活動原由爐主發動，為了避免勞民傷財，後來每年遊神活動改為三年一次，至今已舉辦了五次。2012年將進行第六次眾神出遊活動。

　　自2009年間，該廟只在六月初六三王爺誕及十二月初九或初十答謝神恩擺宴席，數量約60至90桌。宴席中有標福品的儀式，由信眾自由投標，籌到的款項有一部分捐給當地的華校、老人院等，以回饋社會。廟慶標福品的活動，在柔佛州的寺廟似乎很盛行，也許是受比鄰

---

13 引文為劉順強於2000-2001年間與蔡明酒的訪談。見劉順強，〈士乃老街——河婆人過番〉，劉順強「花雨夜」網誌，http://blog.yam.com/skliew，2012年7月18日。

的新加坡民間信仰慶祝神誕的形式所影響，因為在吉隆坡並不怎麼盛
行。由於時代的改變，村民的行業已不局限在農耕行業，尤其二十世
紀80年士乃新村的周邊逐漸發展成一個輕工業區，而柔佛州的飛機場
也在70年代在距離士乃村十分鐘車程的地方建立。要言之，許多橡膠
園也逐步被砍伐來建設輕工業、機場及花園住宅區。加上娛樂的多元
化，步不出戶者有之，以前村民在早上割膠後下午即悠閒地聚集在咖
啡店、社團及神廟等場所獲得消遣娛樂，而此現象也逐漸改變。此
外，經濟發展也吸引了外來人口，包括外勞的移入，客家村的特色也
相對的模糊。同樣的，廟宇以前的角色，也在蛻變中。目前所見，能
吸引村民到三山國王廟祭拜者多為上了年紀的村民，神誕廟慶帶老攜
幼的情景已不如前。加上教育的普及，前來求神問事指點迷津的也逐
漸減少。然而，據蔡明酒說，三山國王廟神明經常顯靈，在神誕慶典
舉辦時屢出「真字」，不少居民因此發了一筆橫財，故吸引了許多信
眾前來祭拜（黃文斌、張曉威，2010: 19）。[14] 這又反映了信眾普遍
的心理需求。

三、譚公信仰

由於「客家人」是一個廣義的名詞，因此三山國王也許是某些客
家地區的民間信仰而不是全體客家人的共同信仰[15]。除了三山國王，
譚公信仰也是客家人比較傳統的信仰，由於在西馬來西亞半島設有譚
公廟者多在惠州客家人的地區，故我們認為譚公信仰應與惠州客家人

---

14 〈考察報告（二）〉，記錄者：葉燕雯，日期：2010年1月23日，時間：10:30am-12:00pm，地點：士乃
三山國王廟。

15 劉還月（1999: 216）指出：「除了潮州、揭西、梅縣泮坑山等地的居民視三山國王為守護神之外，其他
地區的客家人大多不以牠為守護神。廣西客家民間信仰，與廣東客家大體相同。他們認定的保護神是土
地神。」

較有密切關係[16]，雖然在砂拉越不同的地區也有河婆客家人祭拜[17]。張維安認為譚公信仰算是馬來西亞客家民間信仰的特色之一。他指出砂拉越石隆門的礦工曾先祭拜譚公才去反抗英國殖民政府統治，這在「台灣客家社群中，並沒有這麼明顯，在台灣客家移民的歷程中也沒有扮演如在馬來西亞那樣的角色」（張維安、張容嘉，2011: 18-19）。在士乃、泗隆及古來新村皆有譚公廟，原為「家廟」[18]，後也開放讓信眾祭祀。由於士乃新村譚公廟的歷史及可書性不足，故本文只是選擇古來及泗隆村的譚公仙聖廟作論述。

譚公到底是誰，至今還有不同的說法。有人認為是唐末五代道士福建泉州人譚峭（李天賜，2007: 80-81）或元末明初惠州大嶺鎮人譚德（1368-1381）及明代廣東惠州藍田瑤族首領譚觀福。綜合上說，客家人所祭祀的譚公應為譚德或譚觀福的可能性較大。譚德的傳說事蹟如下：

> 譚德（1368年-1381年），人稱譚公。生於元朝末至正二十八年（1368年）農曆四月初八佛誕日，惠州市惠東縣大嶺鎮人。三歲時父母雙亡，由外婆撫養，在多祝鎮麥田村長大。相傳七、八歲時已能呼風喚雨、降龍伏蛇，十三歲時在九龍峰「羽化」。當時羽化登仙之地，現被稱之為「得道亭」。傳說譚公得道後，擁有呼風喚雨和治病救人的神力，經常治療患病的鄉民，又幫助附近的漁民預測天氣，深受敬仰，其後村民更設廟供奉這位漁民的保護神，譚公也成為了廣東一帶著名的「海神」。譚公生性純樸善良，智慧超人，為人熱心，積善好德，

---

16 劉崇漢指出：「目前在西馬設有譚公廟的地方包括吉隆坡增江南區、增江北區、大同華文小學內、森美蘭芙蓉、檳城亞逸淡、浮羅及威省大山腳等地」（劉崇漢，1999: 204）。

17 李天賜（2007: 84）指出黃建淳《砂拉越華人史研究》一書中載：「石隆門開埠以來，向為客家人的天下，又以河婆人居大多數。」筆者不確定該地祭祀譚公者是河婆客家人，還是惠州客家人為多。

18 本文的「家廟」僅意指原屬於自家祭拜的神明，後來開放予社區民眾祭拜的廟宇。由於這些廟宇多由家族成員繼承廟產，故以「家廟」形容之，而非中國傳統宗族概念下的「家廟」或「宗廟」。

他有「稔葉為魚施力」、「杯茶化雨救羅城」、「唐牛好馭」、「定風救船」等神蹟，更為惠州民間廣泛傳頌。

明太祖洪武十六年（1383年）群眾為紀念譚德，在他登仙的地方建「得道亭」。明宣德九年（1434年）建九龍峰祖廟，供人祈拜。清咸豐四年（1854年）惠州翟火姑起事，圍攻惠州城，譚公顯靈託夢祐助守城官兵。朝廷賜「敕封襄濟譚公仙聖」權杖；惠州知府獻有「神恩廣被」匾額。[19]

　　至於譚觀福的傳說事蹟則比較以歷史人物式的流傳。萬信指出：「譚觀福，為廣東惠州藍田瑤族首領，明朝時率領族人反抗官府壓迫，後陣亡，族人立『譚仙廟』祭之，稱譚觀福為譚仙公。另一傳說指譚仙是瑤族譚姓的祖先，譚氏族人立峒主廟，主神即為譚仙。」[20]筆者認為，以上兩種傳說，譚公是譚德的傳說似乎比較合理，不僅有神性事蹟，又有官府贈送匾額使其傳說也帶有歷史性質。

　　古來的譚公廟稱為「譚公仙聖廟」，是古來當地歷史較悠久的民間廟宇，為一間典型的家廟。根據現任壇主楊于生的口述，該譚公仙聖廟的創辦人為陳橋蓮。早在1923年，她從中國攜帶木製的譚公仙聖牌匾，乘船南來馬來亞，隨後在古來現今的新街場開設神壇，譚公信仰遂逐漸成為當地居民的信仰之一。

　　該廟前身乃由樹皮草蓋而成，直到1948年英殖民政府為對抗馬來亞共產黨宣布進入緊急狀態，將靠近山區農耕的華人遷移在控制範圍內的「古來新村」，陳橋蓮才將廟宇搬遷至古來新村。1996年其曾外孫楊于生接任壇主之位。同年，譚公仙聖廟成立理事會，由理事會管理廟宇。與此同時，理事會也制定兩年一次的理事改選條例。為此，廟務從個人管理趨向有組織性的群體領導，從而掀開了神廟的新篇

---

19 〈譚德〉，見《維基百科》，http://zh.wikipedia.org/wiki/%E8%AD%9A%E5%BE%B7。2012年2月16日。
20 〈細說譚公誕（三）〉，見《萬信網誌》http://ng928.mysinablog.com/index.php?op=ViewArticle&articleId=1700591。2010年2月16日。

章。

　　譚公仙聖廟在每年農曆四月初八皆會大事慶祝譚公成仙之日。據楊于生口述，早期舉行慶誕時，有傳統焚燒紙紮品的儀式，同時也會聘請道士前來做法事。如今已無聘請道士做法事。此外，該廟於農曆六月廿六慶祝譚公仙聖的寶誕。過去慶祝神誕儀式較簡樸。自楊于生接任壇主後，在獲得理事會成員的支持下，決定每年籌辦連續五天的神誕慶典。值得注意的是慶神誕的節目除了酬神戲外，晚上九時後則由歌手駐唱，同時也演唱馬來歌曲供友族欣賞（黃文斌、張曉威，2010: 3）。[21] 可見當地有馬來族群雜居，這也是民間信仰廟宇嘗試打破族群藩籬，趨向多元的現象。無獨有偶，泗隆村譚公仙聖廟在1977年1月6日曾租借桌凳予友族辦喜事。事實上，該廟於1972年6月22日的會議記錄上，清楚地記錄了當時已有「桌凳互助會」專門處理桌凳租借用途，而該廟1975年的會議記錄已誌明有「管理桌椅」正副理事一職。[22]

　　此外，在舉辦神誕慶典時，無論是古來村還是泗隆村的譚公仙聖廟都會撥款給當地的華文小學及老人院，體現了取之社會，用之社會的精神。泗隆村譚公仙聖廟每年都會舉辦晚宴，大約宴開70至80桌，有標福品活動等，籌到的款項都會捐給華小，約馬幣500至3,000元左右。泗隆華文小學正好就在譚公廟的後面，廟宇與學校的關係密切。值得一提的是泗隆譚公仙聖廟的重大事情，不一定都由廟方委員單方面決定，而需經過當地村民同意才能進行。根據該廟於1979年的會議記錄，工作委員會曾召開全村村民大會，讓村民投票決定是否拆除該廟舊廚房。[23] 從以上一事來看，管理譚公仙聖廟不僅僅是委員會的責

---

21 〈考察報告（一）〉，記錄者：林德成，日期：2009年12月26日，時間：2:45pm-3:30pm，地點：古來譚公仙聖廟。

22 此資料參考自《泗隆譚公仙聖廟會議記錄》（頁15、27、53）。

23 此外，我們也見到1973年5月22日的《泗隆譚公仙聖廟會議記錄》（頁23）記載：「議程：（二）該日全村共壹佰零四人投票。贊成〔照？〕往年一樣隆重慶祝之贊成票共九十一張，贊成自由上香者十二張票，廢票二張。」

任，也是泗隆村民的責任。另外，委員會也會適時向村民交代廟方的一些舉措，力圖達到公開化及透明化的標準。由此可見該廟與泗隆新村人民互動頻密。由於早期泗隆村有86%是務農的客家人，目前變化不大但已逐漸面臨輕工業入侵的挑戰。[24] 譚公信仰為惠州人較傳統的信仰，因此，泗隆村譚公廟自然扮演了凝聚村人的角色，也成為該村人民重要的代表信仰。

另一方面，古來村譚公仙聖廟除了供奉譚公外，也祭祀三清上聖，這是該廟後來才加以供奉的神明。依據楊氏說以前該廟是沒有祭祀三清祖師的，因一位扶乩有供奉，故後來他們也加入此三位神明。三清祖師為道教崇拜的最高神，原為道教三位神明，至宋代以後成為三位合稱（黃海德，2004）。三清祖師的信仰也與惠州人有歷史淵源，惠州西湖之元妙觀即有三清殿，該觀始建於唐代貞觀年間，為全真派龍門派道觀。[25] 可見，惠州人與三清祖師有關係，故譚公仙聖廟加入三清上聖也很合理，也見客家人對神明多元化的包容特性。

四、觀音信仰

觀音信仰不屬於某一個籍貫群，然而據我們考察古來新村五間較有代表性的寺廟所見，其中有三間主祀神是觀音。[26] 馬來西亞客家人與觀音信仰到底有怎樣的關係值得進一步探討。張維安與張容嘉（2011: 6-8）曾引述王琛發及駱靜山的研究，指出在吉蘭丹布賴客家

---

24 泗隆村雖然距離士乃只有幾公里的路程，但它沒有士乃面臨城市化、靠近高速公路等致使人口增長而造成客家色彩逐漸模糊的衝擊，因為泗隆村仍在郊外及被橡膠園所圍繞。至於日後是否會改變則很難斷定，因其周邊也開始有許多新興工廠。另外，泗隆村有一個特殊的現象，不管有幾位孩子出外謀生，每家一定有一位孩子留在村裡，因此村不缺年輕人口，這是其村能保留傳統民間習俗的關鍵原因之一。

25 據〈惠州元妙古觀簡介〉記載：「1938年惠州淪陷，日寇將三清大殿、王皇樓等一炬焚燒，剩下偏殿殘屋數間，道觀凋零」（轉引黎志添，2007: 307，註272）。此文字記錄是否正確，由於無法查證，我們暫存疑。因依據日本軍占領馬來亞的經驗，他們雖無惡不作，惡名昭彰，但卻甚少見聞日軍燒毀寺廟的事情。

26 這五間廟包括觀音堂、雲山宮（主祀觀音）、萬仙廟（主祀觀音）、譚公廟及龍岩廟。

村的水月宮及一些觀音寺廟，如金寶古廟等皆有客籍人士的祀奉及資助，包括十九世紀末檳城客籍僑領張弼士（1840-1916）及其朋友亦曾大力資助福州鼓山湧泉寺的妙蓮（1824-1907）和尚在檳城鶴山興建與觀音信仰相關的極樂寺。據筆者有限的知識所知，著名古廟而祀奉觀音菩薩者，如馬六甲的青雲亭（1673）、檳城廣福宮（1800）及新加坡天福宮後殿（1842）皆比較與閩南社群有密切關係。無論如何，這不表示客籍人士與觀音信仰無密切關係，例如筆者的家鄉雪蘭莪州加影鎮錫米山新村為一客家村，閩籍居士李天吉（1939-2010）於1976年要在此創辦淨妙佛教協會時曾觀察村民的信仰，發現大部分村民是祭拜觀音的，故他們夫婦決定在此成立佛教會並推動觀音法門。又如，馬來西亞惠州客家人也有因信奉觀音而不可吃牛肉的觀念。也許，觀音信仰已普及在中國人的社會裡，無論閩客人士皆有眾多信徒。我們所考察的古來新村正好也反映這一點，其中較古老的寺廟如觀音堂（1933）、雲山宮（1937）及著名的萬仙廟皆祀奉觀音菩薩為主。雖然，士乃新村也有佛教兼容民間信仰的觀音亭（1988），但是在古來縣九個新村之中只有古來新村是同時有三間代表性的寺廟是祀奉觀音者。

值得注意的是古來觀音堂及雲山宮是同一性質的觀音廟。住持及住眾都是帶髮修行及持素的女居士；皆有領養貧苦人家的小孩。古來觀音堂，由於歷史較悠久，當地居民稱之為「老觀音堂」，以區別鄰近的雲山宮觀音堂。根據自小在觀音堂長大而現在是住持的陳興華女居士敘述，古來觀音堂的香火是源自中國廣東省梅縣。1933年陳慶（宣）女居士從梅縣攜帶只有三歲的陳興華南來馬來亞，同時也攜帶了一尊觀音塑像到古來落腳，並有意在此建立觀音堂（黃文斌、張曉威，2010: 6）。[27]

---

27 〈考察報告〉（一），記錄者：葉燕雯，日期：2009年12月28日，時間：9:00am-10:00am，地點：古來老觀音堂。

陳興華在接受訪談時表示由於1941年日軍南侵，致使古來的新育華文小學停課。復校後，校方有感於學校空間太小，難以容納與日俱增的學生人數。在商議後決定將學校搬遷至附近空間較大的地方，繼續辦學。約1947年，擁有前學校地段的地主，允諾老觀音堂在該地建立。我們一踏入觀音堂，即見「觀化世情心自在，音聽佛法海無聲」的楹聯懸掛在廟正大門兩側。

此觀音堂值得注意的大概有兩點。其一，該堂在早期與佛教的關係密切。例如，我們見到懸掛在廟裡牆壁上有該堂於1956年加入新加坡佛教總會及1960年代（確實年份模糊無法辨識）加入位於新加坡的世界佛教社的會員證書。至1989年，觀音堂又加入馬來西亞佛教總會成為會員。

另一個值得注意的地方是該堂在慶祝觀音誕時，前來觀音堂祭拜的信眾除了古來區以外，也有來自不同地區的信眾前來膜拜，其中包括：新山、新加坡、吉隆坡等地的善男信女。再者，前來觀音堂祈福保平安的不僅只有華人，也有一些印度友族前來祈福。目前，該堂主要的堂務是為信眾提供祈福服務，包括點油燈及看通書擇吉日等。在我們進行考察時，還見善信前來祈福。此外，我們亦見有婦人在折蓮花紙，相信亦為信眾祈福之用。

在觀音堂不遠處有一間雲山宮觀音堂，陳興華表示她們雖同為觀音堂，但是基於香火來源的地點以及師公的不同，故雙方沒有交流或聯繫。然而，我們無法知道老觀音堂的祖師是誰，只是知道第一代住持陳慶（宣）來自廣東梅縣。

根據雲山宮的現任（第3任）住持黃德心（1959-）女居士所敘述，古來雲山宮觀音堂於1937年由來自廣西省昭平縣的黃金（1901-1996）女居士所創立，原取名為「雲山寺」，並於1977年易名為「雲山宮」。黃金將「雲山寺」易名為「雲山宮」，其主要該寺常引來出家人到此掛單，住持認為該廟皆帶髮修行之女居士，為了避免出家眾前來掛單，故有易名之必要。早年黃金與廣東省大埔縣人的堂妹黃

英（1913-？），一同從中國南來。當時柔佛州普遍種植橡膠樹，她們抵達柔佛後受雇為膠工，以割樹膠維持生計。後來黃英南下新加坡創建觀音宮而隨後黃金也在古來新村二巷尾創建雲山寺（黃文斌、張曉威，2011: 70-71）。[28]

　　新加坡四馬路的觀音堂與古來雲山宮有往來。據黃德心表示，雲山宮曾有齋姑在四馬路觀音堂居住過。目前懸掛在古來雲山宮的「慧德堂」一匾，其名字即為新加坡四馬路觀音堂替古來雲山宮所取的「堂號」。雖然如此，雙方僅限於活動的往來，四馬路觀音堂並不干涉或管理雲山宮。

　　黃金在1937年初創時即任住持，有意行善領養孩子，故一些貧苦家庭人士也將小孩送給雲山寺寄養。該廟未來的住持人選也皆從這些孩子中挑選出來。第二代住持為葉佑娘（1927-1990），法號景蓮，便是在該廟長大的孩子。葉佑娘後改名為曾四妹，於1957年時已是雲山寺的當家。黃德心表示，葉佑娘在1990年去世，而黃金也在1996年病逝，她才接任住持。由於她年幼時，兩位前輩很少向她提起雲山宮過去的事蹟，故她對於該廟早期的歷史不甚了解。1957年時，雲山寺曾經在1957年《馬來亞獨立大典紀念冊》特刊上登廣告祝賀國家獨立日，故有一篇略介紹黃英居士的資料。依據黃德心說，該文章所提到的雲山寺創辦人「黃英居士」，其實應該是「黃金居士」，因為出錢刊登廣告祝賀者為「黃英」，故撰寫人將雲山寺創辦人看成是她。如此看來，該文中提到「現年五十八歲」者應為黃金居士，但卻誌明廣東大埔人，這與黃德心所言她是廣西昭平人有別。

　　由於該廟原為齋姑修行的道場，故有收養女孤兒的傳統，但沒有硬性規定長大的孩子不可出嫁。據黃德心表示，在該廟撫養長大的孩子不少，其中亦有成長後出嫁為人妻者。在黃金居士主持的年代，有

---

28 〈考察報告〉（十），記錄者：沈潤遠，日期：2011年4月10日，時間：9:15am-10:30am，地點：古來雲山宮。

五至六位女孩出嫁，一至二位居住在新加坡，二位定居本地。雖然這些孩子已出嫁，但是與寺廟的關係還是非常密切。她們也會感恩圖報，每當慶祝廟誕缺乏人手時，她們也會前來協助。如今廟裡有五位被領養的孩子。孩子們都已就讀於小學，所有學費皆由寺廟負責。

雲山宮早期並無理事會，為了合法化便於2004年註冊。寺廟的運作並無大更動，還是由住持打理廟內大小事務。雲山宮主要供奉觀音菩薩，常年活動計有每年三次的觀音誕、地藏菩薩誕、新年祈福與年終還神。雲山宮在慶祝每年三次觀音誕時，皆開放供大眾進香膜拜及舉辦自由餐，信徒可自由捐款，而前來參與者有400至500人左右。該廟並無進行其他寺廟常見的共修活動，只是提供住戶作個人修行。黃德心說她每天早上會做早課，念誦《卸藏觀音普門品經》或《星辰寶懺》。此經書從黃金居士傳至她，已有數十年的歷史。雲山宮觀音堂後方懸掛著祖師的照片及安置神主牌。據黃德心說大部分的神主牌是已往生信眾的子女所安置，目前雲山宮已不再接受安置神主牌。此外，該廟內有平安符及門符供予信眾奉請。

雲山宮觀音堂的香火來源何處目前不得而知。唯一可以獲得的資訊是該廟與新加坡四馬路觀音堂有來往。目前雲山宮仍然在後廳懸掛一張祖師及其弟子的合照。該照片上有以下的一段文字：

> 江祖號允恭。廣東嘉應州人。翁幼學儒。樂善好施。喜莊老之言。訪玄至叻。遇至人。號南山。授道修真。後遊至粵西有鑊鄹峰即隱焉。得金液煉形之法。形神俱妙。迨應運度人。南返開創馬六甲道場。乾坤景附。中外歸心。何其身有生滅。預示涅槃時當宣統二年庚戌歲。清和既望。示意吾將歸矣。汝等毋怠厥志。至念日晨寅刻。寂然坐化於叻坡天德堂。呈報洋官醫生看驗。曰淨如金玉。其形如生。慈眉朗目。此真仙也。嗣以全坡警聞齊集。瞻仰慈容。禮拜獻花。男女參拜數萬眾。各各讚嘆不已。擁擠之盛難以形容。左出右入如是三晝夜。身正端

然始行奉安焉。謹跋。
天運歲次乙未年蒲月吉旦後學道眾拜撰

　　此段文字記於乙未年（1955），乃由後學眾弟子所撰，並清楚地
交代其祖師為廣東省嘉應州人江允恭（？-1910）。他曾到過新加坡
（叻）[29] 學道，「遇至人。號南山。授道修真」。江允恭後來到粵西
修行，得道後南返馬六甲辦道場，並於宣統二年（1910）在叻坡（新
加坡）的天德堂去世。目前筆者尚無法查到更多有關江允恭的背景資
料。據雲山宮住持黃德心所言，該廟前輩曾學道於新加坡四馬路觀音
堂。目前與四馬路觀音堂有歷史淵源的新加坡如切觀音堂（1919）乃
李南山祖師所創。[30] 因此，我們大概可以肯定真有李南山此人，而江
允恭曾在新加坡向他學道。為了弄清楚這些觀音堂的關係，筆者考查
了幾間觀音堂：馬六甲老街區雞場街的觀音堂（1894）及崇德堂
（1902）、新加坡如切觀音堂及古來雲山宮觀音堂與新加坡四馬路觀
音堂的關係。最後可以確定李南山為四馬路觀音堂的創辦人，其堂號
為「天德堂」。依據筆者與如切觀音堂住持周育民居士的訪談，他指
出李祖師曾為如切觀音堂取名為「天覺堂」。至於馬六甲的兩間觀音
堂乃李祖師的後學，即江允恭所創辦。[31] 上述引文中提到江允恭「南
返開創馬六甲道場。乾坤景附」，這個兩個道場即是觀音堂及崇德
堂，一為男性道場（乾），另一為女性道場（坤）。卓瑜進（2010：
14-25）曾針對馬六甲老街區的三間觀音廟作研究，他依據兩間寺廟
的碑文指出崇德堂為馬六甲聞人曾江水（1875-1940）所捐獻。曾氏
因其母生病喝了崇德堂的符水而痊癒，為了報答準提觀音的庇佑以及

---

29 新加坡早年稱為石叻，乃取馬來文Selat之音譯。
30 有關如切觀音堂的資料可參閱http://www.kuanimtng.org.sg/default.aspx?type=c&uc=aboutus。瀏覽日期：
　2012年2月28日。
31 筆者曾與新加坡如切觀音堂住持周育民電話訪談獲得上述資訊。日期：2012年2月27日。時間：下午6點
　03秒至6點8分16秒。

陳雁貞姑太的恩惠，於光緒壬寅年（1902）購買了一間屬劉姓家族的娘惹（Nyoya）舊屋，並且加以裝修，送給江騰蛟以及陳雁貞，以便作齋堂讓馬六甲持齋的女士居住。其實，江騰蛟即是江允恭，號化雨，諱聖清大夫。[32] 馬六甲觀音堂又名「天一堂」，當崇德堂成立後，男女齋堂的分界自此開始。

上述的這些觀音堂皆為持素及帶髮修行的「齋公」及「齋姑」所居住，與明清流行的先天道派有關。由於早期馬六甲崇德堂及新加坡如切觀音堂皆與新加坡四馬路觀音堂有來往，而如切觀音堂清楚地指出他們乃信仰「釋儒道三教合一」的「先天道」。由此，我們大致可以斷定古來雲山宮觀音堂的香火乃屬於「先天道」一派。

事實上，「先天道」乃屬於俗稱「齋教」一派，是個主張三教（儒釋道）同源的一種宗教。臺灣有龍華、金幢、先天三派，三者均傳自大陸。此三派多以觀音、釋迦牟尼佛為本尊。此外，他們皆鼓勵「持齋」，而先天派與其他兩派不同之處是「禁婚娶，採絕對素食」及較具儒教色彩（慈怡主編，2004: 6549-6550）。由於先天派的齋姑觀音堂「禁婚娶」，故她們便領養貧苦人家的小孩，這不僅是一種善行又可防老。由此看來，觀音信仰在新馬地區的傳播，其中一個因素乃因先天道派或齋教的關係，而在這個過程女性禁婚持齋修行及領養貧苦孩童，形成另一種有別於出家修行的宗教組織。當然，先天道派並非專屬於客家人，只是我們見到古來村的兩間觀音堂皆是屬於此類。

古來村的另一間主祀觀音的廟宇是「萬仙廟」。顧名思義，該廟乃供奉諸多神明之廟宇。據廟內神像背後牌匾的記錄，廟內供奉的神明計有：玄天上帝、斗母娘娘、王母娘娘、哪吒師傅、大伯公等諸神，然而，主神為觀音娘娘，也被稱為佛母娘娘。萬仙廟，就是典型

---

32 江騰蛟為江允恭此資訊乃由戚常卉教授見新加坡四馬路觀音堂特刊所提供，筆者特此鳴謝。筆者亦從網站查獲此資訊。見http://pmgs.kongfz.com/detail/3_295517/，2012年9月2日。

的釋、道及民間信仰互相融合的廟宇之一，從大門兩旁的對聯「萬神聚集傳善果，仙佛畢至授福田」就可知曉。這種佛教、道教、本土創造的神祇等兼互並存的特色，體現出該地佛教、道教相互融合的特點，也反映當地華人民間宗教信仰的多元性與開放性。

萬仙廟始建於1931年，當時有一群熱心村民在獲得該地的黃梨園園主應允後，即在園內以亞答及木板搭建起一座簡陋的神廟。在1967年萬仙廟喜獲五名前來還願善信的巨額捐款，再加上其他信徒的慷慨捐助之下，神廟進行了首次的翻新工程，昔日簡陋的面貌變得煥然一新，而奠定了現在所見廟宇的基本規模。

1995年該廟正式註冊合法宗教團體，理事會也於同年成立，並規定每兩年改選一次。自此，萬仙廟便由眾理事攜手管理及處理神廟諸事務。為了響應州政府的號召，萬仙廟自設立理事會後，另外加設一美化委員會，負責神廟一切美化工作。1999年，該理事會籌建觀音塑像、假山瀑布、涼亭，獲得諸善信不吝捐款而得以完成，而2003年再次進行美化工程。經過數次的擴建及美化，萬仙廟愈加富麗堂皇，甚至被柔佛旅遊促進局列為向國內外觀光客的介紹景點[33]。理事們也表示，萬仙廟在2000年成立婦女組，致使該廟的組織結構更為完善。

基於廟內主神為觀音娘娘，慶祝觀音誕已成為該廟重要的常年活動。每年農曆六月十九日，理事會都會舉辦觀音誕慶祝活動，整個社區熱鬧異常。他們頗為自豪的表示，開辦的筵席有100餘席之多。場面之大可想而知。此外，宴會現場也會進行籌款活動，所獲款項皆捐助予當地的華文小學。除了慶祝觀音誕以外，該廟每年也會舉辦酬謝神明活動，其中包括邀請傳統戲班表演、卡拉OK歌唱比賽和舞龍舞獅等。至於萬仙廟的日常活動，要數每月農曆十五的乩童問事最受信眾歡迎，可見尚有許多信眾尋求神明指點迷津（黃文斌、張曉威，

---

33 此根據《民生報》1999年4月24日報導。

2010: 1）。[34]

從神廟保存的多張證書即可看出萬仙廟對於教育與慈善活動之支持，尤其是華人教育，神廟更多次熱心慷慨解囊。廟宇也提供場地供村民學習「護身學」。據聞此護身學源自臺灣，能讓村民學習調理身體，為一養身之功法。除了護身學外，廟宇也提供場地給予舞獅團作為練習場地。這一系列活動的推行，強化了神廟與村民的互動，也體現了神廟與信眾之間的密切聯繫。

值得一提的是，該廟除了「齊天大聖」以外，其他諸神如「三奶娘娘」也是乩童扶鸞的神明之一，並非只局限於一位神明而已，這點也與萬仙廟供奉眾神的特點相同。據悉，附身的神明不同，使用的語言也不同，如齊天大聖使用華語、三奶娘娘使用客家話（黃文斌、張曉威，2010: 2）。

由此看來，萬仙廟雖以觀音為主祀神，然而其宗教風格與其他兩間觀音堂有很大的差別。觀音堂屬於家廟，萬仙廟比較像是一個社團，扮演一個讓民眾活動及聯誼的地方。這些民間信仰與客家的關係並不明顯，除了創辦人及村民為客家人。

五、洪仙大帝信仰

洪仙公或洪仙大帝信仰是另一個在古來縣華人新村值得注意的信仰，因為其知名度及影響越來越廣，方興未艾。其中如新港村、加拉巴沙威村（下稱沙威村）、武吉峇都村（下稱峇都村）及士年納村都有供奉洪仙大帝，而新港及沙威兩村更以洪仙大帝廟聞名。據我們考察獲得的資料，沙威村的洪仙大帝香火乃源自新港村，而峇都村玄天廟所供奉的洪仙大帝之香火則來自新山的柔佛古廟（黃文斌、張曉

---

34 〈考察報告〉（一），記錄者：葉燕雯，日期：2009年12月26日，時間：2:00pm-2:45pm，地點：古來萬仙廟。

威，2010: 23）。[35] 由此可見，洪仙大帝信仰為古來及新山流行的信仰之一。再者，沙威村的洪仙大帝廟更有健全的現代化組織，該廟理事會不僅管理廟務，也發展及管理義山（塚山）、承辦幼兒教育（幼稚園）及舉辦許多文教與康樂活動以造福村民。在古來縣九個新村中，有許多村寺廟都有祀奉洪仙公，然皆屬配祀神，而主祀又有歷史及特色者當歸新港及沙威村的洪仙大帝廟。洪仙大帝廟以新港村歷史最悠久，而沙威村的發展組織最完善。因此本節我們只以這兩間廟作討論。

依據安煥然（2011: 211）的說法，洪仙大帝是新加坡及柔佛一帶地方性的神明，為「三腳白虎」的化身，自神跡傳開後，開始獲得民眾的祀奉，新加坡有順興古廟，又稱洪仙宮。他指出洪仙大帝非專屬某個方言群，在新加坡有福建紹安、在柔佛州亦有潮籍人士祀奉。唯獨目前尚未在中國找到其神緣出處。由於這是新加坡及柔佛州一帶的民間信仰，而目前在古來縣所見其祭祀者皆為河婆客家人。然而，胡錦昌（2009: v44）指出傳說中的洪仙大帝為廣東省大埔縣人，為人善良，樂於助人，一日遇三腳虎騎之而化為仙。由於傳說中的洪仙公沒有真實的姓名，故我們視此為民間傳說。也許，華人南來拓荒時，常發生老虎噬人事件，村民膜拜洪仙公之後，虎患漸減，洪仙公因而變成新加坡、馬來西亞柔佛州一帶民眾所崇拜的神明。目前在新港村與沙威村祀奉洪仙公者多為廣東省揭西縣河婆鎮人，難免令人懷疑洪仙公的神緣傳說應該是揭西縣而非大埔縣。由於無法在中國找到神緣出處，而據目前所見，除了河婆客家人祀奉洪仙公外，也有福建人和潮州人供奉洪仙公。在客屬之中有潮州客與福佬客，加上新加坡以福建人居多，故閩潮人祭祀洪仙公也屬自然之事。例如，柔佛古廟的洪仙大帝神像在遊神時即由福建幫所負責。

---

35 〈考察報告〉（二），記錄者：葉燕雯，日期：2010年1月24日，時間：2:00pm-2:45pm，地點：武吉苔都玄天廟。

新港新村祭拜洪仙公的傳統，與二十世紀初前來開芭種植黃梨的村民有密切關係。新港在開發前一片荒蕪，前來開墾的先輩，生命時常受到老虎的威脅，鑑於此就在該地請了洪仙大帝前來坐鎮。根據該廟資深理事彭漢明（1931-）追憶早期的狀況時說：「新港約在1928年，就開始種植黃梨，洪仙大帝廟在那時就已存在了。」雖然建廟的時間無從稽考[36]。此外，據該廟吳永輝（1939-）主席、黃其祥秘書暨理事們的口述，蓋因當地老虎橫行，英國人為保村民員工之安危，基於此緣由允許村民創建洪仙大帝廟。該半英畝大之廟地由英國園丘公司（Fraser Ladang）所捐贈，同時該公司也為洪仙大帝廟修建道路。在緊急法令前，該廟已是香火鼎盛，信眾繁多，並且屢次出現洪仙大帝頻顯靈的傳說。《古來掌故》一書提到：「新港附近皆為荒山大芭，人們在這裡開墾芭地時，有人在外買了牛肉回到公司吃，可能是剩下的牛骨腥味，迄夜間，竟引得連續多晚出現白額老虎，虎視眈眈，吼聲震天，嚇得人們心驚膽寒，幸而未有人受傷。」（梁文華，1979: 36）新港村民相信這是洪仙大帝在顯靈。此外，根據我們口訪得知，有一些人不相信白虎出現是洪仙大帝的顯靈，就在村內試吃牛肉，結果即刻腹痛不止，經過這起事件後，村民都相信這是洪仙大帝在靈驗。此後全村人幾乎都不敢在村裡吃牛肉（黃文斌、張曉威，2010: 11）。[37]

至於為什麼洪仙大帝不喜歡人們吃牛肉則不得而知。若與惠州客家人信奉觀音不可吃牛肉看來，也許他們認為牛是對人們有貢獻的動物，故不忍心見牠們被宰殺。另一個可能是華人或受馬來西亞的印度人影響，印度人視牛為神聖動物而不吃牛肉。此外，據筆者的經驗推測，牛在二十世紀70年代以前還是馬來西亞主要的運輸工具之一，加上本地的牛肉有很重的腥味，故華人不喜歡吃牛肉是很普遍的事。由

---

36 根據《南洋商報》在2006年2月12日報導新港洪仙大帝廟在1891年創立，惟不知其根據。
37 〈考察報告〉（一），記錄者：葉燕雯，日期：2009年12月28日，時間：10:00am-11:00am，地點：新港洪仙大帝廟。

於中國大陸或台灣吃牛肉是普遍的事情，與馬來西亞華人的飲食習慣有差異，故筆者推論馬來西亞華人不喜歡吃牛肉乃受上述的在地因素之影響。

除了上述洪仙大帝顯靈的事蹟，據新港洪仙大帝廟理事們口述，在第二次世界大戰前，每年的洪仙大帝誕辰，由古來開往約二英里的新港火車都會在洪仙大帝廟前停站，讓信眾前往膜拜。有一次洪仙大帝寶誕，火車不讓信眾在新港洪仙大帝廟下車或乘搭回返，結果有一節火車廂竟在該廟前附近脫軌翻覆。事後每當該廟誕辰時，開行的火車便會在該廟前停站，方便善男信女前往膜拜（黃文斌、張曉威，2010: 11）。甚至理事們還說，在日侵時期村民為保性命而逃難至神廟附近，負責搜索的日軍到此地時卻未發現一人，因此村民逃過一劫。他們深信是洪仙大帝保佑的緣故。因此可見，新港村洪仙大帝廟的香火所以旺盛，乃因村民深信這些事蹟是洪仙公的顯靈。目前，不僅村裡的人民膜拜洪仙公，甚至沙威及士年納的村民也不辭行路之苦，前來新港膜拜洪仙公，祈福消災。

新港村洪仙大帝廟曾於1972年進行整修，1978年獲得土地局批准五畝空地，1989年獲得合法註冊。[38] 據目前所見，該廟最大的特色在於曾於2003年投注80萬重資進行為期三年的美化環境工程，包括建設：假山瀑布、八卦池、仿古長城、亭子等。美化工程竣工後，該廟變得煥然一新，四周美景引人入勝，吸引了許多本地及新加坡信眾前來運動及參觀。此外，該廟不僅只有華人善信前來祭拜，就連錫克族也會前來膜拜，廟中部分石凳子和八卦轉運池乃由該族兄弟兩人所捐贈。可見洪仙公威名早已跨越種族的藩籬，紮根在信眾心中。

---

38 馬來西亞社團註冊局把註冊社團分為13類，宗教團體為其一。馬來西亞曾分別於1966年和1984年制定《1966年社團法令》（Societies Act 1966 & Regulations）和《1984年社團條例》（Societies Regulations 1984），賦予馬來西亞內政部管理國內社團，並根據以上法律、規章處理商會的註冊、變更、終止、對違法行為進行行政制裁等，沒有按時提呈年報的神廟社團組織可能會被對付，所面對的刑罰也相當嚴重。參考自洪祖秋，〈神廟與社團面對的年報〉，http://ang49.blogspot.com/2012/04/blog-post_14.html，2012年7月17日，原刊登於《星洲日報》12-4-2012「大柔佛」版。

新港洪仙大帝廟的組織結構及廟誕慶典活動，與其他廟宇無太大差異。該廟每逢農曆十一月廿一日為洪仙公慶祝成道日。然而，近幾年該廟的洪仙大帝金身被請去古來鎮上慶祝寶誕，理事們才改慶元宵。據悉，每年元宵節早上，洪仙大帝聖駕就會在善信暨理事的護駕下，從廟宇出發繞境一圈。洪仙公金身所到之處都會引起信眾爭相進香，祈求洪仙大帝的庇佑。2010年的遊神活動甚至還吸引超過五百人的參與。早年遊神的路線會越過火車軌道，近年來顧慮到信眾的安全而取消。除了遊神活動外，也會表演傳統酬神戲，供村民消遣娛樂。鑑於近年來演唱流行曲的歌舞演出深受善信歡迎，理事們也會邀請紅星前來助興。

　　由於每年舉辦神誕耗資不少，理事們也頗懂開源之道，即在神誕前先準備110至120對燈籠供信眾投標，藉此籌集慶祝神誕的經費。此外，善信們出席平安宴皆需樂捐香油錢馬幣20元，由於善信常攜老帶幼踴躍出席平安宴，宴席筵開100桌之多，故造成每年舉辦宴席都會虧損馬幣1、2萬元，所幸虧損金額可以由燈籠投標活動的經費填補。較為特殊的是，該廟有「借利」的習俗，即信眾（或稱借利者）向神廟討個紅包，金額由信眾要求，額數從馬幣2元至28元不等，今年所借的金額，明年必須退還兩倍。神廟每年借出馬幣1萬元之多，雖然會遇到欠而不還者，所幸每年收回的金額皆超額而略有盈餘（黃文斌、張曉威，2011: 19-20）。[39]

　　神廟除了開放供善信膜拜外，也扮演著華文教育暨社會慈善推廣者的角色。據廟宇裡保留的證書，該廟曾經捐助中國青海地震、四川大地震、古來殘障兒童協會等。此外，該廟也秉持重視教育的精神，積極參與華教的捐款活動，受惠的學校有寬柔古來分校、新港華小等。牆上掛滿「熱心教育」、「為善最樂」、「熱心公益」等數十個

39〈考察報告〉（九），記錄者：江炎凱、溫子茹、蘇韻淇，日期：2011年1月9日，時間：3:00pm-4:30pm，地點：新港洪仙大帝廟。

的旗子、證書、清單，都是洪仙大帝廟熱心教育、回饋社會的最佳佐證。由此可見，該廟扮演了宗教、教育及社會福利之功能。

在緊急法令時期，居住在郊外的村民被迫遷入新村，由英殖民政府加強管制，村民的人身自由受到限制。有鑒於此，沙威村民有人獻議將洪仙大帝請來該地坐鎮。1952年該村善信便從新港洪仙大帝另請一支分香到沙威新村，以方便善信們膜拜。士年納新村也曾因村民前去膜拜洪仙公遭火車撞倒之事，善信也另請了洪仙公香火至該村的大伯公廟。自此後，這兩個新村就擁有了洪仙公的分香。

沙威村洪仙大帝廟是目前古來再也縣九個新村裡在當地最具規模及有組織性的廟宇。早在多年前，管理加拉巴沙威洪仙大帝廟的前輩們已了解置產業的重要性，並為此做出長年規劃。該廟目前有管理義山及幼稚園等機構，可謂與當地村民的互動密不可分。洪仙大帝廟的理事會秉持著為村民謀求福利，致使該廟凝聚了整個村民的發展力量，成為該村發展史上不可或缺的組織機構。依據我們考察所見，洪仙大帝廟在該村的社會功能已遠遠超越了其宗教功能。

自洪仙大帝廟香火分設至加拉巴沙威村後，村民們終可免兩地奔走祭祀之苦。洪仙大帝廟於1968年重建成磚瓦建築。該廟於1976年成立信託理事會，主要為負責管理神廟的產業和福首理事會的款項。在信託理事會成員努力下，該廟於1986年獲批准為合法註冊宗教團體，並藉此推動廟宇屬下的福利事務計畫。其中包括：一、發展義山；二、發展四維幼稚園分校；三、成立慈善機構及獎學金；四、統一集體慶祝神誕；五、發展修建神廟。

1987年，信託理事會在沙令附近購置了一塊七英畝的地段，並於1990年獲當局批准該地段作為發展義山之用。該義山也於1992年正式啟用，為該廟目前主要的經濟來源之一。另外，信託理事會於1977年創立四維幼稚園。該幼稚園曾因無固定教室而數度搬遷，迄至2000年，信託理事會向土地局申請一畝的土地作為建立幼稚園課室之用，並已於2002年竣工，正式啟用。這在在顯示該廟理事會組織能力強

及能幹，更重要的，他們關心村民的教育及社區福利。這個新村有90%以上是河婆客家同鄉，我們沒見到廣府、福建、潮州、海南等籍貫方言群的會館組織，只有血緣性的宗親會館，如黃氏宗親會、張氏宗親會等。這種現象在馬來西亞是較少見的。也許，正因為大家都是河婆同鄉，故比較有向心力，再通過洪仙大帝廟將大家組織起來，凝聚力就更加強了。

由於發展日益壯大，該信託理事會於1990年正式成立會所，為村民提供活動場所，其中包括有近十位導師的書法班、為年長者提供強身健體的外丹功班等。1993年，該信託理事會開始每年頒發會員子女學業優異獎勵金。1998年，沙威圖書館正式成立，藏書高達數千冊，提供了當地中小學生與社會人士一個學習與閱讀的場所，也提升了當地閱讀與學習風氣。

隨著時光流逝，該廟宇已顯陳舊，以及遭白蟻侵蝕而造成逢雨必漏的窘況。該理事會於2005年議決推行「發展修建神廟」計畫，並於2008年3月動工。他們曾經到處籌款，群策群力，最終募得馬幣約130萬建築費。新廟建築於2010年1月3日落成。新廟宇的啟用，再進一步擴大為村民服務，也促進更多的地方文化活動。加拉巴沙威洪仙大帝廟眾理事的同心協力及無私奉獻，無疑是促使該廟成功的最大要素。

六、大伯公信仰

古來縣的亞逸文滿、士年納、士乃新村都有大伯公信仰的存在。本節只是選擇亞逸文滿村（下稱文滿村）及士年納村作為論述，因為文滿村的大伯公廟是最古老及香火最旺盛的大伯公廟，堪稱為該地的地標，而士年納村的大伯公乃文滿村的分香。

文滿村大伯公廟早在1930年前已創廟，迄今已超過七十年的歷史，而其供奉的大伯公最特別的是黑臉的大伯公。據我們觀察，其廟宇格局是以大伯公廟居中間殿，右殿是善緣亭，左殿則是觀音庵。據

悉，當時文滿新村除了大伯公廟以外，新村裡還有觀音廟。在90年代之前，兩間廟已合建成現今的大伯公廟。

大伯公廟正殿，擺放了數張供桌。神龕上大伯公居中，左右兩旁分別是玄天大帝及大歲爺。在大伯公神龕左右對聯寫著「神功浩蕩物卓民康，廟貌巍峨地靈人傑」，至於觀音塑像的牆壁上也掛了「南海飛來」的匾額，是在1964年慶祝觀音誕時善信所贈送。居中而坐的大伯公像，身披藍袍站姿。據理事告知，曾有扶鸞者表示大伯公有文武之分，文滿村的黑臉大伯公乃屬於「武」大伯公，故其塑像乃呈站姿（黃文斌、張曉威，2011: 11）。[40] 此外，殿裡其他配祀的神祇還有哪吒三太子、玄天大帝、華光大帝、五路將軍、黃天來將軍、梁周文將軍、大爺伯二爺伯等。基本上，大伯公廟供奉的神祇是屬於民間信仰及道教的神明。

大伯公屬於土地神，又有各種稱謂包括伯公、大伯公、福德正神、福德老爺、土地公、社神、社公、社官等。大伯公信仰在馬來西亞流傳已久，主要分成兩種說法：第一，大伯公信仰與客家人有關，屬於華僑先驅的祖靈崇拜（安煥然， 2003: 5-6；陳波生、利亮時，2006: 60-61；王娟，2008: 76-79）。最早的客屬大伯公廟是檳州的海珠嶼大伯公廟（1810），相傳是馬來西亞最早的大伯公廟，由惠州、嘉應、大埔、永定、增城五屬客家人的代表共同管理（轉引張維安、張容嘉，2011: 357）。根據碑文顯示，大伯公為張理。第二個說法是大伯公為地區守護神，屬於土地崇拜信仰。在馬來西亞，大伯公作為主祀神明極為常見，學者推測全馬應該超過300間以上，其中砂拉越州以58間居冠（張維安、張容嘉，2011: 357-360）。在柔佛州，大伯公信仰也是普遍的民間信仰之一。古來縣的文滿村及土年納村的大伯公廟，似乎也與客家人脫離不了關係。只不過古來縣裡的文滿新村所

---

40 《考察報告》（九），記錄者：阮湧和，日期：2011年1月10日，時間：2:00pm-3:30pm，地點：亞逸文滿大伯公廟。

主祀的大伯公，其神像造型與平日常見的坐著手持玉如意、白臉大伯公神像不同，其神像造型為站姿與黑臉，別樹一格。

　　據文滿村大伯公廟諸位耆老口述，該廟的塑像乃由一名中國廣東東莞人漂洋至馬來亞時所攜帶。早在1930年代，大伯公廟就建立在目前文滿新村的對面山頭。當時不過是簡陋的木板小廟，供附近的居民膜拜。一直到了二十世紀50年代緊急法令時期，居住在對面山頭的村民遭到英殖民政府的迫遷，大伯公廟也無可豁免，隨著居民搬遷至現址（黃文斌、張曉威，2011: 11）。大伯公廟理事表示，60年代時眾人集資在大伯公廟附近搭建了一座戲台，因早期村民缺乏娛樂活動，廟會舉辦的活動常常能吸引村民熱烈的參與。因此每逢酬神大戲的演出，附近的村民自備椅子前來霸位，欣賞大戲的演出。[41] 該廟後因大伯公英靈顯赫而威名遠播，吸引了不少其他新村的村民前來膜拜，其中包括士年納及沙威新村的信眾等。

　　二十世紀60年代，士年納村民為了方便膜拜大伯公，便從文滿村大伯公廟另請一支香火到該新村。自此，聞名的黑臉大伯公也開始在士年納村有了分香。不過，士年納的大伯公金身並非黑臉大伯公，而是常見的白臉大伯公塑像。據文滿村大伯公廟理事們透露，他們感到最高興的事莫過於該廟在1991年取得註冊成功，成為合法宗教團體之一。自50年代以來，村民至少三次集資修葺廟宇，最近一次是在1995年進行修葺工程。經過修建後，該廟更添姿彩。近年來吸引更多信眾，甚至鄰國新加坡的遊客也前來一睹黑臉大伯公的風采。

　　每年農曆十月初二為大伯公誕，神廟到了這一天就會大事慶祝一番。爐主與信眾們都會前來盛祭神明，神廟也會舉辦一系列的活動，如：過平安橋、演酬神戲劇、舉辦卡拉OK歌唱比賽等。此外，舉辦平安宴暨標福品，更是不可少的活動之一。該廟曾在1998年進行首次的遊神活動，之後相隔十一年（2009年）才有第二次遊神，故該廟並

41《東方日報》南馬新聞，2009年11月21日，洪志達接受報章訪談時的談話。

不常舉辦遊神活動。除了大伯公誕，每年三次的觀音誕（即農曆二月十九日、六月十九日、九月十九日）也是神廟的慶典之一，同樣深受信眾的歡迎。從神廟裡張貼著不少的觀音寶誕通告即可知一二。

文滿新村大伯公廟設有理事會掌管廟務。該廟設有廟祝及乩童，對於乩童的挑選與繼承，理事們透露並沒有一定的標準或形式，這一切延續傳統的擲筊方式進行，聽神旨意來挑選乩童。該廟廟祝與乩童為同一人，其職務除了要替信眾看病外，也從事民間俗稱的「擇日」工作。有不少信眾因為擔心結婚、搬家有相沖或不吉，而前來求助。

除了扮演村民心靈寄託者的角色外，大伯公廟對於華文教育的援助也頗為熱衷，捐獻了不少錢資助學校。根據神廟裡掛上的感謝狀，受惠的學校有萬邦華小、寬柔中學、拉曼大學等，身兼萬邦華小董事的諸位理事，也曾集資捐贈萬邦華小兩間課室。根據理事們的敘述，該廟每年都會捐獻馬幣5、6,000元給當地的學校與社團。此外，神廟也設立獎勵金給予萬邦華小的優秀生。文滿村大伯公廟曾在1997年獲得柔佛政府頒發非回教宗教組織外觀與整潔比賽第三名，是少數獲得這種殊榮的神廟之一。

士年納大伯公廟似乎沒有文滿村來得有規模。據知該廟約於1946年，由一批熱心的居民籌建，當時神廟坐落在士年納外的橡膠園裡。1948年緊急法令時期，強迫郊區外的華人搬入新村，大伯公廟也不可豁免，從橡膠園遷移至士年納新村，自此落地紮根。早期的士年納大伯公廟，乃由亞答葉與木板搭成的簡陋小屋，現今已改建為水泥的神廟。

據該廟理事表示，在緊急法令時期，士年納村民並沒有人因此而喪生，他們認為這是大伯公顯靈庇護（黃文斌、張曉威，2010：22）。[42] 足見大伯公信仰已深入民心，成為村民不可或缺的心靈寄託

---

[42] 〈考察報告〉（二），記錄者：葉燕雯，日期：2010年1月24日，時間：10:00am-11:00am，地點：士年納大伯公廟。

之一。約在1950-60年代，坐落在士年納馬華區會會所附近的觀音庵，也遷移至大伯公廟旁邊。這正好與文滿村的大伯公廟的發展歷史情況相呼應。大伯公廟的面積有4段（英文俗稱lord），面積頗大。單層屋子的大伯公廟位置居中，觀音庵及忠善壇分居兩側。廟裡的擺設簡單，大伯公塑像前的桌子，擺放觀音娘娘的符咒及大伯公、洪仙大帝及觀音娘娘印章。該廟理事表示，忠善壇乃他人借用此地安神，與大伯公及觀音庵並無直接關係。觀音庵只有觀音神像一尊，並無其他神明。觀音庵原有尼姑主持，如今尼姑已不再駐守。

經過數十年的歲月洗禮，原本簡陋的大伯公廟已殘破不堪，間中曾進行了數次的擴建及維修。根據廟裡遺下的信眾捐款芳名牌區，大伯公廟曾在1971年進行維修擴建。在一批高瞻遠矚信眾的努力下，該廟在1979年就向政府爭取為合法的宗教組織，並在1982年就獲得註冊局批准。至於神廟的常年活動，他們透露每年的農曆十月初二為大伯公誕，當天神廟會大擺筵席，大約有20至30桌。標福品的籌款活動也會在當天進行。怡情的娛樂節目自然少不了露天電影、卡拉OK等。

大伯公廟有扶鸞的宗教服務。在緊急法令時期，新村的診所還不普及，獲得醫藥援助並不易，乩童不僅能替村民排紛解難，而且又能治療疾病，因此深受村民的信賴。神廟不止扮演著村民生活的心理療效，也扮演醫療者的角色。惟在醫藥逐漸發達，求醫途徑便利的情況下，乩童的醫療者角色才逐漸被取代，如今神廟只提供善信問事的服務。此外，大伯公廟、觀音庵都設有籤桶供善信求籤，據說頗為靈驗。該廟早期設有解籤服務，俗稱「解籤佬」，每日皆駐守在桌前替人解籤解惑。如今解籤佬已不需每日報到，只有在農曆初一、十五才為信眾提供解籤的服務。

該廟供奉的主神為大伯公，陪祀的神明為當地村民普遍膜拜的洪仙大帝。理事們笑言大伯公廟曾發生的一段小插曲。據說，較早前大伯公塑像原與洪仙大帝供奉在同一神台上，寓意兩神同等的地位。某日才獲乩童扶鸞告知，大伯公廟的主人為大伯公，主客有別，故大伯

公塑像不應與洪仙大帝置於在同一神台上。至此以後，理事們才將洪仙大帝塑像略降一臺階，安置在較低的檯面（黃文斌、張曉威，2010: 108）。[43]

七、結語

古來再也縣華人新村以客家人占多數，然而我們很難界定這些民間信仰的「客家性」。若以客家人比較「硬頸」或固執，以及有「革命精神」傾向作為「客家性」觀之，我們也約略見到其所祭祀的神明有類似的傾向。例如，士乃村三山國王廟主祭的神明為三王爺，而非大王與二王爺，乃因其比較英勇善戰之故。此外，砂拉越石隆門的客家人在反抗英國人時，也先行祭拜三山國王及譚公爺，以團結族人的案例。再者，文滿村祭祀「武大伯公」及新港村祭祀本土化的洪仙大帝乃為了鎮壓虎患等，這些多少反映出客家人吃苦開墾的戰鬥性。類似的客家「戰鬥」精神，似乎與台灣祭祀義民廟有相似之處，反映出客家人的性格講究「正義」，為正義而戰鬥。上述古來縣各新村所供奉的神明也具備這種特殊精神。當然，三山國王與譚公都是來自原鄉的香火，非衍生於本土。然而，其奮鬥的精神與馬來西亞早期客家移民刻苦奮鬥開發錫礦及開發山芭進行墾殖有一定的相關性，如採礦區的芙蓉與吉隆坡的惠州客家人即祭祀譚公，墾殖區的士乃村及新港村就分別祭祀三山國王及洪仙大帝。

縱觀這些新村的民間信仰，其功能主要為村民提供了精神寄託與娛樂。如上所言，第二次世界大戰後，因政治意識形態分歧問題，馬來亞政府於1948年實施緊急法令，將生活在山區墾殖的華人迫遷至「新村」裡，以杜絕馬來亞共產黨的武裝鬥爭獲得「民源」。新村華

---

43 〈考察報告〉（八），記錄者：沈潤遠，日期：2010年12月6日，時間：1:00pm-2:00pm，地點：士年納大伯公廟。

人面對英國殖民政府的管制及馬來亞共產黨的兩面治安威脅，加上務農體勞的辛苦，身心更加感到迷茫與苦悶而需要精神寄託及娛樂。因此，我們所見到新村的廟宇有許多是時代的產物，華人新村的建立，將「人」從郊外搬遷到指定的地點建村，而「神」也隨人一起搬遷。可見人神共處是草根華人社會極為普遍的現象。另一方面，我們也看出華人除了物質生活需求外，心靈也需要有所寄託，尤其面對生活上許多的不確定性，更使他們需要通過神明的指引來獲得生活平安及精神安頓。這些民間信仰促成了廟宇的建立，無論是從「家廟」變公廟，如古來與泗隆村的譚公信仰；或從中國請來香火而需建立公廟，如士乃村的三山國王廟；又或原鄉為修行人而籌建新道場，如古來村的觀音堂等。這些廟宇的建立象徵著華人在此落地生根，也為當地村民提供了一個精神寄託的家園。此外，從這些新村的民間信仰，我們還是可以看出客家人信仰的多元性及包容性。除了本文特別討論的三山國王、譚公、觀音、洪仙大帝及大伯公之外，如在前言所言，此地區尚有真空教、媽祖、黃老祖師、關帝聖君、玄天上帝、城隍爺、三清玉皇、齊天大聖等等，不一而足。由此觀之，此地區的「客家」與「客家神明」就很不突顯。也許，這些客家村民因為面對開墾農作的辛苦及住在新村隨時面對英軍與馬共軍的雙重威脅與壓力而感到心靈不安，故民間信仰自然興盛不已。無論如何，村裡神明的多元性，只是說明他們沒有排斥及接受多元神明的共存，顯示客家人對神明的容忍與包容性。

這些寺廟的成立，為村民們提供了一個聚集互動的場所。在娛樂缺乏的年代，寺廟又提供了一個演酬神戲、廟會等娛樂的場所。甚至，提供場地辦喜事擺酒席。可見這些新村的廟宇不僅提供了宗教的功能，也扮演社會功能。此外，從士乃村三山國王廟及新港村洪仙公廟，我們也見到印度及錫克族前來祭祀及捐助神廟，或者古來村譚公廟在廟慶時唱馬來歌，泗隆村租借桌椅給馬來族婚慶等。在在說明一些神廟的功能及活動有跨種族的和諧現象。

二十世紀80年代之後，我們見到許多廟宇都會捐助教育，無論是華文小學、華人民辦中學、學院及大學，如新港村洪仙公廟、文滿村的大伯公廟等。有者則自行辦教育，如沙威村的洪仙大帝廟便經營幼稚園。再者，這些廟也進行一些文化活動，如書法班、舞龍團、舞蹈班、氣功班等，如沙威村洪仙大帝廟及古來村萬仙廟等。更甚者，神廟也扮演了社會慈善角色，如古來村觀音堂雲山宮領養貧窮小孩或孤兒。至於娛樂方面，我們也見到這些神廟為了適應時代的需求而唱卡啦OK，邀請歌星在神誕駐唱等。這些諸種的業務與活動，正與會館鄉團等所扮演的社會功能相同。在早期十九世紀中葉，華人移民社會的廟宇與會館（社團組織）所扮演的社會功能，基本上是有差別的。廟宇比較強調心靈慰藉、求平安及醫療，雖然也兼顧一些慈善工作；會館則比較傾向為同鄉尋找就業機會、聯誼及安葬等福利。然而，時值二十世紀80年代之後，我們發現兩者的社會功能已逐漸相似。也許，目前的華人社會正有此需求，故神廟也走向「社團化」的發展。這種現象與社團組織向政府申請註冊成為一個「合法團體組織」有密切關係，因為作為一個合法註冊的團體，該組織的理事會必須向政府提呈年度報告，如此一來常年活動報告也就成為一項重要的內容，也是政府評估一間合法組織的指標之一。這是目前我們見到民間信仰廟宇新的，也是未來的發展趨勢。

參考資料

王娟，2008，〈新加坡客家人的禮俗和神靈信仰初探〉，黃賢強主編，《新加坡客家文化與社群》。新加坡：新加坡國立大學中文系等出版。

王琛發，2006，《馬來西亞客家人的宗教信仰與實踐》。吉隆坡：馬來西亞客家公會聯合會出版。

安煥然、劉莉晶編撰，2007，《柔佛客家人的移殖與拓墾》。柔佛：南院學院出版。

安煥然，2003，〈淺談新馬的大伯公信仰〉，《本土與中國：學術論文集》。新山：南方學院出版社。

──，2009，〈馬來西亞柔佛客家人的移植及其族群認同探析〉，《台灣東南亞學刊》6卷1期，頁81-108。

李天錫，2007，〈紫霄真人成神與譚公信仰在馬來西亞的傳播〉，《華僑大學學報》，第1期（總第74期），頁80-85。

林美容，1991，〈台灣民間信仰的分類〉，《漢學研究通訊》，10(1): 13-18。

房學嘉，2008，《客家民俗》。廣州：華南理工大學出版社。

卓瑜進，2010，《觀音信仰──以馬六甲老街區之青雲亭、崇德堂和觀音堂為例案》。拉曼大學中文系大學部畢業論文（未出版）。

胡錦昌，2009，《柔佛廟宇文化》。生活出版社。

陳波生、利亮時，2006，〈客家人與大伯公的關係：以新馬為例〉，林緯毅主編，《民間文化與華人社會》。新加坡：新加坡亞洲研究學會。

劉還月，1999，《台灣的客家族群與信仰》。台北市：常民文化出版。

劉崇漢，1999，〈西馬客家人〉，收錄賴觀福主編，《客家遠源流長──第5屆國際客家學研討會論文集》。吉隆坡：馬來西亞客家公會聯合會出版。

黃文斌、張曉威，2010，《古來縣華人新村編撰計畫》年度報告①（2009年12月～2010年12月），馬來西亞拉曼大學中華研究中心。

——，2011，《古來縣華人新村編撰計畫》年度報告②（2011年1月～2011年12月），馬來西亞拉曼大學中華研究中心。

黃海德，2004，〈試論道教「三清」信仰的宗教內涵及其歷史衍變〉，《世界宗教研究》，第2期。

梁文華，1979，《古來掌故附古來縣九新村概況介紹》。古來廣肇會館贊助出版。

張維安、張容嘉，2011，〈馬來西亞客家族群信仰〉，收錄蕭新煌主編，《東南亞客家的變貌：新加坡與馬來西亞》，頁3-38。台北：中央研究院人社中心亞太區域研究專題中心。

慈怡主編，2004，《佛光大辭典》第7冊。北京：北京圖書館出版社。

黎志添，2007，《廣東地方道教研究：道觀、道士及科儀》。香港中文大學。

鄭琪玉，2004，《客家人的守護神——三山國王》。台北：稻田出版有限公司。

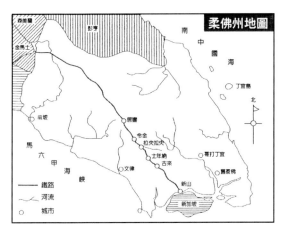

圖一：柔佛州地圖

轉引自安煥然，〈馬來西亞柔佛古來客家聚落〉，收錄於蕭新煌主編，《東南亞客家的變貌：新加坡與馬來西亞》。台北：中研院人社中心亞太區域研究專題中心，2011，頁187。

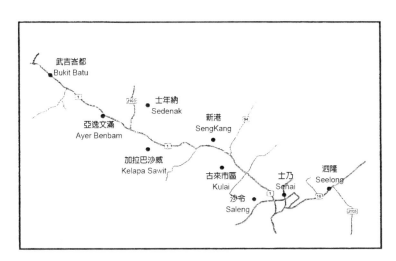

圖二：古來再也縣地圖

轉引自安煥然，〈馬來西亞柔佛古來客家聚落〉，同上，頁191。

One Deity, Many Ways: A Comparison of Communal Rituals in Two Chinese Settlements, Sarawak

Elena Gregoria Chai Chin Fern (蔡靜芬)[†]

Abstract

This paper documents one of the most celebrated communal rituals of two Chinese settlements in Sarawak Malaysia, the anniversary of the Thai Pak Kung. Although there are more than 68 documented Thai Pak Kung temples in Sarawak, this paper analyses thoroughly only two of them. Historically and as practiced to date, the anniversary of the Thai Pak Kung in conjunction with its birthday are held statewide on either the 2nd day of the 2nd lunar month or the 29th day of the 3rd lunar month. The difference in dates is a manifestation of the diversity of local beliefs of Thai Pak Kung. Furthermore, there is no proper doctrine on this belief, with knowledge normally passed down from earlier generations or presented by the highest ranking priests who preside over the Thai Pak Kung in each of the individual temples. This paper shows that every temple differs in the way rituals of the processions in conjunction with the anniversary are done. It is envisaged that this paper will lay ground to a better analysis of the communal ritual in future when the scope of study is widened. In this paper, Tabidu and Kota are two settlements inhabited by majority Chinese of the Hakka ethnic group. The Thai Pak Kung temples erected by the local people observe the anniversary of the deity but there are some stark differences in the celebration, such as the ways the

---

† Faculty of Social Sciences, University Malaysia Sarawak

processions are held. Despite the close proximity of these two temples, the actual dates of the celebration are different. Historical set-up of the settlements are factors that create a distinct diversity between the Thai Pak Kung deities of Tabidu and Kota. There are recent efforts to standardize the celebration to fall on one date, in order to gain more recognition for the religion.

Introduction to Chinese Religion in Sarawak

Malaysia in general is a country where its people practice multi-culturalism, made up of various races but dominated by the Malays (50%), followed by Chinese (24%), Indigenous communities (11%), Indians (7%) and others (8%). In Sarawak, the largest state in Malaysia, the population is about 2.5 million people in 2010. Of this, the majority is the indigenous Dayak, Melanau and Orang Ulu (50%), followed by Chinese (26%) and Malay (21%). The major religion in Sarawak is Christianity. The Chinese communities are mostly followers of the Chinese religions as well as other Christian faiths. In order to have a better understanding of the Chinese population and their faiths, let us study the categorization of the Chinese religions in Sarawak.

In Malaysia as a whole, Chinese are generally considered as believers in Buddhism, Taoism, Christian faiths. The complexity of Chinese religion was difficult to grasp even by the Malaysian government. This is proven when the census taken in 1970 (Table 1) showed that a majority of Chinese in Sarawak (31.6 per cent) were Buddhist, followed by 25.8 per cent who had no religion, 23.5 per cent with Unknown religion and 18.9 per cent were practitioners of the Christian faiths. Less than 1 per cent of Chinese in Sarawak were Muslims in 1970.

In Table 1 which shows the census result of the Sarawak Chinese religion in 1970, there were three main religious categories recognized by the government at that time. They were Islam, Christian and Buddhism. Interestingly, more than one quarter of the Chinese population were grouped into the "No religion" category. Equally, the same number of people were grouped in the "Unknown" category. Together, these two categories made up close to half of the Sarawak Chinese population in 1970 who had no clear

Table 1: The Religion of Sarawak Chinese in 1970

Religion among the Chinese	Population	Percentage (%)
Islam	465	0.19
Christian	45,329	18.92
Buddhism	75,664	31.58
No religion	61,753	25.78
Unknown	56,358	23.53
Total	239,569	100

Data source: Statistic Department Malaysia, (1970). 1970 Population and Housing Census of Malaysia, vol. 1 – basic population tables, part xiii - Sarawak

indication of their faiths or beliefs.

It is sensical to note that about one third of them were of Buddhist faith, considering that the Chinese arrived as immigrants to Sarawak from China in the late 1800s. The Chinese are strong followers of the belief systems. Considering that they ventured from their homeland in China to travel southwards to new regions such as peninsular Malaysia, Indonesia and Borneo, they would have brought with them their guiding gods during the journey. Therefore, the high percentage of Chinese in the 1970 population census does not really reflect the actual situation. The "No religion" and "Unknown" categories demonstrated a lack of understanding of the government towards the belief of the Chinese and it also portrayed the complexity of the religious affiliation of the Chinese.

In the 1980 and 1991 population censuses (Table 2), the categories of religious affiliation were diversified, and new categories of "Hindu", "Confucianism/ Taoism/ Other traditional religion", "Tribal/ Folk religion" and "Others" were added. It is uncertain how the breakdown for these extra categories was achieved but the exercise shows that the government has given recognition to these religions. It could also reflect the diversity of religious faiths among the people of Sarawak and/ or the need to properly categorize religions to take into account the high percentage of the "No religion" and "Unknown" categories as shown in the 1970 census.

Table 2: The Religion of Sarawak Chinese in 1980 and 1991

Religion among Chinese	1980		1991	
	Population	Percentage (%)	Population	Percentage (%)
Islam	813	0.23	1,917	0.43
Christian	84,121	23.36	121,148	27.42
Hindu	172	0.05	285	0.06
Buddhism	120,247	33.39	167,222	37.53
Confucianism / Taoism / other traditional religion	79,322	22.03	94,147	21.13
Tribal / folk religion	2,968	0.82	1,440	0.32
Others	3,245	0.96	763	0.17
No religion	68,996	19.16	57,450	12.89
Unknown	No data	-	176	0.04
Total	359,884	100	445,548	100

Data source: (i) Statistic Department Malaysia, (1995). Population and Housing Census of Malaysia 1991, State Population Report – Sarawak. Department of Statistic Malaysia, Kuala Lumpur; (ii) Statistic Department Malaysia, (1981). Population and Housing Census of Malaysia 1980, State Population Report – Sarawak, Part 1. Department of Statistic Malaysia, Kuala Lumpur

In Table 1 and 2, the figures show that generally, most Chinese in Sarawak professed themselves as Buddhist, with over 30 per cent in all the census years in 1970, 1980 and 1991. The representation of Chinese practicing the Buddhist faith has remained stable over these three decades, if not increasing slightly.

In 1980, when two other categories were added to the census' religious affiliation categories, which were "Confucianism, Taoism and Other

Traditional Religion", "Tribal or Folk Religion", the percentage in the categories of "No religion" dropped. In 1980, 19.16 per cent of Sarawak Chinese had no religion. In 1991, the figure was 12.89 per cent, a significant drop from 25.78 per cent in 1970. A more drastic drop could be seen in the category of "Unknown", from 23.53 per cent to 0.04 per cent in 1991 and null in 1980. In 1980, the percentage of Sarawak Chinese practicing "Confucianism, Taoism and Other Traditional Religion" was 22.03 per cent and in 1991, the percentage for the same faith was 21.13 per cent. So it is suffice to say that those who said that they practiced "Unknown religion" in 1970 were actually those who were practicing the belief in "Confucianism, Taoism and Other Traditional Religion" before the category was added in. The percentage for "Tribal or Folk Religion" for both census years is rather insignificant as it only stood at less than 1 per cent.

Within the category of Buddhism itself, the figure may not reflect the actual percentage of people who actually practiced the faith. The actual number may be much lower than reported. Soo (1990: 29) in his study about the religions of the Chinese in peninsular Malaysia, wrote that "Those Malaysian Chinese who continue to list themselves simply as 'Buddhists' may be motivated to do so in order to avoid being seen as 'superstitious'...". Based on the account by Soo, it cannot be denied that those who proclaimed themselves as Buddhists were possibly also practicing other Chinese beliefs. In the category of mixed religion of "Confucianism, Taoism and other traditional (Chinese) religion", there were over 20 per cent practitioners in the 1980 and 1991 censuses. In order to disassociate with superstitious beliefs, many of the Chinese conveniently classify themselves as Buddhist, thus inflating the figure.

Table 3: The Religion of Sarawak Chinese in 2000 and 2010

Religion among Chinese	2000		2010	
	Population	Percentage (%)	Population	Percentage (%)
Islam	7,467	1.35	4,037	0.70
Christian	192,918	34.88	210,306	36.41
Hindu	608	0.11	154	0.03
Buddhism	249,334	45.08	320,270	55.44
Confucianism, Taoism and Tribal/ folk, other traditional Chinese religion	59,734	10.8	19,197	3.32
Others	1,327	0.24	987	0.17
No religion	33,794	6.11	17,754	3.07
Unknown	7,909	1.43	4,942	0.86
Total	553,092	100	577,647	100

Data source: Statistic Department Malaysia, (2001). Population and Housing Census of Malaysia 2000, State Population Report – Sarawak. Department of Statistic Malaysia, Kuala Lumpur; (ii) Statistic Department Malaysia, (2011). Population and Housing Census of Malaysia 2010, State Population Report – Sarawak. Department of Statistic Malaysia, Kuala Lumpur.

In Table 3, the two categories of Confucianism/ Taoism/ other traditional religion and Tribal / folk religion are merged as one. From the initial five categories of Chinese religion in census 1970, it increased to nine categories in the 1980 and 1991 censuses, but were then reduced to eight categories in the subsequent censuses in 2000 and 2010. The increase in the numbers of categories and subsequently merged again, shows that the context of Chinese religion in Malaysia is not well understood.

Back in Sarawak on more local context, the need for recognition of these people under the mixed religion category has grown stronger. While conducting field work in Sibu, one of the major cities of Sarawak consisting predominantly Chinese population, I had a conversation with the chairman of Sibu Yun An Ting Tua Pek Kong[1] Temple Association. At that time in 2009, Sibu proposed the first state wide Tua Pek Kong Celebration, which they aimed to make it an annual event. During my interview with him, the chairman noted that he envisioned introducing the Tua Pek Kong faith as an official faith, trying to cast away the superstitious image of the traditional belief. In a gathering, he made a statement to a group of committee members from temples all over Sarawak, that he inspired that one day in near future, the anniversary of Tua Pek Kong and its celebration can be declared an official public holiday in Sarawak[2]. He made this statement based on the fact that there the Tua Pek Kong faith has set its foothold in Sarawak and has become well received by a large population. Furthermore, there are over 68 recognised Tua Pek Kong temples in Sarawak, with perhaps many more sprouting up in the future and many more undocumented.

Scope of this paper

In this paper, I cannot cover the full range of Chinese religious experience in Sarawak. The focus is on two settlements, namely Tabidu and Kota[3], in the outskirt of Kuching, the capital city of Sarawak whereby I exemplified the experience of the Chinese communities, their religions and beliefs. The paper examines close the Thai Pak Kung[4] beliefs of the local people. I use the terms Tua Pek Kong and Thai Pak Kung inter-changeably. Tua Pek Kong is the official term used by the government, while in the article,

---

1 Tua Pek Kong is an official term adopted by Sarawak and is pronounced in the Hokkien and Teochew dialect.
2 I was invited to the meeting in Sibu and managed to witness the event and listened to the speech made by the chairman on that day. (Date of interview: 15 January 2009. Venue: Sibu Yun An Ting Tua Pek Kong Temple)
3 The name of the villages has been changed for privacy purpose.
4 Thai Pak Kung (大伯公) is a Hakka term. In Mandarin, it is pronounced as Dà bó gōng.

I revert to using Thai Pak Kung to reflect to the Hakka study.

Considering the complexity of the understanding of Chinese religion, this paper aims to relay this notion. Such complexity has been discussed and debated widely by renowned sinologists such as Maurice Freedman, Arthur Wolf and Robert Smith. Freedman (1974: 2) asks "How precisely to consider Chinese religion as a whole?" He then answers it by (ibid) "...one might predict from first principles that a society so differentiated by social status and power would develop a religious system that allowed differences in beliefs and rites to complement one another or...that allowed religious similarity to be expressed as though it were religious difference." Smith (1974: 325) counters by saying "It is equally likely that this society may instead have treated religious differences as though they were religious similarities."

Discussions were generated from the viewpoints of other researchers who have conducted similar research topics, the local people from the affected regions especially the spiritual specialists who have extensive background and experience in rituals and finally, my personal views. Literatures from other researchers provided background information for argument points, either refuted or substantiated by the local spiritual specialists. I give my personal transparent analyses where possible, taking into consideration the ideologies of other informants and researchers.

Research areas – Tabidu and Kota

This paper is based on the cases of two settlements, Tabidu and Kota that are situated nearby each other which I have good access to. These two sites are significant considering they celebrated the Thai Pak Kung separately but decided to jointly host the event in 2011. The actual names of the settlements have been changed to preserve anonymosity.

Tabidu is located along the Kuching-Serian Highway and is approximately 35 km from Kuching city. There were 2,518 occupants from 471 households, comprising 97 per cent Hakka, according to the population census carried out in 2000. The community in Tabidu was resettled under the Hammer Operation, whereby they were moved from an old settlement to the present location by the government in the 1960s. The operation involved moving people who were mostly Hakka farmers who lived between the 15th and 24th mile[5] of the present highway. Before the highway was built, there was a smaller road passing through many small settlements of Hakka, Malays and Bidayuh up to Serian.

Historically, the Thai Pak Kung temple was speculated to be built by the first Chinese settlers at around 1900s at what was then, the old settlement. According to one elder villager from Tabidu who turned 98 years old in 2012, the temple started as a small worship place with only an incense burner at the same spot where the current temple is now. The temple then was very simple, constructed with palm fronds in the beginning before they were replaced with zinc sheets. These zinc sheets were placed on the top and on both sides of the incense pot to protect it from the weather. Visitors had to cross a small stream using a shaky bridge to reach here. The Thai Pak Kung deity statue was moved there only a few years later.

The earliest grave in the cemetery nearby the temple was traced back to the year 1907, indicating the approximately time of the early settlement of people here. Places of worship and cemeteries are common indicators of the earlier history of a settlement. The current temple building, made of concrete was re-constructed in 2003 and the stream had been filled up.

---

5 Old metric measurement is used because the term is more familiar to the local people, and is still being used extensively.

Kota is situated nearer to Kuching city, about 10 km away from Tabidu. In this article, Kota refers to the bazaar itself, which has 234 shops. The people are primarily made up of Chinese of Hakka and Teochew ethnicity. From the population census carried out in 2010, there were 181 households and 928 occupants, most of them living in shops (1st floor) in the bazaar. In the 1960s, there were only four rows of shops comprising a total of 33 shops, mainly selling groceries to the local people who came from the interior. Today, the town has expanded many folds but the old rows of shops still remained, many of which have been renovated and their structures changed from wood to concrete.

Based on accounts from some of the most senior citizens residing here, the early history of the Thai Pak Kung temple in Kota was believed to have started when an early migrant from China called Mr Bong moved the incense burner from his house at Mile 11 to its present place at Kota (Figure 1). The time was traced back to between 1920s to 1930s. There is no written record on this, but the accounts related to me by the senior citizens were reliable, who provided consistent information based on their memories or stories told to them in the past.

Similar to Tabidu, the temple in Kota started without any statue of the deity. The early temple had only an incense burner which contained ashes of a temple in China which was brought over here by Mr Bong. In the beginning before it was moved to Kota, the temple at Mr Bong's house consisted of an altar for worship of which the incense burner was placed. The residents nearby would frequently visit the house to pray. When Mr Bong decided to move to Kota, he brought the incense burner along and built a new temple. It consisted of a simple makeshift structure built out of palm fronds, which was later replaced with zinc sheets to protect it from the weather. In the early 1940s, a proper structure was constructed and had since undergone three renovations, and the latest was done in 2000 (Figure 1). The earliest grave situated in the cemetery in front of the temple dated way back to 1932.

Figure 1: Thai Pak Kung temples in Tabidu (left) and Kota (right)

Thai Pak Kung celebration

One of the most important celebrations every year among the Chinese communities of Tabidu and Kota is the anniversary of Thai Pak Kung. The Chinese communities in these two settlements as well as the surrounding settlements acknowledge the importance of Thai Pak Kung and the need to commemorate the anniversary in grand scale. This shows the global acceptance of the same god. However, there is one very obvious difference in the celebrations carried out by Tabidu and Kota. The actual dates for the celebration are different. In Tabidu, the celebration falls on the 2nd day of 2nd lunar month as was observed in 2007 and 2009. In Kota, the celebration is held on the 29th day of the 3rd lunar month. The date of the celebration is consulted with the high priest and has been passed down from many years ago. Hence, it is followed by the current followers.

Celebration in 2011

The Thai Pak Kung anniversary celebration is an annual event organized by Tabidu and Kota and is participated by a large congregation, often taking up many hours of preparations. In 2011, there was a major change affecting the celebration, which also marked the third year the annual celebration has been carried out. The chronicle of major events affecting Thai Pak Kung celebrations in Tabidu and Kota is presented in Table 4.

The 3rd annual Thai Pak Kung Celebration in 2011 was hosted by the Kota Thai Pak Kung temple (哥打巴達旺十哩福德大伯公廟 *Fuk Teck Ta Pek Kong Miao*). As Kota normally holds the celebration on the 29th day of the 3rd lunar month, the celebration was fixed for that day. For the first time, Tabidu has decided to shift the celebration from the normal 2nd day of 2nd lunar month to follow suit Kota's date. As a consequence of changing the date of celebration, there was no major celebration and procession in Tabidu as most of the manpower had shifted to helping Kota organize the grand celebration. Nevertheless, the anniversary of Thai Pak Kung was still observed in Tabidu on a smaller scale, whereby devotees presented their offerings at the temple only. The changing of date and mode of celebration was first decided by the local organizing committee, and then consulted with the gods by a spirit medium.

In Tabidu, the celebration is handled by a spirit medium by the name of Mr. Chen. He has been the caretaker of the temple and intermediary of Thai Pak Kung for many years. Two years prior to changing the date when the idea was proposed to Tabidu by the Sibu Yin An Ting to make the celebration simultaneous at state level, the people of Tabidu showed no interest. They could not accept the change of date at that time. In my conversation with Mr. Chen, I asked if shifting of the date and mode of celebration would anger the

Table 4: Chronology of the annual Thai Pak Kung celebration in Tabidu and Kota as witnessed by the author

Year	Tabidu	Kota
2008	Thai Pak Kung procession started from temple, moved along old settlement road, Tabidu bazaar, all housing lanes in new settlement. Lorries and buses were used, and followed by foot procession in the bazaar.	No observation done by author.
2009	Thai Pak Kung procession was held and celebrated for seven days. All deities, including Datuk Kong were paraded and placed at the newly built community hall. 2009 marked the first year Datuk Kong was taken out of his altar and paraded.	No observation done by author.
2011	No grand celebration and procession as most of the manpower had shifted to Kota to prepare for the grand scale celebration of Thai Pak Kung.	Grand scale Thai Pak Kung anniversary celebration held after visits were made by Taiwanese academicians and Jin Men temple delegation from China. 2011 marked the State level celebration which was hosted by Kota. The celebration lasted for 14 days. Makeshift temple at the centre of Kota bazaar was constructed during the celebration.

god. He replied that he has "communicated" with Thai Pak Kung over the change and the situation was considered settled. In view of this, the celebration was shifted to the new date, marking a major change in the history of celebration of Thai Pak Kung in Tabidu.

Worshipping Datuk Kong

Besides Thai Pak Kung, a localized god called Datuk Kong has significant foothold in the beliefs of the people in Tabidu and Kota. As Datuk

Kong was also presented in the anniversary celebration of Thai Pak Kung, I have dedicated some discussion on this matter.

In the vicinity of both the Thai Pak Kung temples in Tabidu and Kota, there are altars erected for the worshipping of Datuk Kong. This is a localized version of the gods, associated with a Malay god by the local people. The name itself, "datuk" is a Malay word for "grandfather" which is synonym with the "respected one". Datuk Kong is a belief followed in countries in Malaysia and Singapore (Sakai, 1993). Because of its affiliation with the Malay's belief and hence their religion, Datuk Kong is perceived to be fasting during the holy Ramadan month of the Muslim calendar. However, the Datuk Kong in the temple in Tabidu does not fast. According to the villagers here, Datuk Kong is a god therefore he does not have to fast. In Kota, the situation is different. The Datuk Kong in temple here fasts during fasting month. During this period, which lasts one month, no food or drink are offered. On the auspicious Hari Raya Aidilfitri[6], just after the first azan[7] which is usually heard transmitted by loudspeaker from a nearby mosque, both the Datuk Kong from Tabidu and Kota are presented with conventional Malay dishes such as curry, rendang and satay.

The Datuk Kong altar

In Tabidu, the altar of Datuk Kong is located at the same site and joined together as one unit with the Thai Pak Kung temple. The Datuk Kong altar is situated at the left wing of the building. In Kota, the altar of Datuk Kong is situated a distance away from the main building complex that houses the Thai

---

6　The celebration comes after observing one month of fasting by the Muslim community. Hari Raya Aidilfitri is the first day of the new lunar month.

7　Morning call for prayer.

Pak Kung. It is situated approximately 100 m from the main Thai Pak Kung temple, at the front part leading to the temple. Here, a separate altar is built to house Datuk Kong. Behind the altar is a frangipani tree, locally known as *bunga mawar*. This species of tree is usually planted in Muslim cemeteries. The presence of the frangipani tree signifies the close association of Datuk Kong with the Muslim faith.

Datuk Kong's participation in the Thai Pak Kung procession

During the grand celebration of the Thai Pak Kung anniversary, Datuk Kong is normally asked to join in. In 2009, both Thai Pak Kung and Datuk Kong were paraded in the procession in Tabidu. I was informed that Datuk Kong had agreed to join in the celebration for the very first time in 2009. In the previous procession held in 2007, Datuk Kong was not part of it. The spirit medium whom I enquired about said that Datuk Kong is a very temperamental and troublesome god. This could be the reason why he did not join in the procession as it was difficult to receive his acceptance to participate. However, the situation was different in 2009, whereby Datuk Kong related to the spirit medium that he would like to join the procession for the first time. Therefore, for the purpose of the procession, an extra makeshift temple was constructed for Datuk Kong. It was situated in the middle of the new village hall (Figure 2).

In Kota, Datuk Kong did not join in any of the Thai Pak Kung anniversary processions. Here, it was related to me by the spirit medium that inviting Datuk Kong to join in the procession was and has been a difficult affair. The characters of both Datuk Kongs in Tabidu and Kota bore some similarity, that they are troublesome. The term "troublesome" here possibly connotes to being difficult to please.

Figure 2: A makeshift temple for Datuk Kong

Engaging counter pollution methods

During the Thai Pak Kung anniversary procession, the deities were paraded along significant routes to the makeshift temple. Therefore, they had to leave their usual altar at the temple. The handling of any memorabilia accorded to the gods must be done with care. It is believed that the deities are pure but human hands that handle them are not. Therefore, these "unclean" hands should not pollute the pure body of the deities' statues. There are various means to counter these pollutions. One of the most commonly used methods was through cleansing oneself with water containing the *mat cho* leaves (Figure 3). Before handling the deity's statue, devotees cleaned their hands with this water.

The use of the *mat cho* leaves in water to clean hands was not observed in both the Thai Pak Kung processions in Tabidu in 2007 and 2009. Instead, devotees only warded off impurities along the path taken during the procession. This was also a type of counter pollution and was performed by

Figure 3: A container filled with water and stalks of *mat cho* leaves used in cleansing rituals

the men leading the procession. They each carried a bucket of water containing some stalks of *mat cho* leaves and burnt fu (talisman). As they walked, they sprinkled the water into the air and onto the road to cleanse the road off impurities before the deities were paraded through.

Other forms of counter pollution processes were also applied before the procession began. For the procession to happen, the statue and incense urn of the deities were transferred from the altar onto a sedan chair, whereby they were to be paraded later. When these statues and incense urn were being moved, one man tossed into the air and onto the items, handfuls of rice that was mixed with salt and placed inside a red bucket as devotees were summoned to carry each deity (Figure 4). This was to ward off any impurities that may come into the paths of the deities as they were being shifted. The detailed process of transferring the deity onto the sedan chair is described as below:

Figure 4: Rice mixed with salt was tossed when the statues and incense urn were moved

A spirit medium was in charge of transferring the deity's statue. He started off by seeking consent of the deity, through tossing of the divining blocks to find out if the deity concerned has descended into the golden body (金身) or the statue. The diving blocks were made up of two kidney shaped wooden blocks with two non-identical surfaces, one side which is flat and another is rounded. Upon tossing the blocks, any combination of two non-identical surfaces[8] signifies that the deity has descended from heaven into the golden body.

After the sign that the deity had descended into his golden body was obtained, the master of ceremony made an announcement. This moment was regarded as the auspicious time for the devotees to carry the deity into his sedan chair, which was already in place at the front

---

8 Should the dividing blocks show identical sides, the spirit medium will toss them again. The process is repeated until opposite sides are obtained, and all devotees who are present in the temple will be asked to kneel down until the divining blocks show a favourable answer.

of the temple.

In the temple, there were also a few other deities residing there. In Kota, the Ta Sheng Fuo Zu[9] (大聖佛祖) deity, an important subsidiary deity sat on the left side of Thai Pak Kung. The right side of Thai Pak Kung was Chieng Tien Shang Ti[10] (玄天上帝). Which deity was to be transferred first must follow a structured order. The first deity to be transferred was Ta Sheng Fuo Zu. When the announcement was made, the devotees started to wash their hands in the cleansing basin (a basin that was filled with *mat cho* and a towel). The cleansing of hands in the cleansing basin before handling the deities statues was observed only in Kota and not in Tabidu (Figure 5). From the opposite side whereby the devotees were moving into the front of the altar to get ready to carry the deity, rice with salt was sprinkled abundantly towards the direction of the main altar where the deities were. After sprinkling the rice three times, the process stopped. Likewise, the actions were repeated when the subsidiary deity Chieng Tien Shang Ti and Thai Pak Kung were transferred from the altar to their sedan chairs.

Among some of the other differences observed in Kota but were not practiced in Tabidu were the use of other types of paraphernalia in temples to counter pollutions. In Kota, a sieve used by the local people during padi dehusking process (Figure 6) was observed being hung on top of the Thai Pak Kung altar. Such sieve was not found in Tabidu temple. According to the spirit medium of the temple, the sieve is to protect the deities from other forms of pollutions that may harm or come into close contact with them.

---

9 In Mandarin pronunciation.
10 In Mandarin pronunciation.

Figure 5: Water filled with *mat cho* leaves for cleansing ritual before handling of deity's statues in Kota

Figure 6: A sieve which was hung on top of the Thai Pak Kung altar as one of the counter pollution paraphernalia

Communal ritual

Communal ritual is a cultural product of a society which represents who the people within the society are. In a case study of the Hakka in Tabidu (Chai, 2009), the people choose to believe that the deity is the guardian of their ancestors who first came to this settlement in Sarawak. It is a historical product that tells about the people's link to their predecessors.

A collective voice that calls for a better representation of such communal ritual has recently become stronger. The Sibu Yun An Ting Tua Pek Kong Temple Committee first came out with the idea to unite all the Thai Pak Kung temples in Sarawak. The reason was to get the official recognition from the Malaysian government for their beliefs. They are aiming to get Tua Pek Kong birthday recognised as a public holiday. The same committee also hoped that one day, a devotee of the Tua Pek Kong can proclaim his or her religion openly, under the category of Tua Pek Kong religion itself.

In the earlier part of the text, the historical beginnings of Thai Pak Kung were explained. The people of Tabidu in particular have very close affiliations to their histories of origins. However, over recent years, communal ritual and a need for better uniform representation of the Thai Pak Kung faith has become stronger and overtook the traditional practices, as in the case of unifying the different dates of the Thai Pak Kung anniversary celebration.

The culture of the society is also formed by the social group to which they belong. In the case of Tabidu, the people first arrived from other parts and set up homesteads. The temple was built as a form of identity of the community. The Thai Pak Kung celebration itself is a rite which is followed by the people. Over time, this rite equate to their strong beliefs. Many people do not know the significance of the practices during the celebrations, but they followed fully because they are already regarded as the norm and "correct" actions.

The original Thai Pak Kung temple of Tabidu is still located at the same site where the old settlement was. An offshoot group of younger generation have decided to set up another temple nearer to the current Tabidu settlement, giving reason that the old temple is too far from the town and that less people have made the effort to patronize it. The setting up of new temple reflects the dynamism of Thai Pak Kung, of which the same deity representing by the same original community can form an off-shoot to be placed into a new temple. The same situation was also noted by DeGlopper (1974) in his account of ritual contrast between the towns of Erhlin and Lukang in central Taiwan, which presented a unique case study of how the different population set up affect the religious affinity of the people. This a very old case example but I have found it very similar to the set up in my study areas. DeGlopper's had wanted to know how the skewed population ratios for these two towns influence how temples were built or renovated and that a lot of money were contributed by the people themselves. He obtained the answers that the search for generalizations must begin with the histories of a particular place which is still being valued upon by the people.

Lukang cherishes its temples as tangible links with the past and eschews the competitive aspects of public rituals as a way of expressing solidarity vis-à-vis an unappreciative world. Similarly, in the cases of Tabidu and Kota, whereby both sites show similar level of ritual fervor, there appeared to be differences in the way they carried out the Thai Pak Kung rituals. By looking deeper into the histories of these towns, one of them had a controversial past while the other town did not. Tabidu was once regarded as a "black area" where communist insurgencies were rampant. The local people did not like to be associated with this piece of event of their past. Only the history of the original locality of the Thai Pak Kung temple is still greatly remembered, which led to the older generation still maintaining its location but the younger ones decided to construct a newer temple.

Although Kota had little histories related to communists, it was not a prosperous town until mid-1990s when the area was upgraded into a municipality. In the beginning, Kota was a small town with only two rows of shops, comprising of Hakka and Teochew people doing business. Furthermore, it could be considered as situated too near to Kuching, the capital city. Hence, it did not serve much as a stopover town for the rural people. Instead, these people would usually travel to the 7th Mile town, now known as Kota Sentosa.

Localized diversity

DeGlopper (1974: 46) wrote about the importance to stress on the common pattern or core that is found in all places, whereby he said that local diversity is not accidental events and ritual is has no determinate relation to the particular community that supports it, and thus giving the appearance of a more local colour than in fact exists. The birth of Thai Pak Kung propagated from the local people's admiration and exaltation of a local hero, as described in the case of Bau and West Kalimantan. There, past heroes and prominent personalities who had played significant influence on the early lives of the people, such as those who pioneered gold mining activity were regarded as the Thai Pak Kung, asserting the notion of localized belief.

Luo Fang Po was a Chinese pioneer who developed gold mine and died in 1795 in West Kalimantan. He is regarded as the Thai Pak Kung of that area. In the Bau town in Sarawak, during the thriving gold mining activity, Liew Shan Pang headed the rebels to fight against the Brooke's government. He died in 1857 and is regarded the Thai Pak Kung of Bau.

In Tabidu, local belief also constituted to what was passed down from the earlier generations that have kept the community bounded. After some time, along with the rich historical past, the beliefs in Tabidu become more diverse, absorbing the changes the community had to undertake in relations to their social and economic situations. This is also noted by DeGlopper (1974) who emphasized that Lukang's peculiar ritual style is related to its past but is also correlated with other social changes. In the case of Tabidu, the tradition of the place and people is upheld strongly, making it the biggest event of the past. These traditions are traced back all the way to their root where life started at the temple. During the Thai Pak Kung anniversary procession, the people showed reverence to the deities of the temple by parading them around the site of the old village. The procession also passed by the graveyard situated about two miles away so that the forebears buried there were granted respect and "shown" the procession.

The Thai Pak Kung anniversary celebration is also carried out annually in Kota. The year 2011 was celebrated in grander scale as Kota was nominated as the host of the state level Tua Pek Kong celebration. The event was very lively. Among the floats were lorries decorated colorfully and ferrying young girls dressed up as ancient Chinese fairies, and boys in ancient kung fu warrior costumes, lion dance bands, and flower girls carrying lanterns. Other troops from as far as Kuching city, Serian and Bau were invited to grace the occasion. The involvement of outside troops in the celebration in Kota was not something new as it has been practiced throughout the years.

On the other hand, the annual Thai Pak Kung anniversary celebrations in Tabidu were very much a local affair and no outside troops were involved. The celebrations did not have decorated lorries and attractive looking floats. Instead, only a few cars with minimal decorations took part. Compared to Kota, the celebrations in Tabidu were very much toned down. The focus of the procession was not to create a carnival like atmosphere but to parade the deities to "go around" the road along the old settlement, passing by the graveyard, before finishing at the site of the new Tabidu settlement and its bazaar. At the new settlement, the procession "toured" around the entire settlement by going through each of the housing lanes. There are altogether five housing lanes in the Tabidu.

How the celebrations were carried out in Tabidu and Kota reflected the historical beginning of these settlements. The celebrations exemplify that the present mode in the people's presentation of their ritual life is firmly connected to their past. Kota is a new and booming bazaar whereby many people started moving there from nearby areas such as Kuching or Serian to set up or expand their businesses. From then on, more shops were built and business started to mushroom and expand.

Historically, the demography of Kota were more diversed, comprising people from outside the area. They may not have the significant hardship beginning as experienced by the people of Tabidu, who had to experience forced relocation. The occupants of Kota can be considered as outsiders to the area. Therefore, they are indirectly and inadvertently considered outsiders to the temple and deity. Their main historical linkage is their own decisions to relocate to Kota to seek better economic wellbeing. On the contrary, the people of Tabidu have very close affiliation to their temple because the temple also marks the origin of their history. The temple itself is the tangible link to their past. It is the link to the history of the earlier settlers and also the creation of the community. For many years after they were forced to relocate to another area, they left the temple behind, but never forgotten about it.

The loose link between the people of Kota with their temple is manifested through the extensive use of "anti-pollutant" rituals during Thai Pak Kung procession (see Table 5). Devotees cleansed and purify their hands with *mat cho* water before handling the deities. This elucidates their fear of polluting the deities. Devotees in Tabidu did not perform this act. Here, the deities are considered an integral part of the community. They only use the *mat cho* water to cleanse the road, by sprinkling them to ward off luring spirits along the road where the deities will be passing by, a practice also performed by the devotees in Kota. The cleansing processes were more intensely applied to the surrounding areas outside of the temple. Local people handling the deities were treated with less suspicions.

Conclusion

The rituals performed by the devotees of Kota as compared to Tabidu during the celebrations and processions of Thai Pak Kung reflected the loose link the people of Kota have towards their temple and deities. Despite similarly of worshiping the same Thai Pak Kung god, the devotees of Kota and Tabidu performed their rituals differently. One clear distinction is the dates of the anniversary itself.

Nevertheless, the influence of communal ritual has become stronger than traditions, as demonstrated by the willingness of the people of Tabidu to adhere to new changes to follow suit Kota's celebration of Thai Pak Kung anniversary on a new date. One may argue why such strong historical bondage the people of Tabidu have towards their temple could eventually be nudged, to the extent of acknowledging a new date of celebration? I believe the lack of a doctrine in Thai Pak Kung belief is the weak point that could not lay a strong foundation towards a proper recognition of this faith, or religion as others may like to term it. Efforts to make it an official religion may take much longer effort and time.

Table 5: Comparisons between Tabidu and Kota in the Thai Pak Kung anniversary celebrations

	Tabidu (2007 & 2009)	Kota (2011)
Organisers	Temple committee members, villagers	Temple committee members, villagers
Leader	Keeper of temple, also a spirit medium from Tabidu	Temple committee chairperson and assistant; Spirit medium is from a nearby village.
Preparations before procession	• Starts early at around 6 a.m. • Spirit medium initiates contact with deity through chants and offerings • Devotees prepare deities' seats made from bamboo into a carriage or khiàu (轎). Three khiàus are made for the three deities of the temple.	• Starts around 6.30 a.m. • Spirit medium initiates contact with deity through chants and offerings • Spirit medium chanted while writing on talisman, flags. • Devotees prepare deities' seats made from bamboo into a carriage or khiàu (轎). Three khiàus are made for the three deities of the temple.
Transferring the deity	• Spirit medium throws divining blocks to check for readiness and seek permission of deity to transfer from altar to khiàu • When permission is granted, the spirit medium carries the kim shin (金身) onto the khiàu • Two other deities, namely Ńg Kwuk Sien Shi (五穀仙師) (God of Agriculture) and Vông Lo Sen Shi (黃老先師) (God of Virtue) who reside next to Thai Pak Kung in the temple are also transferred to their respective khiàus.	• Spirit medium throws divining blocks to check for readiness and seek permission of deity to transfer from altar to khiàu • When permission is granted, all devotees cleanse their hands in *mat cho* water before handling the deities. • The Ta Sheng Fuo Zu (大聖佛祖) deity and Chieng Tien Shang Ti (玄天上帝) deities reside on the left and right of Thai Pak Kung respectively. • As the statues of the deities are being moved, devotees sprinkle three tosses of rice mixed with salt towards the altar onto the statues

During procession	• The route starts from the temple, moves along the old village road, passes through the cemetery, moves along the new highway to Tabidu, meanders along the housing lanes and then back to the temple. • *Mat cho* water is sprinkled onto the road along the path to cleanse off impurities. • Parade includes vehicles with little decorations. • Mostly people from Tabidu itself.	• The route starts from the temple, passes by the cemetery just beside the temple, moves through the smaller road leading to the main road, meanders along the roads in front of the many rows of shops, then to the temporary makeshift temple at a parking lot. • *Mat cho* water is sprinkled onto the road along the path to cleanse off impurities. • Parade is made up of lorries beautifully decorated, with people performances and dressed-up icons. • Participated by congregations from Kota, Kuching, Serian and Bau.
Other paraphernalia		• A sieve, used by the local people during padi dehusking process, is hung on top of the Thai Pak Kung altar.

In many religions, there are localized versions of their beliefs. How the rituals are performed cannot be regarded as unconformity or confusions among the faith believers. These are in fact localized diversity, changes that have evolved to take into account the local surroundings and set up. In Tabidu, the people have very close affiliations to their temple and deities, something not readily seen in Kota. People also form their own perceptions of gods, their versions very much based on their beliefs.

References

Chai, E., 2009, "Our Temple, Our Past: Memories of the Past and Social Identity of A Hakka Community in Sarawak". Paper presented at 43rd Conference of the Japan Society of Cultural Anthropology, Osaka, Japan. 29 May - 31 May 2009.

DeGlopper, Donald R., 1974, "Religion and Ritual in Lukang", in Arthur Wolf ed., *Religion and Ritual in Chinese Society*. California: Stanford University Press.

Freedman, Maurice, 1974, "On the Sociological Study of Chinese Religion", in Arthur Wolf ed., *Religion and Ritual in Chinese Society*. California: Stanford University Press.

Sakai, Tadao, 1993, "Chinese Religious Practices and Customs in Malaysia and Singapore", in Cheu Hock Tong ed., *Chinese Beliefs and Practices in Southeast Asia*. Kuala Lumpur: Pelanduk Publications.

Smith, Robert, 1974, "Afterword", in Arthur Wolf ed., *Religion and Ritual in Chinese Society*. California: Stanford University Press.

Soo, Khin Wah, 1990, "The Cult of Mazu in Peninsular Malaysia", *The Contributions to Southeast Asian Ethnography*, No. 9, Dec 1990.

Statistic Department Malaysia (1970) Population Census.

Statistic Department Malaysia (1980) Population Census.

Statistic Department Malaysia (1991) Population Census.

Statistic Department Malaysia (2000) Population Distribution and Basic Demographic Characteristics, Population & Housing Census of Malaysia 2000.

Statistic Department Malaysia (2010) Population Distribution and Basic Demographic Characteristics. Population & Housing Census of Malaysia 2010.

Appendix

Inscription on the notice board placed at Thai Pak Kung temple in Tabidu

The above plaque translates to:

Notice to all devotees

1. Prohibited to place statue, incense pot, candle stand, oil etc.

2. Prohibited to go into trance.

3. Preserve the inside and outside of temple in original environment and outlook

4. Together protect the inside and outside of temple in good, clean condition.

5. Those wishing to donate money or "add oil money", please proceed to Tabidu Old Folk's Leisure Centre from 8-11 am.

6. This temple's deity's birthday is on the 29th day of the 3rd month of the lunar calendar.

Thank you for your co-operation.

Thai Pak Kung Temple Association Committee

1st December 2010

Hakka in Engkilili, Sarawak: Community and Identity*

Daniel Chew†

Abstract

The objective of this research is to examine the social and cultural characteristics of the Hakka as a Chinese dialect group living in Engkilili, in the Malaysian state of Sarawak.[1] In Engkilili the Hakka are a minority residing among the Iban majority community. The Hakka have a strong primordial sense of self identity, and have retained their Chinese cultural characteristics in speaking the Hakka dialect and Mandarin, and following Chinese religious practices. Chinese religious practices are kept, and help convey a sense of identity and belonging to Engkilili. A major cultural celebration for the Hakka and other Chinese, the 10th day of the lunar new year observance for inviting deity blessings, illustrates this sense of

* This research was supported by a grant from the Chiang Ching Kuo Foundation, Taiwan, awarded in 2010, and field-work was undertaken when the author was with the Institute of East Asian Studies, Universiti Malaysia Sarawak (UNIMAS) in Kota Samarahan, Sarawak. A draft of the paper was written when the author was a Visiting Research Fellow with the Research Centre for Humanities and the Social Sciences, National Tsing Hua University (NTHU), Taiwan from April to June 2011. I thank Chang Wei An of NTHU for arranging this visiting fellowship.

† Visiting Research Fellow, Institute of East Asian Studies, University Malaysia Sarawak

1 The valuable comments of Lim Khai Thiong and Danny Wong on this paper at a workshop "Multiculturalism in Monsoon Asia: Chinese in Southeast Asia and Beyond" held at the National Tsing Hua University in Taiwan on 16 to 17 June 2012, are acknowledged. I have also benefited from comments on a draft of this paper presented at seminars held at the National Tsing Hua University, National Chiao Tung University and National Chi Nan University, Taiwan in June 2011, and at Universiti Malaysia Sarawak (UNIMAS) in Kota Samarahan, Sarawak in November 2011. I am thankful too, to Abdul Rashid Abdullah, Jayl Langub, Sanid Said and Lam Chee Kheung, from the Institute of East Asian Studies, UNIMAS for their friendships and assistance, and for the many discussions I had with them. The comments of Richard Shatz who read a draft of the paper are appreciated. Thanks are due too to Goh Kaw Sze, Cynthia Chin and Yeoh Cheng Huat for fieldwork assistance, and to Pauline Yeo for translation work. Many people in Engkilili, notably Kapitan Bong Jin Choon and Kapitan Liew Ah Ban gave their generous assistance. The usual disclaimer applies.

Map of Engkilili

Source: Google Maps

identification, an adherence to Chinese cultural values, and to the place of belonging, Engkilili.

The Hakka adapt to the wider environment around them as a minority living together with their numerically stronger Iban neighbours, showing a willingness to learn and speak Iban, and inter-marry with Iban spouses. While adapting to the Iban, the Hakka have not lost their facility with the Hakka dialect and the mastery of Mandarin. It can then be said that the Hakka in Engkilili represent an example of Chinese settlement and adaptation in Malaysia where the Hakka dialect is retained, and other languages, Mandarin and Iban are acquired.

The Hakka acculturation to the Iban is a two way process. There is Iban acceptance of the Hakka as their neighbours, a high incidence of inter-marriages, and an interest in taking part in and observing Chinese cultural practices such as the 10th day of the lunar new year observance for deity blessings. There are no ethnic rigid boundaries which separate the Hakka from the Iban.

As a case study, this research has highlighted the social and cultural experiences of a Chinese Hakka dialect group in Engkilili, Sarawak, where Chinese adaptations have taken place, and by the same token, their majority Iban neighbours have also adapted to them.

Introduction

Sarawak has a multi-ethnic population of 2.4 million according to the 2010 census, made up of Chinese, Malay, Melanau, Iban, Orang Ulu and other smaller groups. The Chinese make up about 25 per cent of the population, with the Hakka being the second most numerous dialect group after the Foochow, followed by other dialect groups, Hokkien, Teochew, Cantonese and others. The story of the Hakka in Sarawak, hailing from China's Guangdong province, is very much a part of the history of Chinese migration and settlement in Southeast Asia. The Hakka are characterized as a people with agrarian and rural backgrounds, and this influenced their choice of destinations to settle in when moving to Southeast Asia. In Sarawak, the Hakka have shown this inclination in occupying rural and semi-urban areas away from the towns .

Hakka from the Hopoh sub-group began moving into Engkilili in a rural and hilly, undulating part of Sarawak around the mid-19th century and continued to do so in the first half of the 20th century. Kuhn (2008) suggests a three-pronged approach in studying the Chinese overseas, which are time, place and circumstances. The long term historical period, the *langue duree* period of Hakka sojourning and settlement in Engkilili has become a term of reference for the Hakka who identify with the legacy of a gold mining *kongsi* dating back to the mid-19th century. A diachronic framework is useful in understanding the adaptations of the Hakka to Engkilili. The geographical space which the Hakka journeyed to in Borneo was in the tropics where the pull attractions of drawing the Hakka were gold mining, then followed by riverine trading and agriculture. The circumstances which the Hakka found themselves in were moving into a spatial environment where there were indigenous Iban, and Teochew, people like themselves who had journeyed to the south seas. The conditions of living under a quasi-colonial Brooke regime (1841-1941), then under Japanese Occupation (1942-45), followed by an interlude of British colonial rule (194-63), and finally with independence in Malaysia after 1963, are extrinsic factors in influencing the Hakka sense of belonging in Sarawak, Malaysia.

In a study of this nature on the Hakka in Engkilili, it is imperative to research on the Hakka and their neighbours. The work of Tien Ju-Kang (1953) on the Chinese in Sarawak in the early 1950s, which included a sociological analysis of the rural nature of the Hakka, hardly mentioned the presence of indigenous communities among whom the Chinese lived. Leach (1954) had a different approach in his study of the Kachin and Shan in Burma in examining a social and cultural system of relationships and networks which linked the two groups. In the words of Kuhn, "it is hard to understand the experiences of Chinese overseas without trying to understand the lives, traditions and attitudes of the non-Chinese among whom they settled " (Kuhn, 2008: 4).

The interactions of long established Chinese communities in Southeast Asia with indigenous Southeast Asians where acculturation takes place, have been researched by Tan (1988) in Melaka, Malaysia and by Skinner (1957) in Thailand. In Melaka, a distinctive language based on the mixing of Hokkien and the local Malay language emerged, accompanied by other cultural traits like cuisine, dress and music influenced by indigenous cultures. In other port cities in Southeast Asia such as Singapore and Batavia which like Malacca had Chinese traders, mixed communities emerged from inter-marriages between Chinese men and indigenous women.

In Thailand, the absence of cultural boundaries eased the assimilation of Chinese into Thai society. The Chinese did not just conduct trade at the Southeast Asian coastal ports but had ventured further afield and Borneo was the destination of Chinese attracted to the presence of minerals. Sarawak under the Brooke Raj had gold which attracted the Hakka to the interior of Bau and Engkilili. In this research paper, a different situation can be observed, although not unique to Sarawak. Over in Kalimantan were similar communities of Hakka who were engaged in gold mining.

In the literature on the Chinese who through inter-marriages appeared to have acculturated to the indigenous communities, language and religion have been identified by Tan (2004) as contributing towards the dynamics of acculturation. According to Tan (2004: 48) "Firstly, the instrumental aspect of a culture, as represented by language as a medium of communication, is easier to be acculturated and even replaced, whereas the symbolic aspect of a culture, as represented by a religious or worldview is more resistant to change." In my research on the Hakka in Engkilili, I look beyond language and religion, to include the dynamics of history, community and social relations between the Hakka and Iban.

Near to Engkilili just across the Indonesian land border in West Kalimantan, the Hakka have maintained their identity and language despite adverse political and social conditions, forming alliances with indigenous Dayaks through trade and inter-marriages (Heidhues, 2003). Carstens (2005), in her long term study of the Hakka in Pulai, Peninsular Malaysia who retained their Chinese cultural identity despite inter-marriages, described her work as a case study of local Hakka Chinese identity which has been unconsciously reproduced in a new environment. Hakka communities in different parts of the world show differences in the expression of their identities. Hakka identity broke down in Kwan Mun Hau, Hong Kong and Pulai Malaysia It re-emerged in mainland China and Taiwan. In Shung Him Tong Tsuen, Hong Kong and Calcutta Hakka identity persisted (Constable, 1996). This research will show Hakka identity and adaptation in another local setting, similar to but at the same time different from conditions in West Kalimantan. The Hakka in Engkilili encountered more conducive social conditions which allowed for the continuity of their identity and acculturation to the Iban. While Iban women through inter-marriages became part of the Hakka community in Engkilili, at the same time the Iban did not abandon their links to their natal families.

The study of the Hakka here is grounded in historical research and ethnography, examining extant archival materials to trace the footsteps of Hakka journeying to Engkilili, and using ethnography to gather empirical data on the ground. "Past and present illuminate each other reciprocally" (Braudel in Tosh 2000: 248) and this approach with the past and present forming a continuum is used here. After laying out the historical background from available empirical evidence on the Hakka mining for gold, farming and trading, and analyzing their relationships with the Iban, ethnographic data is collected to describe the present circumstances of the Hakka, including their interactions with the Iban and the Teochew. An event, the 10th day Chinese new year deity procession, is covered to highlight the continuity of Hakka identity, and the Iban receptivity to Chinese religious values. The story of Hakka farmers and small traders living in a multi-ethnic setting remains largely hidden and unwritten. This research is aimed at addressing this gap, notwithstanding the limitations in available archival sources.

The objective of this research is to examine the social and cultural resilience of the Hakka given their long period of settlement in Engkilili, where they are a minority living alongside the indigenous Iban. The research questions to be asked are what the social and cultural characteristics of the Hakka that enable them to maintain their community and identity in a rural part of Sarawak. This necessitates an analysis of Hakka as a collective group and as individuals in their social interactions and relations with their indigenous neighbours.

I Physical and Demographic Setting

Engkilili describes a present-day district in the Sri Aman division of Sarawak. The name Engkilili is said to be derived from a slightly sweet and reddish fruit. However the Hakka and Teochew have known Engkilili by another name, "*Sang Ti Tou*" (top of the ladder), possibly a reference to Engkilili being situated in the upper reaches of the Lupar river (Tay Chek Pin, 1996: 1). Sri Aman division is now largely a smallholder agriculture and plantation area overshadowed by its more developed neighbouring Kuching division where the state capital Kuching sits. Back in the past under Brooke quasi-colonial rule (1841-1941), the Sri Aman division enjoyed prominence as an Iban heartland, and still does.

The modern state of Sarawak had its beginning with an English dynastic family of the Brookes acquiring the territory as a semi-colonial possession in 1841 by intervening victoriously in local disputes on behalf of Brunei suzerain overlords. Nineteenth century Sarawak on the northwestern portion of Borneo was a sparsely populated land, lending itself to popular western images of a tropical frontier teeming with exotic flora and fauna (see Beccari, 1986 [1904]). In the 1750s, Hakka miners journeyed to west Borneo or Kalimantan to mine for gold, setting up companies known as *kongsi* which grouped together to form federations. The role of the *kongsi* has been documented in Yuan (2000) and Heidhues (2004). Descendents of the miners in Engkilili trace their roots to west Borneo which coincide with documentation in English sources on a mining *kongsi* in Marup, Engkilili.

The scope of this study is confined to the historical site of Marup, where gold mining was undertaken, the linear villages of individual homesteads and farms stretching out from the Engkilili township or bazaar, and including Engkilili district itself. The Hakka population is estimated at about 1800, and there are a few hundred Teochew and other Chinese, all living in approximately 400 households, spread out across 5 villages, the town and a government built "low cost" housing estate. As a settled community that evolved over time, the Hakka have lived alongside the majority Iban group who presently make up more than 90 per cent of the population of 23,000 in the Engkilili district which derives the same name as Engkilili town. The Iban, like the Chinese are a rural community. Although Engkilili is used interchangeably for town and district, for the purposes of this report, the name refers to the wider context or district of Engkilili unless specific reference is made to Engkilili town.

The Iban, who form the majority ethnic group in Engkilili, migrated from the Kumpang river tributary which is adjacent to the Batang Ai watershed in Sarawak, settling in the area around Engkilili and Lubok Antu (Sandin, 1994). They are a longhouse dwelling community residing along river banks, and in the past were engaged in the collection of jungle products for sale to Chinese traders, and in the swidden cultivation of hill rice. While much more is known about the Iban in the lower reaches of river basins and their conflicts with each other and with the overlords of Sarawak during the Brooke era (1841-1941), very little has been said or studied on the Iban in Engkilili. What will be useful here to note are some general observations about the Iban which have relevance for this paper. Firstly, there were symbiotic economic relationships which were conducive to social relationships, between the Chinese and Iban (Chew, 2004 [1990] and Pringle, 2010 [1970]). Secondly, there is the Iban attention to *adat*, "the embodiment of universal order, the normative rules and understandings that regulate human affairs and govern relations between humankind and the unsee supernatural world and everyday visible worlds" (Sather, 1994: 31). In the context of this paper, I will discuss Iban perceptions and attitudes towards Chinese religion.

II Historical Backdrop: Miners, Traders and Farmers

The origins of gold mining in Marup, Engkilili have been documented through oral and written sources by local researchers (Liu, 1991; Goh and Tay, 1996). The scarcity of written sources does not permit a comprehensive reconstruction of the past, and there are gaps in our understanding of the ethno-history of the Hakka in Engkilili. Mining in Marup was in the hands of a Fifteen Shares *kongsi* which although led by charismatic leaders, appeared to work like a cooperative partnership of miners pooling together their resources, work and gold ore diggings. This type of working and living arrangement in the gold mines in Marup and Bau had its origins in West Borneo dating back to the 1750s when Hakka, invited by local overlords, set up these *kongsi*. These *kongsi* were arrangements set up to cope with an alien environment. Borneo was a frontier environment where the Hakka needed local indigenous acquiescence to extract the gold ores (Brooke [1990], 1886). Establishing a company, a *kongsi*, to take collective care of miners' needs fulfilled the miners' sense of sharing, security and belonging. In West Borneo, and in Bau, Sarawak, *kongsi* grew and combined to form even bigger autonomous federations which challenged and fought each other, and against the intrusion of western colonial powers, the Dutch in West Borneo, and James Brooke in Bau, Sarawak. The founders of the Fifteen Shares *kongsi* fled from inter-*kongsi* warfare in West Borneo and sought refuge in Marup sometime around the mid-19th century (Liu, 1991; Goh and Tay, 1996).

Besides mining for gold in Marup, vegetable gardens were kept.[2] When the mines were exhausted towards the end of the 19th century, the miners switched to farming.[3]

Gold mining in Marup declined by the end of the 19th century but has left a legacy which continues to shape the collective and individual identities of the Hakka. A *kongsi* hall is still standing, and although having gone through several renovations (Goh, 2006), has retained its essence, a central hall which houses deities honouring the protector deity of the Fifteen Shares *kongsi*, the god of three mountains, and other deities, and two empty adjacent rooms of an old office and armoury.

Despite a short period of mining operations in the second half of the 19th century, the residual influence of the Fifteen Shares *kongsi* on Hakka can be felt in the leadership role played by descendents of the miners who have formed a Marup Chinese Trust Fund Committee which looks after the *kongsi* temple hall and its assets of two shophouses, and organizes the hungry ghost festival on the fifteenth day of the seventh lunar month at the *kongsi* temple hall, and takes part in the lunar new year 10th day deity procession.

Almost everyone living in Engkilili knows the existence of the Fifteen Shares *kongsi* temple hall and can vaguely associate it with the past heyday of gold mining while there are others who claim ignorance or show no interest. The Fifteen Shares *kongsi* in Marup is more associated as a place to go for picnic excursions in the adjacent streams. While the mining legacy remains in social memories, it is in trading and farming where there are continuities to the past.

A permanent site for the Engkilili shophouses was identified in 1920.[4]

---

2 Sarawak Gazette (SG) 12 May 1887, p. 87.

3 SG, 1 December 1893, p. 174, SG 1 February 1894, p. 22 and SG 1 November 1900, p. 208.

4 SG, 1 April 1920, p. 23.

Teochew traders had been trading along the Batang Lupar from its lower reaches at Simanggang right up to the up-river hinterland at Engkilili and Lubok Antu according to late 19th century Sarawak Gazette records. Rivers connected people and places, and administrative centres and trading outposts were strategically sited along rivers. The Brookes, who persuaded the Brunei overlords to let them rule Sarawak, like their Brunei predecessors, depended on trade for revenue taxes, and to control the movement of people along rivers. The intermediary role of traders was given to the Chinese. In the Lupar river basin where Engkilili was located in its upper reaches, Teochew traders took upon this middleman role. The traders sold items like salt and cloth to the Iban. In turn, the Iban sold jungle products to the Chinese. This trading relationship linked the Teochew to the Iban and bound the two groups together in ways which were unintended by the Brooke administrators who tried to keep the communities apart. There were Brooke decrees which forbade Chinese traders from "living among Dayaks", from setting up shop in remote Iban longhouses, ostensibly to prevent the Chinese from cheating the Iban.

Having shophouses at designated places by government orders, usually within reach of a government station was a way of ensuring that traders could be watched over, and to ensure that fair trading practices were carried out which did not disadvantage the indigenous Iban customers (Pringle, 2010 [1970]., Chew, 2004 [1990]). At Engkilili, there was a Brooke station, Fort Leonora which played this supervisory role over trade. Despite a head start and monopoly by Teochew traders, Hakka also went into trading[5] as petty traders and set up shops at Marup.[6]

---

5   SG, 1 November 1893, p. 174.
6   SG, 2 May 1892, p. 91.

Although there were official concerns over the Chinese, the economic relationship between trader and native customer had a social dimension which bridged ethnic boundaries. Traders learned to speak Iban, and set up shop in longhouses which were frowned upon and decreed illegal by the authorities. One Hakka trader Jap Nam Joon remembered growing up in the vicinity of a longhouse from the age of 8 years when his father acquired a piece of land next to a longhouse to set up shop. Jap spoke Iban fluently. An Iban longhouse, Rumah Lio, adopted the Jap family as fictive kin. Indeed Chinese traders who wished to set up shop in Iban longhouses or wished to establish close social relations with Iban were aware of this process of symbolic adoption. In the words of an informant, it is an *"abang-adik"* (elder brother-younger brother) relationship which facilitates social dealings when Hakka and Iban are in close contact with each other, either economically or socially. When I asked the Iban at Rumah San Samaju, Lubok Antu where *Kapitan* Liew had courted his Iban wife, what they thought of him then, one Iban elder said they accepted him.

Traders observed a tradition of allowing native customers to stay at the back of or on the top floor of shophouses when they came down to the bazaar to trade. This could be due to the long boat journeys that had to be undertaken and an overnight stay might be needed for the next day's return journey. When the Iban brought their jungle produce to the shops to sell, they put their trust in the shopkeepers to determine the value of the products.[7] Chinese new year was a time for visits by Dayaks and the exchange of gifts. Dayaks would arrive bringing live fowl, and would be feted and plied with food gifts. According to Tay Chai Ling, "Chinese new year was a time of celebration for the Iban too, and not only for us."

---

7 Interview with Ms Tay Chai Ling, Engkilili.

The positive social relations extended to Chinese traders, both Hakka and Teochew, marrying Iban spouses, a subject dealt with in a later part of this paper, *Crossing Over: Inter Ethnic Relations*. Hakka miners from the Fifteen Shares *Kongsi* married Iban spouses as well, from names which Goh (1996: 67, 69) identified in a donors' list for renovation work in the kongsi hall in 1873.

The depth and intensity of economic and social relationships between the Chinese, Hakka and Teochew, with the Iban meant that different groups of people co-existed at a place where ethnic and cultural differences did not keep them separate. Ethnic boundaries were broken down with social relationships and marriages, and with economic symbiosis between the Chinese trader and indigenous client.

While the traders, both Hakka and Teochew, had positive social relationships with the Iban, relations between the Hakka and Teochew were more variable, marked by conflict, rivalry and eventual acceptance, a characteristic of Chinese dialect groups living together on the Chinese mainland and overseas. The Hakka in Engkilili have always been a larger group in comparison to the Teochew. There were more Hakka in farming than in trading in the early days of settlement in the late 19th and early 20th centuries. Farming activity started to pick up around the 1920s with demand for planting rubber.[8] Pepper was another cash crop in demand (Shi, 1999, 126). According to Wilson Chai[9], the 1920s to the 1930s was the peak period for the movement of Hakka from Hopoh county to Engkilili and he estimated there were 1000 to 1500 families. High pepper prices were recorded in 1924 and 1935 and in the early 1950s (Shi, 1996). The type of trader-

---

8 SG 1 April 1926, p. 95 and SG 1 May 1926, p. 21.
9 Interview with Wilson Chai, 15 June 2010, Sri Aman.

farmer relationship in colonial Sarawak described by Tien Ju-Kang (1953) which was dialect group-based where farmers only dealt with traders of the same dialect group to get credit terms and sell their produce, did not apply in Engkilili, as Hakka traders were fewer in number. The arrangements were for the traders to give credit advances to the farmers for their planting needs, and the eventual crop harvests would then be sold to the creditor traders. Hakka farmers were free to choose which traders to go to irrespective of dialect group. Such arrangements were not necessarily free of tension and conflict. In the 1930s, there was conflict between pepper farmers and traders on the breach of credit terms. The complaint from the traders was that the farmers refused to pay back the debts they owed (Shi, 1996: 125). The farmers threatened to burn down Engkilili town and traders wanted to go on strike, but government intervention averted the crisis from blowing over.

Over time, dialect group tensions have decreased, and in matters of religion there was co-operation, in the support given by Simanggang Teochew for the upkeep of the Fifteen Shares *kongsi* house (Goh, 1996). Dialect group barriers are further broken down by education, in the Chung Hua primary school, marriages, and by social mixing in the shops, markets and farms. Today both Hakka and Teochew concur that dialect divisions are now not as prevalent as in the past.

Agricultural smallholdings are still kept and farmed in the five Hakka villages. The sizes of the farms range from one to two, five and up to 10 hectares. Vegetables and fruit trees are grown, and the produce is sold to the nearby bigger towns, Sri Aman, Betong and Sarikei. However, the market for the farm produce is small, and one farmer complained that there is competition from farmers near Kuching who also send their produce to the same markets in Sri Aman, Betong and Sarikei. Farming on a small scale with farmers growing similar types of vegetables and fruits for a small competitive market does not generate lucrative financial returns. A few enterprising farmers are trying out oil palm growing on their small farms but the size of the farms is a handicap. Some farmers rent land from the Iban or else ask their Iban kin to buy land on their behalf. Chinese are not regarded as indigenous to the state and are not allowed to own native customary rights and native land which only communities regarded as native can own. This is a legacy inherited from the Brooke government which is still in force today. It does not appear possible to rely on farm incomes alone and families have to rely on off farm incomes or remittances from children working in the bigger towns. Farmer Kuan who is 40 years old and has worked on orchards in Australia, supplements his livelihood by collecting produce from other farmers on his pick-up vehicle. The farmers are an ageing group in their fifties and sixties, and few youngsters show interest in agriculture as a means of livelihood.

With farming a major livelihood, and with smaller numbers of people in trading and other occupations, class distinctions do not appear to be prevalent in Engkilili. Indeed the headmen of the villages are farmers and serve on temple boards such as the Marup Chinese Trust Fund Committee which looks after the Fifteen Shares *kongsi* temple hall. Descendents of the *kongsi* pioneers, given the privilege to serve on Marup Chinese Trust Fund Board are farmers. The absence of class distinctions contributes to easy social relationships and people mix around easily in public places like the coffee shops, market and town, and with neighbours at home.

While farmers depend on their own resources to plant and sell their produce, the shops which are owned in almost equal numbers by Hakka and Teochew, sell similar merchandise such as foodstuffs and clothes while a number of others are coffee shops which sell cooked food and drinks. The shopkeepers are aware that their businesses are tied to the livelihoods of the

Iban who form the majority of customers. The economic outlook of the town is bound up with the livelihoods of the Iban. Iban depend on incomes from their smallholdings like the Hakka farmers. At the time of my fieldwork, rubber prices were said to be favourable which would leave the farmers with more disposable incomes. But like the Chinese in Engkilili, migration to the towns has depleted the Iban population in the longhouses, leaving only ageing parents and the young dependents behind while the able bodied adults go off to the towns and overseas to work.

III   Social Characteristics

A survey was undertaken to highlight the present social and cultural characteristics of the Hakka in Engkilili for glimpses and insights on the community. The sampling method was purposive in targeting Chinese households. The outside appearance of the houses with talismans and other paraphernalia on the main doors were clues as whether the households were Chinese. Rural communities generally welcome visitors, and even researchers, into their midst and households. This was true at the research site in Engkilili although the author and his research assistants encountered hostility, evasiveness and non-cooperation which reduced the sampling size. The Hakka stay in individual homesteads in 5 villages, the township, and a low cost housing estate. The 5 villages of Jelukong, Mawang, Merio, Marup Atas, and Marup Baroh are made up of individual homesteads with small farms ranging in size from one to ten acres. There are 90 shophouses in the town many of which double up as dwelling units on the top floor. The low cost housing estate is estimated to have about 30 units where the Hakka and Teochew live.

The Engkilili township where the shophouses are located, is surrounded by government offices which administer the district also known by the same name of Engkilili. The government offices are represented by government at the national, state and local levels. The district office under the state government is directly responsible for running the government affairs of Engkilili while some national departments and the local government administer the specialized functions.

Under the district office, the Chinese are indirectly administered with appointed area headmen (*kapitan*) and an overall head (*pemancha*). The *kapitan* and *pemancha* appointments conform to residential areas and economic functions. As trading is recognized as an important economic activity, a Teochew *pemancha* is appointed as the overall community leader. The Hakka are spread out in the five villages, and each village has its own headman, invariably a Hakka. The headmen perform perfunctory functions such as attending government functions and generally looking after village affairs and individual requests. The *kapitan* appointment is a legacy carried over from the Brooke (1841-1941) and colonial (1946-1963) eras while the *pemancha* post is an post-Malaysia (1963-) appointment.

Lockard (1987) in his research on Chinese leadership in Kuching described the "interlocking" nature of leadership where community leaders were also businessmen who served in the clan associations, religious committees and school boards. In rural Engkilili, a similar pattern appears to be the case with *kapitan* who are active in the two dialect group associations, the Teochew association and the Hakka association, the temple committees and school boards. There are two temple committees which play a leadership role, the Marup Chinese Trust Fund Committee which manages the Fifteen Shares *kongsi* hall temple, and the *Tua Pek Kong* (big uncle god) temple committee. There appears to be a dialect group division between the two committees which may suggest some latent dialect group differences. The Marup Chinese Trust Fund Committee is made up of descendents of the

Fifteen Shares *kongsi* and appointed Hakka from the outlying Hakka villages while the *Tua Pek Kong* temple committee comprises mainly Teochew and some Hakka from the town. Both committees play a leading role in the organizing of the 10th day Chinese new year deity celebrations. There are other temples such as the temple of the king of heaven, the temple of the monkey god, and the temple of the heavenly dragon.

Similar to the Fifteen Shares *kongsi* temple and the *Tua Pek Kong* temple committees which reflect dialect group membership, there are two dialect group associations, the Teochew Association and the Hakka Association, their formation being a recent phenomenon. According to a former teacher turned businessman, dialect associations did not exist when he was a youth in the 1940s and 50s. The reason could be due to the small size of the community, and that the school board was playing a key role in leadership functions and looking after communal needs. The Teochew Association was formed in 1961 by conservative Teochew traders concerned with protecting their business interests at a turbulent time when young Chinese were challenging colonialism (Zhou, 1999: 132). Meanwhile, the Hakka Association was only formed in 1978 when it was felt that the community for its numerical strength, lacked an association to look after Hakka interests (Huang 1999: 135). It promoted welfare and educational assistance for members and their children, and organized recreational activities.

An examination of how the Hakka are organized at the individual family level is done through administering a questionnaire in a purposive cluster sample of 81 households in the 5 villages, the township and the housing estate. The questionnaire, followed up by interviews and observations, collected social data on gender, age, marriage, languages, education, religion and out-migration.

As the Hakka belong to a patrilineal society, in these 81 households, 51 male heads of households were interviewed. If the male heads of households were not present, the wives were interviewed, 30 of them.

The majority of respondents in this survey are above 40 years of age, numbering sixty five persons out of eighty one persons. Sixteen persons are aged from twenty years to thirty nine years. See table 1.

Table 1: Gender and Age Groups

	Male	Female	Age Group
	4	4	20 – 29 years
	5	3	30 - 39
	12	10	40 - 49
	16	6	50 - 59
	14	7	Over 60
Total	51	30	

Marriages

In marriages, there is a preference to marry Hakka partners as table 2 indicates, with lesser numbers marrying other Chinese. Among the men, out of 51 persons sampled, 8 married Iban. More will be said about inter-marriages in the section on "Crossing Over: Inter-Ethnic Relations". Although not shown in the tables, 8 male respondents had Iban mothers. There were no examples of Hakka women married to Iban men, although in a separate section in this report on inter-ethnic relations, there is a sole example of a bi-cultural Hakka-Iban lady married to an Iban man.

When asked to what they would prefer to identify themselves as, seventy five persons said they were Hakka. Four respondents preferred to be called Chinese, while two called themselves Malaysians. See table 3.

The readiness to take on a Hakka identity as a preference when asked, is

Table 2: Marriage patterns of Hakka males and females

Married to:

	Hakka	Other Chinese	Iban	Not married	Total
Male	36	5	8	2	51
Female	23	5		2	30

Table 3: Identity Preference

	Identify as Hakka	Identify as Chinese	Identify as Malaysian	Total
Male	48	2	1	51
Female	27	2	1	30

not surprising and can be correlated with objective criteria such as speaking Hakka and Mandarin. The Hakka still speak the dialect at home and in public, and impress upon their children to continue doing so. When asked why they called themselves Hakka, a common answer was that their fathers or their parents were Hakka. Patrilineal lineage and a historical identity of being Hakka influence perceptions of identity. Identity is situational and although it is generally accepted that ethnic Chinese in Malaysia have multiple layers of identity depending on circumstances such as at home, school, state, country and overseas, a strong sense of being Hakka can be discerned in Engkilili. This could be due, not only to the fact of objective criteria such as speaking the Hakka dialect and Mandarin, and of ancestry, but also that the Hakka among the Chinese dialect groups comprise the majority dialect group.

The questions on languages spoken at home, and the ability to speak other languages drew these responses on multi-lingual fluency. Please see table 4. Looking at the top two responses on speaking Hakka, Mandarin and Iban, fifty nine persons claimed to have this multi-lingual facility. Hakka is the language of the dialect group, Mandarin is the language of formal learning acquired in the school, and Iban is the language useful for communicating with the Iban majority group.

Table 4: Languages Spoken

	Male	Female
Hakka, Mandarin & Iban	26 persons	8 persons
Only Hakka & Iban	18	7
Only Mandarin & Iban		2
Only Mandarin	1	3
Only Hakka	1	2
Hakka, Mandarin, Iban & Malay	1	3
Hakka, Iban & Malay	1	2
Only Iban	1	1
Total	51	30

This versatility in languages is a characteristic of rural Sarawak where speaking several or more languages is useful in communicating with people of different ethnic groups. In fact, for the ethnic Chinese in Malaysia it is not uncommon to be fluent in several languages which is necessary for communication at home, in school, the workplace and in public where one encounters people of different ethnicities.

Living in an Iban majority environment and learning to speak Iban has not diminished the importance which the Hakka place on speaking Mandarin. The mastery of Mandarin is acquired through a Chinese primary school in Engkilili. Sixty respondents have had at least 6 years of attendance at the Chung Hua primary school in Engkilili and some were educated in Chinese schools elsewhere. Eight persons had two to four years of attendance at the Chung Hua primary school. See table 5.

Table 5: Chinese educational levels (primary school only)

	Male	Female
6 years of Chinese school	39 persons	21 persons
2 -4 years of Chinese school	6	2
Other types of schools	4	2
No schooling	2	5
Total	51	30

Education

The first institutions to be organized by the Hakka migrants in a new land were schools and temples and it was not unusual for some form of learning to take place at the religious venues. In a rural community, education was highly regarded by those who may not have had much schooling themselves. The first Chinese school in Engkilili was started at the Fifteen Shares *kongsi* in 1870:

> The miners who migrated from West Borneo started a mining company at the foothills of Tiang Laju. The number of people has reached 450. The area produces gold of good quality and in quantity. It appears that the people here are in contentment. Apart from mining gold, they plant rice and vegetables and domestic animals can be seen in great numbers everywhere. The kongsi also runs a fairly large school. After school, older students would help with domestic work such as cutting firewood and carrying water. [10]

There is a gap in the historical sources on how schools evolved in

---

10 SG, 15 October 1870.

Engkilili until the 1920s when commemorative books highlighted the establishment of the first Chung Hua primary school teaching in Chinese in Engkilili town in 1926. In the outlying areas beyond the town there were 8 schools serving the scattered Hakka[11] villages, teaching in Hakka . The 1920s and 1930s were the peak period of Hakka settlement in Engkilili, which explains the presence of 8 village schools and the town school. With pepper crop failures in the 1930s, the village schools closed down one after another, leaving only the town school. The Chung Hua school in town was rebuilt after the end of the second world war in 1945, and for a second time in 1955. The most recent renovation was in 1990 when a three storey building block was built, which remains to this today.

The school has remained a resilient institution because of the community support it receives. According to the principal of the Chung Hua School, Sim Kung Hui, there were 215 Chinese pupils, 78 Iban and 3 Malay[12] in October 2011. See table 6. The high enrolment of Iban students in the Chinese is viewed positively by the principal as an indicator of amenable social relations between the Chinese and Iban in Engkilili, and of the high regard which Iban parents have for Chinese education. The Iban, and even the Chinese for that matter, have a choice in sending their children to a nearby government school where the language of instruction is in the national language, Malay. The reason given by Chinese parents for their children to learn Mandarin is that an ethnic Chinese must know how to speak Chinese, associating language with identity. This attitude is not necessarily shared by urban town parents who have other concerns such as the utilitarian value of language. During the colonial period when English was recognized as a language that opened doors

---

11 Sri Aman Chung Hua Primary Schools Academic Committee, 1998, p. 214.

12 Interview with Sim Khung Hui, 12 October 2010, Engkilili.

to employment in the civil service, children of families such as mine were sent to English schools. Iban parents in Engkilili and even in the rest of Sarawak, who send their children to Chinese schools have favourable opinions on the value of learning Chinese, especially on its social and economic value, and in communicating with the Chinese. The economic ascent of China places even more value on the learning and mastery of Mandarin.

Table 6: Chung Hua Primary School Enrolments by Ethnicity

Chinese students	215 pupils
Iban students	78
Malay students	3
Total	296

The history of Chinese schools in Sarawak has had a chequered past due to political pressure from the colonial government, which was fearful of communist influence on such schools, pressurizing them to switch to English. Eventually Chinese middle schools which did not agree to these policy changes to teach in English were forced to remain as private schools. Chinese school students in Engkilili were caught up with the communist revolutionary zeal, a subject which is still taboo, talked about in hushed tones or not at all, silenced or simply forgotten (Kee, 2006). If the subject was alluded to, it was in understated language.

"After world war two, many colonized lands became independent. Similarly, the Sarawakian people began to strive for independence. During this time, a group of young people got involved in politics to push for independence for Sarawak". (Zhou, 1998: 132)

The subject of fighting for independence by bands of armed young men and women cropped up occasionally, "mountain rats who want to change the government" according to one elderly Hakka. But as quickly as the taboo subject crops up, it is suppressed just as fast. "Don't write it down", I was told by another person when he said how many young men and women were killed in Engkilili during the low level communist insurgency which plagued Sarawak from the period between 1963 and 1990. I was asked to keep away from the subject of communism as I was told "Engkilili is a small place, and people will avoid you and not want to talk to you". The sensitive subject of communism is likely to remain as one not to be talked about, eventually to remain silenced or forgotten although in recent years there is a readiness among the ex-communists to express themselves in self-published memoirs which shed light on why and how idealistic young men and women in post-second world war Sarawak were influenced by communist ideals and who opposed colonialism and the formation of Malaysia.

For many years, Chinese schools were perceived negatively by the government, colonial and post-independent, as a bastion of communism, and also by those who were educated in English, and then Bahasa Malaysia, Malay. The end of the communist insurgency in 1990 in Sarawak, and the modern economic transformation of China after it opened up to global economics, has changed the perceptions of Chinese schools. A mastery of the Mandarin language is now seen as beneficial and those who were schooled in Mandarin feel vindicated in keeping faith in the language.

Some 24 years after the independence of Malaysia in 1963, there was a changeover to teaching into Bahasa Malaysia, the national language, in 1987. Chinese middle schools continued to teach in Mandarin, but at a price, the withholding of official recognition of the Chinese middle school examination certificates. Non-recognition of Chinese school certificates has prevented the school graduates from applying to enter public universities and from recruitment to the public service. Despite these obstacles, Hakka parents in Engkilili continue to send their children to the Chung Hua primary school where they receive 6 years of elementary schooling in Mandarin even though there is the option of going to an alternative government primary school. After six years of Mandarin elementary schooling, students can opt to continue schooling in Mandarin in the middle schools in Kuching, or join the government schools which teach in Bahasa Malaysia. In Engkilili, with its mix of traders, workers and farmers, the stress on learning Mandarin cuts across social strata. Since most children and their parents speak Mandarin, whether a person of Chinese descent can speak Mandarin or not, does not figure at all in self- perceptions of identity, or in how others see them.

This is unlike in the capital Kuching where it does matter whether an ethnic Chinese speaks Mandarin, with a clear distinction between those who do, and those who don't. In Kuching there is a social divide or class division, with professional and English educated families preferring to send their children to English private or government schools, while the working and trading class Chinese prefer to send their children to Chinese schools.

The Hakka and other Chinese in Engkilili have hung on to the Chinese school tradition focused on Mandarin. The language of Mandarin is not a cultural marker which sets the Hakka apart from their Iban neighbours. We next turn to religion as a cultural marker.

Religion

An indicator of Hakka keeping their cultural practices is adherence to religion. As shown in table 7, sixty nine respondents claim to be followers of Chinese religion which is a mix of ancestor reverence, deity worship, Buddhism, and Daoism. Ten people said that they did not observe Chinese religion while two persons were Christian. Religious and cultural practices are both individual and public. At an individual level, there is a range of observances from daily deity worship to praying on the first and fifteenth days of the lunar month, casually visiting a temple when passing by, to asking for blessings when doing something important like going on a long or auspicious journey. The more common observance is on the first and fifteenth days of the lunar month. Thirty out of eighty one persons say they follow individual worship practices at home. This figure is lower than the sixty nine persons who said they are followers of Chinese religion. The reason given for lack of religious practices at home by some informants is limited space for setting up deity altars. Another possible reason is that the respondents only follow the cycle of calendrical major events for worship purposes.

The major cycle of festivals which is observed includes Chinese new year, tomb cleaning, the dragon boat (rice dumpling) festival, hungry ghosts month and the mid-autumn festival. Chinese new year and the hungry ghosts month are public and communal events, and more of what these major festivals mean for Hakka and Chinese identity will be elaborated upon later. Hakka and other elders confidently say that Chinese culture in Engkilili is "bright", implying a continuity of cultural traditions. However, this "brightness" is under threat from the out-migration of youths.

Table 7: Chinese religion

	Male	Female
Followers of Chinese religion	45 persons	24 persons
Non-followers but keep Chinese traditions/festivals	6	4
Christianity		2
Total	51	30

Out-migration

Engkilili, like the rest of rural Sarawak, is suffering from the out-migration of youths. The lack of jobs, education, and a sense of adventure in venturing to the outside world, have encouraged this movement of youths from their homes. In the past, Brunei was an attraction, then replaced by Singapore. Some have even gone further to Australia. Cities in peninsular Malaysia and bigger towns in Sarawak, Kuching, Miri, and closer to home, Sri Aman, are favoured destinations. When parents were asked about this migration trend, a common answer was "the children go where the jobs are". According to 28 year old Chew Sik Choi who was working in another Sarawak town, Sarikei, "youngsters don't see prospects in Engkilili and want to leave".

In February 2011, I was in Engkilili for Chinese new year, and interviewed returning youths working in Singapore and elsewhere in Sarawak and Peninsular Malaysia. Notable among the youths and young adults were two families of siblings working outside Engkilili. The first Chin family of three sisters were working in Kuching and Taiping in peninsular Malaysia, and two more brothers were working in Kuching. The Chin sisters indicated they would be staying where they are as they do not see any job prospects in Engkilili. They were back in Engkilili to be with their parents and "to relax and take a break". Four Sia siblings, who have a Teochew father and Hakka mother, were working in Singapore in skilled professional jobs in accounting, information technology and engineering. Two sisters said "they would rather be back in Engkilili but have no choice because of limited work opportunities". Engkilili youths working in Singapore, who enjoy higher wages and salaries are realistic about the likelihood of not returning to Engkilili to work. Business opportunities are talked about as a reason to return to Engkilili but in reality the small size of the town may not provide the opportunities. Some who have worked outside successfully in jobs or businesses have returned to Engkilili but they are a minority.

The father of the Chin sisters mentioned above, Mr. Chin, left Engkilili at the age of fifteen to work in Brunei for about 15 years in construction work and then moved to Miri for another 16 years, and became a successful contractor in securing big projects in Miri and Kuching. He decided to return to Engkilili because of what he perceived to be business prospects in a petrol station and associated supplies shop. Mr. Chin was to run the business with a partner who unfortunately died before the business venture could take off. Chin decided to stay back in Engkilili in semi-retirement, operating a passenger van service and tapping rubber. He frequents the foodstalls market in the mornings. Another returnee is a Teochew sundry shop owner who has worked for many years in Brunei. Roger Lee who lived and worked in Singapore for 10 years returned to Engkilili to get married and to help out in his father's building construction business.

The likelihood of the youngsters and young adults returning to Engkilili is slim, and one young man, working in Johor Baru was about to settle down as he was running an interior design business, and was buying a house. He has an older brother with a family in Singapore, and another sister, also in Singapore. This is an example of siblings setting up home away from Engkilili. When asked about family ties, informants were insistent on keeping family links and traditions of Chinese new year in Engkilili where their parents were. Other young people that I talked to working nearer Engkilili, in Kuching and Sri Aman gave similar answers.

The re-migration of Chinese from Southeast Asia as a second wave of movement is a potential research area (Kuhn, 2008) and on a much smaller and different scale, Hakka in Engkilili are moving to other parts of Sarawak and Malaysia, and to Singapore. The spreading out of Hakka to other parts of

Sarawak, Malaysia and to Singapore where social and cultural conditions are different, may help to create another kind of identity and pull. For Hakka who are in Kuching, Sri Aman and other towns, it is easier to return to Engkilili for the tomb cleaning ceremonies, other festivals and for a "holiday". Youngsters working in Singapore do not return as often, more likely once a year during Chinese new year. Eventually, families in Engkilili will be like what Kuhn has described of families in China, families spatially separated because of residence and work in several or more places but with a sense of belonging to the original home. In Engkilili, the family and kinship ties are re-kindled at least once a year during Chinese new year, and less so during the tomb cleaning festival, and during periods of crisis like sickness or death. However, when the parents pass away, and if there are no family members and kin remaining in Engkilili, it remains to be seen if the tomb cleaning practices in the first week of April will continue to be maintained.

The social survey indicators show a Hakka community that is able to replenish itself with intra-Hakka marriages, but at the same time inter-marrying with other Chinese and Iban. In terms of cultural identity, there is strong adherence to Chinese religion. There is linguistic ability in speaking Hakka, Mandarin and Iban, which enable the Hakka to keep their linguistic identity as Hakka and Chinese, but able to communicate with their Iban neighbours and friends in Iban. Arguably, the learning of Mandarin reinforces Chinese cultural identity.

IV   Crossing Over: Inter-Ethnic Relations

A consistent feature of social relations between Hakka and Iban over time is inter-marriage. Contemporary observers in the 19th century commented on the incidence of inter-marriages between Hakka miners and

Iban women. A.B. Ward, Resident of the Second Division on a visit to Engkilili in the 1920s reported seeing the mixed offspring of Chinese men and Dayak women, saying that they inherited the "best of their parents' character and features" (Ward, 1966, 37). Inter-marriages continue to this day in Engkilili. Living in close proximity with each other in the past facilitated inter-marriages whether the Hakka or Teochew was a trader or farmer. The legendary hospitality of Iban longhouses encouraged Chinese men to visit, befriend, woo and marry their Iban spouses. When I asked the mixed marriage couples how they met, the common answers were the men were working nearby or at the longhouses.

Carstens (2005), in her study of the Hakka in Pulai in Peninsular Malaysia said that in the early days of the settlement, Hakka men married Temiar and Siamese women and she attributed this to the relatively higher status of women among Hakka who did not practice foot binding and with the ease in which non-Hakka women were accepted into Hakka households. In the case of the Hakka in Engkilili it was not only the acculturation of non-Hakka women into Hakka families that took place. The men also showed a readiness to acculturate to their spouses, in learning the Iban language, and accepting their cultural practices. The children tended to follow the social preferences of the father in speaking Mandarin and Hakka, but also learned the mother's Iban language.

Twenty-nine households identified as having inter-marriages, were selected for interviewing. In these mixed households, both the Iban and Hakka languages were the languages of communication among the parents, between the parents and children, and among the children themselves. Some Iban are not confident in speaking Hakka although they understand it, and reply in Iban when spoken to in Hakka by the husband as I have observed. When I asked a young Hakka husband in his thirties if his wife understands

Hakka, his reply was he spoke Hakka to his wife so that "she will learn to speak Hakka". Alternatively, the husband may just speak Iban to the wife, or there may be a mixed conversation of Hakka and Iban, or a constant switch of languages.

Kapitan (headman) Liew Ah Ban is married to an Iban from Lubok Antu district which is adjacent to Engkilili. In this household there is easy language switching in the family lounge room even though Hakka is spoken most of the time. *Kapitan* Liew speaks in a mixture of Hakka and Iban to the wife. The daughter speaks Iban to her mother, and then the granddaughter appears. The grandmother switches to Hakka to speak to the granddaughter. There is another example of multiple language usage in inter-marriage households. *Kapitan* Kiu Nam Joon has a Hakka father and an Iban mother. The *Kapitan* himself has an Iban wife who does not speak Hakka although he speaks Hakka to his children. He has an adopted Hakka son Lai Soon Chin who is married to a bicultural Iban-Hakka wife who only speaks Iban and Malay. Lai is fluent in Hakka, Mandarin and Iban. When I visited the multi-generation household, Lai's children were conversing in Mandarin among themselves and making glutinous rice dumplings for the dragon boat festival.

The use of multiple languages happens in the market as well. I speak in Hokkien to trader Jap Joon Nam in his shophouse and he replies in Hokkien even though he is Hakka. An Iban customer walks into his shop, buys some sundry items and goes to Jap to pay for his purchase. Jap switches to Iban when speaking to the customer and some light bantering goes on in Iban. I am talking to trader Kua in English in front of his cooked food stall at the market. He sees some people walking past, and grabs hold of their attention by speaking to them in Iban, Hakka or English. Multiple language use and the ability to switch from one language to another, frequently takes place among the Hakka.

The Hakka spoken in Engkilili which is Hopoh Hakka, appears to have remained intact in its syntax and semantics. The language has not become mixed to become another language although in the normal course of conversation, Iban words may be used. When speaking Iban, some Hakka words may creep in. This aspect of socio-linguistics requires further research which is beyond the scope of this paper.

There is a readiness on the part of the Iban to learn Hakka and even Mandarin, and to use the adopted language readily, even fluently. Surong, 49 years old, married to a Teochew trader, speaks Teochew to her husband, and was observed using Mandarin with her grandchild, when I met her at home. This language fluency according to her, was akin to the process of "*masok Cina*" (becoming Chinese), the first time I heard such an expression. When queried where and how she learned Mandarin, she replied, "from the grandchild, her books and from television". Surong's household is uncharacteristic where Iban was not used between the parents, between parents and children, and among the children themselves. The children, when young, spoke Malay to the mother's Iban kin in the longhouse, and only spoke some Iban to them when they were older.

There is a strong emphasis towards learning Mandarin, with 25 families out of the 29 families interviewed, sending their children to Engkilili's only Chinese primary school even though there is the option of enrolling the children in the government schools which use Malay. One respondent, Bong Sin, who is of mixed heritage, with a Hakka father and Iban mother, is atypical in enrolling his four sons in a government school. This stress on mastering Mandarin in Engkilili is consistent, and perhaps even more so at present when the usefulness of Mandarin is associated with the rise of China as a global economic and cultural power.

The Yap household is an example of multiple language usage and emphasis. Yap Hian Fong is a fifth generation Hakka tracing his lineage to the Fifteen Shares *Kongsi*. He is married to Jerma, an Iban for the last 44 years. Despite the lengthy years of marriage, Jerma, although understanding Hakka, speaks Iban to her husband Yap. Jerma and Yap have five children, four sons and one daughter, who all attended the Chung Hua primary school. The children spoke Mandarin, Hakka and Iban at home. The four sons are married to Chinese spouses. The only daughter, Yap Pui Jan, has good enough fluency in Mandarin to be a teacher in the Chung Hua primary school. She is married to an Iban and the children attend the Chung Hua primary school. Yap is an example of a bicultural Hakka-Iban lady married to an Iban man whereas the tendency in inter-marriages in Engkilili is for Hakka men to marry Iban women.

The children of Yap Pui Jan speak Mandarin, Hakka and Iban, as do many bi-cultural children of mixed Hakka and Iban heritage. Yap Pui Jan's children speak Iban to their father as he is Iban, and to their maternal grandmother in Iban too, as she is Iban too. The children speak Mandarin to their maternal grandfather. Like bi-cultural Yap Pui Jan whose identity and that of her children are both Hakka Chinese and Iban, there are examples of two bi-cultural Chinese/Iban to illustrate the fluidity of identity. Sie Shiau Liang has a Hakka father and Iban mother, and is married to a Hakka. Sie admits that her Hakka is not as fluent as Iban and she uses Iban more. Sie's children attend the Chung Hua primary school and speak a mixture of Hakka, Mandarin and Iban at home. Although the Hakka Chinese influence is dominant at home, and there is a deity altar, and the calendrical cycle of festivals is followed, Sie keeps in touch with her maternal mother's kin in Ulu Engkari by returning back for Gawai and critical events such as funerals. Yek Ai Mee comes from Bintulu and has a Foochow father and Iban mother, and is married to a Hakka in Engkilili. Similar to the examples above, a mixture of Iban and Hakka is spoken at home even though Yek is Foochow. The children attend the Chung Hua primary school. Yek and her Hakka husband visit her Iban mother's longhouse to keep in touch with her Iban kin and when asked why, said "it is important and for mutual help". At the time of visiting her house in Engkilili, Yek's Iban kin from Bintulu were visiting her.

The acculturation of Iban spouses to the Hakka households is noticeable in the adoption of religious values and practices. Traditional Iban religion is still observed in Engkilili where Christianity has not made many inroads. Out of 29 Iban spouses who were surveyed, before marriage, seventeen women adhered to traditional Iban religion while ten were Christians, and two followed Chinese religion due to their part Chinese origins. After marriage, there is a religious conversion with twenty three Iban spouses following Chinese religion, while five remained Christian. This conversion is accompanied by the observance of the Chinese calendrical cycle of festivals and religious occasions. See table 8. Iban spouses who choose to remain Christian, even nominally, find it difficult to keep the tenets of their faith as there are no churches in Engkilili except for a Baptist church.

Table 8 : Religion of Iban spouses of Hakka men before & after marriage

	Before marriage	After marriage
Traditional Iban religion	17	1
Christianity	10	5
Chinese religion	2	23
Total	29	29

A syncretic mix of ancestor and deity worship is followed in Hakka households, and Iban spouses are aware of the obligations for worship at home and in communal ritual events which bring together the entire community. Nai, an Iban wife of a Hakka, is an exception as an adherent of the practices. The family home has a deity altar dedicated to *Guan Yin*, goddess of mercy, *Tua Pek Kong* and the king of heaven. She does the offeringstwice every day, on the first and fifteenth days of the lunar month, and during the calendrical cycle of festivals. Nai speaks Hakka, but may switch to Iban when offering her prayers and recite in Iban: *gayu guru, celap lindap, gerai nyamai, lantang senang*[13] (a long healthy, tranquil, cool, content and comfortable life) (Gerunsin Lembat 1994, 6).

The ease with which Nai and other Iban married to Hakka appear to readily adopt Chinese religious rituals and prayers may be explained by the similarity of Iban *adat* (customary law) to the Chinese idea of *pingan*, of asking for blessings and wellbeing in prayers. The main function of Iban *adat* is to maintain a harmonious relationship among members of the community and to preserve the physical and spiritual wellbeing of the Iban longhouse (Lembat 1994). The Iban see no ritualistic difference between *gerai nyamai* and *pingan*. Even Iban who are Christian and follow Chinese prayer rituals do not see any conflict with their Christian beliefs. One Iban lady when asked what her pastor would think of her taking up her husband's religious practices said, "this is between me and God".

The readiness to acculturate and to be absorbed into another ethnic group is a feature of Borneo societies where "whole communities change their ethnic ascription" (Rousseau 1990: 73). The fluidity in crossing ethnic boundaries in Sarawak has been pointed out by Edmund Leach (1954), who although recommending the areas for ethnological research in Sarawak after the second world war, did not suggest on the fluid and mixed ethnic

---

13 This is also a reference to a "state of grace" in which all parts of the universe remain "healthy", "tranquil", "cool" and that the Iban are "content" physically and in spirit. The Iban ask for "a full life-span in contentment, health and comfort". See Jensen (1974: 115).

backgrounds of groups in Sarawak as a subject of study.

While there is acculturation in the Hakka households, the Iban spouses have not abandoned their Iban heritage and their longhouse background, and when Iban festivals like Gawai, the mid-year rice harvest are celebrated, all the twenty six Iban women in the survey sample returned to their natal homes, with the exception of three women whose original homes were too distant in Kalimantan. Surong follows her husband in the cleaning of up of the ancestral graves, praying to her husband's ancestors and to her own Iban ancestors. During the Iban *Gawai Antu* (festival of dead spirits), Surong and her husband will attend the Iban version of the same ritual.

Notwithstanding the fluidity in ethnicity for bi-cultural Hakka/Iban and for those who choose to acculturate, there are official impositions and situational circumstances which may dictate the choice of self-identification. The Brooke government loathed the idea of social mixing although saying that bi-cultural Chinese/native inherited the best characteristics of both cultures. In particular, there was official concern over Chinese traders cheating their indigenous clients and there were prohibitions on traders staying in longhouses. On inter-marriages, the Brookes decreed that the children of such unions had to follow the father's ethnicity and these rulings still apply to this day which causes confusion and creates problems as ethnicity is highly politicized. Indigenous people in Sarawak and Malaysia are called *bumiputeras*, literally meaning "sons of the soil" and groups which are not *bumiputera* and regarded as not indigenous include the Chinese. With government policies of affirmative discrimination to assist economically disadvantaged indigenous communities, *bumiputeras* enjoy privileges such as more opportunities to enter public universities and the public service. The ownership of customary rights and native land, a legacy of Brooke policies to protect the interests of the indigenous groups, prevents the Chinese from ownership of such land.

Taking on an officially recognized ethnicity or race as it is called in Sarawak is mandatory as it is a stipulation in documents like birth certificates. Ethnicity of the children strictly follows the father's ethnicity and not the mother's. In Engkilili, the children of inter-marriages with a Chinese father and Iban mother invariably take on the father's ethnicity. Official categorization of ethnicity is rigid and does not recognize bi-culturalism or allow the choice of ethnicity. As most of the inter-ethnic marriages in Engkilili are between Hakka men and Iban spouses, the children for official purposes are Chinese. Official categories of race classification do not capture the extent of inter-marriages.

Official naming of "race" does not appear to bother the bi-cultural Hakka/Iban or with Iban married to Chinese who are easy with ethnic categories. When Iban spouses of the Hakka were asked what they would prefer to be called, a number said "*Cina*-Iban" (Chinese-Iban), although in the official documents, if the father is Chinese, their ethnicity will be recorded as Chinese.

In everyday social situations, since the Iban spouses can speak Iban, Hakka and in some cases Mandarin, they freely choose to identify as Iban or Chinese when asked about their identity. One lady who understands but does not speak much Hakka said that as she looks like an Iban, she will say she is Iban when asked. An Iban lady Udek, married to a Hakka, said when asked about her ethnicity will reply that she is Chinese as she is married to a Chinese. Another Iban spouse, Ligat, also married to a Hakka, when asked by others about her ethnicity, might reply that she is Hakka or Iban. Iban spouses after marriage can take up residence in either partner's family. This flexibility appears to extend to the situational ethnic identity of the hybrid Iban-Chinese or of Iban married to Chinese.

There is a process to change one's official ethnicity in order to reap the economic benefits of *bumiputera* (native) status by going through the native courts and the district office to certify that one is identified as native by virtue of having one native parent for inheritance purposes for the maternal line, or by giving up bi-cultural children for adoption by Iban relatives in name and not necessarily in reality. This does not appear to be practised in Engkilili. It can also be observed that in Engkilili the inter-marriages are between working class Hakka men and Iban women, and not between indigenous men and Chinese women. Marriages between indigenous men and Chinese women do take place, but mostly in the towns and cities, where the indigenous men with better educational levels work due to more job opportunities. In Engkilili, Serai, an Iban married to a Hakka farmer, has a daughter working as a police woman officer in Kuala Lumpur the national capital city. The daughter is married to a Kadazan from Sabah.

When the Iban and Hakka-Iban women were asked for their views on inter-marriages, their overwhelming responses were in the affirmative; "it is okay"; "in Engkilili, Chinese and Iban live side by side", "good for mutual understanding", and "we live in a mixed society". Three replies from the questionnaires had reservations, "not with food taboos", a reference to marriage with muslims which prohibit the eating of pork. Both Chinese and Iban religions are syncretic and polytheistic, which could be a facilitating factor in inter-marriages. Opportunities for muslim-non muslim inter-marriages are limited as the muslim population in Engkilili is small, forming only one per cent of the population. The Malaysian government has recently launched a policy initiative called "1Malaysia" to mean a multi-cultural population living together which is tolerant and accepts multicultural diversity. "1Malaysia" is a slogan campaign repeatedly aired in the media and promoted by the government. Some Iban married to Hakka such as Regina are adamant that they are already practising multi-cultural tolerance even before the government promoted "1Malaysia." Besides the Iban who are married to Hakka, there are Teochew who are also married to the Hakka.

There are more Hakka than the Teochew in Engkilili, even though the latter play an important economic role, owning about half of the 90 shops in Engkilili. With the breaking down of dialect group barriers, inter-marriages take place between Hakka and Teochew. Out of a sample size of 20 Teochew male and female respondents, half of the marriages are with Hakka., as shown in tables 9A and 9B.

Table 9A: Marriages of Teochew men

Married to Teochew women	3 persons
Married to Hakka women	6
Married to other Chinese	2
Married to Iban woman	1
Total	12

Table 9B: Marriages of Teochew women

Married to Teochew men	4 persons
Married to Hakka men	4
Married to other Chinese	-
Married to Iban	-
Total	8

"Becoming Dayak"

So far the discussion has been on the acculturation of Iban women to Hakka society. There is an obverse process of Chinese men who may choose to go "native". The archival sources in the Sarawak Gazette are replete with references of Brooke abhorrence for Chinese men who decided to "live among the Dayaks" either to facilitate trade in the longhouses or because of marriage to Dayak women. "Living among the Dayaks" in the longhouses was a punishable offence that incurred prison sentences. As mentioned in the preceding section, the Brookes believed that the Chinese traders would cheat the Dayaks if they lived among them. Despite these edicts, the Brookes were unable to stem the social mixing and inter-marriages of Chinese and Dayaks. In Lubok Antu, in the upper reaches of the Batang Lupar beyond Engkilili, the social relations between the Chinese and the Iban resulted in a mixed Hakka and Teochew Chinese-Iban community fluent in speaking Iban and losing its linguistic facility with dialects and Mandarin.

An astute government official noted:

> Very few of the Chinese community there can speak any Chinese dialect and practically none can write it. Up to the present, the Chinese community there has considered itself to be Dayak to all intents and purposes.[14]

When a former senior servant friend knew that I was researching on the Hakka in Engkilili he suggested that I study the Chinese in Lubok Antu. His rationale was that the Chinese in Lubok Antu spoke Iban to each other. Together with Jayl Langub, I made several trips to Lubok Antu to get data from the government district office which was responsible for overseeing Engkilili, and to conduct preliminary investigations. There was a particular shop which sold Iban *ikat* (woven cloth) and other touristic paraphernalia that I stepped into at each visit, and I soon got to know the Teochew-Hakka

---

14   SG, 12 April 1951.

trader, Tay Chie Pen, who is in his early forties. His life story and that of his family is a representation of others, Teochew and Hakka, who have acculturated into the bigger Iban community in Lubok Antu.

Tay Chie Pen is a fourth generation Tay, a lineage that stretches back to 19th century Simanggang and whose widely dispersed clan members have spread out to Engkilili and Lubok Antu. Tay's paternal grandfather Tay Peng Hak had married a Hakka woman Bong Nyit Ping from Engkilili. Tay Chie Pen's father, Tay Lek Sui also married a Hakka, Liew Say Fah. The father only spoke Iban but observed certain Chinese customs such as Chinese new year. My informant Tay Chie Pen said the reason for his father to marry a Hakka was at the grandfather's insistence, so that the children could learn to speak Hakka and Teochew. Tay Chie Pen's multi-lingual mother could speak Hakka, Teochew and Iban. The mother spoke Iban to the father as this was the only language he understood. She spoke Hakka to the son. The son learned Teochew from his paternal Tay cousins.

When I was asking Tay Chie Pen about his life story and family tree, he had an animated discussion with his father in Iban. Tay Chie Pen who is widely travelled, having worked in Kuching and Brunei, can speak Teochew, Hakka, Mandarin and Iban. While we were having our discussion, Tay Chie Pen spoke Mandarin to his wife Hii Mui Chen, a Foochow from Sri Aman. So I asked where he learned to speak Mandarin, and he replied from his wife. Their children learn Mandarin from the mother.

Tay Chie Pen used a quaint expression *"Cina Pelandok"* to describe acculturated families like his, *Cina* meaning Chinese, and *Pelandok* is mousedeer. Tay described *Cina Pelandok* as similar to the Melaka Peranakan (acculturated Chinese) in Peninsular Malaysia. The experiences of the *Cina Pelandok* in Lubok Antu warrants a separate study in itself as they appear to have different cultural experiences from the Engkilili Chinese and other acculturated Chinese in other parts of Malaysia.

What this extended Tay household speaking multiple languages illustrates is an ongoing process of acculturation to their Iban neighbours, but because of concern with losing facility with dialects and Mandarin, there is a readiness to "re-sinify" by learning Mandarin. It is the insistence of the Hakka on keeping the dialect and Mandarin alive which sustains their identity in a rural district in Sarawak. In fact I did not come across any Hakka in Engkilili who could not speak Hakka and almost all, with the exception of some elderly Hakka, could speak Mandarin.

Inter-marriages between the Hakka and Iban cross ethnic boundaries but cultural identity for the Hakka remain strong as in Tay's example above, and in the keeping of religious traditions. For the children of inter-marriages, they speak Hakka and Iban, and go to the Chinese school. For the children, while their fathers would insist on them learning Hakka and Mandarin, learning the Iban language is not neglected because of the mothers' influence. The Iban spouses of Hakka men make a conscious choice to follow the religious practices of their husbands. How religion plays an important part in the lives of the Hakka, is examined in the next section.

V   "The Ritual Community": Chinese New Year 10th Day Deity Celebrations

Scholars have described Chinese religion as a complex system of traditional beliefs and practices which are observed individually and publicly, a syncretic mix of traditions in ancestor worship, Buddhism and the philosophies of Confucianism and Daoism (Tan 1990: 3-4). There are individual practices which are carried out at home and at temples and public places for the community. The communal celebrations such as Chinese new year draw together the Hakka and the Teochew, attract the participation of Chinese in nearby towns, and the interest of the wider Iban community. In my discussions and interviews with Hakka, I asked them about the major community celebrations in Engkilili. Chinese new year, in particular the 10th day deity celebration was frequently mentioned. The celebration of Chinese new year is an individual occasion for family reunions, and for the community to get together as a "ritual community" (term from Tan ibid) in a collective act of devotion. But Chinese new year is an event that transcends to the Iban. The notion of *communitas* (common living) (Turner 1969: 69) is useful here, for in a singular ritual of the deity procession, we witness a gathering of individuals and groups who come together for a ritual and spectacle. When Hakka, Teochew and Iban are asked about the significance of the deity procession, two reasons are given, the sacred and secular.

According to community elder Mr. Kuah, a Teochew:

The 10th day Chinese new year celebration is a Chinese custom that has been handed down by our ancestors. The purpose is to ask for blessings from the deities. Iban also take an interest in taking part and in watching. It is fun to watch and also an occasion for them to receive blessings.

The origins of the lunar new year celebrations are to ask the deities for blessings for the new year. The lunar new year 10th day celebrations started as two separate celebrations. The Fifteen Shares *kongsi* temple was one of the main organisers. It had a patron deity, the king of three mountains, a deity from Hopoh county first carried over to west Borneo, and subsequently brought over to Marup. Previously the Fifteen Shares *kongsi* temple had its celebrations on the twentieth day of the lunar new year. Another major organizer of the event was the *Tua Pek Kong* (big uncle god, also known as earth god) temple in Engkilili town, a temple mainly managed by the Teochew traders. The temple previously had its celebration on the 10th day to commemorate the anniversary of the *Tua Pek Kong* temple . Both temple committees got together and decided to hold a single celebration on the 10th day, and other temples, the monkey god temple, the heavenly dragon temple, and the king of heaven temple joined in. These temples although having their main protector deities, have other deities as well. Other smaller temples in houses, and even from as far as Sri Aman, Lubok Antu and Kuching take part. Since 2009, the 20th day celebrations have been scaled down in size. This 10th day celebration of the lunar new year is entirely organized by the local community, financed by the temples, associations, sponsors and individual donations, with no government financial aid.

I was in Engkilili for three days from 11 to 13 February 2011. Engkilili is a small, quiet town with about 90 shophouses, with a row of old timber shophouses fronting the river and two small blocks of newer shophouses. There is a market with cooked food and drinks stalls. The shops and businesses stir to life in the early hours of the morning from about 7 am onwards. People come to the market and shops to buy their necessities and spend their time in the coffee shops and market for meals of noodles and coffee. This burst of activity and life in the morning is short lived for by late morning, and certainly by noon, the shops are deserted and the market is closed.

The afternoon of 11 February 2011, the eve of the 10th day lunar new year celebrations is like any other day, except for a small crowd of people gathering at the *Tua Pek Kong* temple, making preparations for the event. The *Tua Pek Kong* temple is the centre for the event, where the procession of deities begins and ends, after going through the streets of the town. The temple would receive deities from participating temples on 11 February, while some other temples send theirs on the actual day, 12 February. Buntings and flags decorate the temple and sheds and on the open grounds in front of the temple. In the temple and two sheds are food and wine offerings and giant joss sticks. There is an open stage next to the temple for karaoke entertainment as there is a social aspect to the event, that of entertainment. Further away from the temple, in the market vicinity are tents for vendors to sell their wares, cooked food and drinks. The enterprising vendors want to make use of the opportunities to earn some money when thousands of spectators turn up in Engkilili.

During the late afternoon of 11 February, lorries ferrying the deities, spirit mediums and their temple committees and supporters are slowly driving into the compound of the temple. The lorries have with them groups of youngsters belonging to lion dance troupes who beat their drums and cymbals, lending a frantic and noisy atmosphere. A small crowd of Chinese and Iban starts to gather, a forerunner of a much bigger crowd the next day. Not all the deities can be housed in the *Tua Pek Kong* temple and they are distributed between the temple and the sheds. At the temple, spirit mediums begin to slash their tongues with thin swords. More deities will arrive the next day from outside Engkilili and from cults with no temples, the shrines in house compounds.

What was notable about the spirit mediums was the presence of three women including two sisters in an otherwise male domain. Those helping out in the preparations at the *Tua Pek Kong* temple and other temples were men. Carsten's (2005) observation about public religious activities in Pulai was that it was men who were in the public view while the women remained in the domestic realm, hidden from sight. In Engkilili the presence of women spirit mediums might indicate a less strict division of gender roles. Indeed some girls took part in the procession as drummers and cymbal beaters, and the lead drummer for the night's procession was a young woman.

Spirit mediums play a big role in the lives of the Chinese in Engkilili where as intermediaries they intercede on behalf of individuals who want to be cured of illness or who seek answers to personal and spiritual problems. Tay Cie Pen is a medium's assistant in Lubok Antu. As an assistant, Tay passes on the messages and answers from the medium to the requesters. Even though Lubok Antu is a small place, the sessions are held nightly from around 8 pm to well past midnight, and the clients are both Chinese and Iban seeking intercessions on personal matters. Madam Yap has two daughters who are spirit mediums dedicated to and serving the *Kuan Yin* (goddess of mercy) and *Nacha* (child god) deities both of whom took part in the Chinese new year deity procession.

The build-up to the big occasion of the 10th day of the lunar new year continued on to the next day 12 February 2011. The morning crowd started to gather in front of the temple and around the market where there are food stalls. Around 9 o'clock in the morning the first of the lorries with the deities, spirit mediums and supporters arrived, accompanied by a deafening crescendo of drums and cymbals from the lion dance troupes. Deities that were housed the day before in the *Tua Pek Kong* temple and in the temple are carried to the sedan chairs to be carried on foot or placed in lorries. More deities arrive this morning and each has its own band of supporters. One spirit medium, a plum jovial young man belonging to the sky dragon temple attracts a lot of attention as he invites and challenges bystanders to drink wine from a bottle, and he also drinks, appearing drunk to the amusement of the spectators. A big mixed crowd of Chinese, Iban and Malays, distinguished by the head covering veils of girls and women, has gathered in the temple vicinity and along the roads leading to and around the town. When the signal is given to start, firecrackers hung down from bamboo poles are lit, adding to the loud crescendo of lion dance drums and cymbals. When the din of the firecrackers dies down, the procession is about to start. Some spirit mediums are at the back of the lorries, while others prefer to walk. Groups of young men carry sedan chairs with the deities, which as if on cue will run on the road when signals or signs are received by the men, according to an observer . Many people will be walking on foot following the procession. The spirit mediums sit forlornly at the back of the lorries and will sometimes get off the vehicles to walk. The blazing mid-morning sun does not affect the crowd. The long procession then begins to wind its way around the town. By mid-day the procession winds its way back to the *Tua Pek Kong* temple where it began. The morning procession ends but the second procession at night is the finale, much bigger and grander.

When I asked why there are two processions, I was told the morning procession was to clear the path for the deities for the evening's procession "when the heavens open up" and the gods shower their blessings on Engkilili. In the mid-afternoon, a long line of cars, stretching a few kilometres are parked along the only main road into Engkilili town. Police officers on duty guide drivers to where they park their cars. I arrived around 5.30 pm thinking that I will be early, but I was wrong A much bigger crowd of thousands of Chinese and Iban, much bigger than in the morning, has gathered in the temple vicinity, along the roads leading to the town and in the town itself. Many of the spectators are from outside Engkilili. There is a secular aspect to the evening's celebrations. The karaoke stage is blaring out loud music in competition with the drums and cymbals of lion dance troupes. The temporary food and drinks stalls, and other stalls selling clothes and household items, are open and busy serving customers.

The procession is more elaborate this time, with more deities and their supporters, more spirit mediums, groups of men carrying empty sedan chairs with the deities, and corporate supporters with their decorated lorries. A dragon dance troupe from Chung Hua primary school is given the honour to lead the procession. The mixed crowd of thousands of Chinese and Iban lining up the roads and in the town patiently wait. There is a fireworks display lighting up the sultry night sky. Much like the morning's procession, the beating of the drums and cymbals of the lion dance groups create the mood for the night. Some spirit mediums walk and the groups of men carrying the sedan chairs, with deities and some without, would suddenly dash out and run on the road upon receiving signs or prompting from the deities. More people, Chinese and some Iban, appearing to be not necessarily associated with the spirit mediums, join the procession unlike in the morning when people who marched with procession had some role to play. In front of some shops are tables of offerings where spirit mediums stop and accept the offerings. The spirit mediums enter into some shop premises for the same purpose. It takes about two hours for the procession to wind down, and part of the crowd moves on to patronise the temporary stalls. When the procession is over, the deities are brought back to where they are housed in the temples or houses. The karaoke entertainment at the stage next to the Tua Pek Kong temple takes over when the procession is over. The next morning the town is quiet, with litter from the night scattered about. I visit the Fifteen Shares *kongsi* temple in Marup around noon where a group of men had gathered. The purpose of the gathering, as we were told by the temple elders and committee leaders, was to send the deities back to the heavens. In the kitchen next to the temple, one of the men cooked in two large woks, chunks of pork and chicken meat. At a small table, some men were gambling away.

This biggest event of the year for the Engkilili community organized and funded by the Hakka and Teochew, with association, corporate, temple and individual contributions, brings together the Chinese in Engkilili as a ritual community. Fifteen deities were counted during that night's celebrations. Some residents said Engkilili which still retains much of its agrarian character is a spiritual place, with many shrines dedicated to the deities, which appear to the spirit mediums, and even on one occasion to the Dayak community according to an informant.

The Hakka elder added:

> Engkilili is unique in that many deities that have shrines have appeared to the mediums on their own accord, unlike in other places deities are invited or certain rituals are done to invite or attract them. For some reason Engkilili stands out. Many other small towns have their own special procession days but few or none like Engkilili because of its attractiveness to deities.

An Iban lady, married to a bicultural Iban-Hakka, commenting on what the procession meant to her said:

> In fact, one of my mother-in-laws' grandson took an active part in this year's procession. He wants to be a medium. His name is Ah Chin and he works as a carpenter.

After seeing Iban taking part in the procession, and comprising a big proportion of the spectator crowd, I set out with my Iban speaking colleague, Jayl Langub[15], to find out more about Iban interest in a Chinese ritual event.

---

15 I am grateful to Jayl Langub for his assistance in conducting the Iban interviews and for sharing his insights on the Iban.

We visited a forty- door Iban longhouse, Rumah San Samaju in Lubok Antu district which is about fifteen minutes' drive from Engkilili. We held an open discussion on the *ruai* (verandah) of the longhouse. with residents who come freely to sit down and talk. After some ice breaking remarks, the discussion is on the 10th day Chinese new year deity celebrations. The Iban know it is a religious event in asking for "prosperity" and well-being. In the late afternoon, many will get ready to go to Engkilili, lock up their doors and leave, except those who are old, sick, infirm or very young. They go to enjoy the occasion, to feel good about the atmosphere of the lion dances, the procession and the presence of spirit mediums.

One Iban woman said:

> Lots of Iban attend the deity procession. They know it is religious, asking for prosperity. Iban go to enjoy the occasion, to feel good about the atmosphere the whole activity creates. It just makes one feel good, feeling of *gerai nyamai*, *lantang senang*. They like to pull the whiskers of the lion. If one can pull the whiskers the first time, sign of luck. If can't pull, don't try the second time, it means luck is not on the way.

This "feel-good" and "fun" reason is similar to what a Hakka elder said earlier about the event. For a small place like Engkilili which does not have avenues for entertainment, people look forward to the occasion. At this Iban longhouse most residents are Christian but they see no conflict between attending a Chinese religious occasion and Christian beliefs.

An Iban lady married to a part Hakka, and who has accepted the Chinese belief system was more explicit about the reasons on going to watch the celebrations:

I go to the 10th day celebration every year. It is part of an activity that a believer has to attend. Also it is partly a big social event that Chinese and non-Chinese attend in a small town like Engkilili. Of course it is about the gods coming down to earth to offer blessings. As an individual who embraced the belief I go to get blessings. The whole event gives a sense of calmness and peace, the notion we Iban call *gayu guru, celap lindap, gerai nyamai, lantai senang* (a long healthy, tranquil, cool, content and comfortable life). I don't take active part, just an ordinary spectator. My family members also attend the event regularly.

Similar to the Chinese wish for prosperity, luck and blessings, the Iban hope for prosperity can be said to be similar to the Iban complex of attitudes which Sutlive classifies as luck, "the imponderabilia of life, both good and ill, which are fully felt but little understood." (Sutlive, 112). This communal event symbolizes the "*communitas*" of Engkilili, drawing people from Betong, Lubok Antu and Sri Aman, bringing together Chinese and non-Chinese as a single ritual community, celebrating the passing of an old year and asking for blessings for the new year. Sutlive noted that "the Iban [are] the most responsive of the indigenous people to the presence of other people and their values " (Sutlive, [1988], 1978, 113). Like Chinese religion which is syncretic, the Iban, whether believers in traditional Iban *adat* or converts to Christianity, accept the religious values of the Chinese deity celebration.

This event allows the Hakka and Teochew to assert a public Chinese identity. The Hakka and Teochew live on the rural periphery of Sarawak with the majority of individuals keeping their livelihoods as smallholding farmers and small traders. In the big local event they celebrate once a year, the Chinese transform themselves liminally from a peripheral status to a central position where they enjoy public cultural recognition of who they are in

Engkilili, which does not threaten the non-Chinese but is in fact well received by them. The event is not seen as a threat by the state either. For a period of time during the communist insurgency from the mid-1960s until 1990, the celebrations were banned by the government. This public ritual and spectacle, despite the small numbers of Hakka and Teochew, looks likely to continue in the future.

It might be asked, during the rest of the year, what happens when there is no collective event or celebration to draw people together. I have argued in the earlier part of this paper that conducive social relations between the Chinese and Iban, which resulted in inter-marriages and acculturation, bring people together.

Conclusion

The Hakka and their descendents who have settled in Engkilili since the 1850s have remained resilient in maintaining their Hakka identity in this rural district of Sarawak. The Hakka have a strong primordial sense of self identity and have retained their Chinese cultural characteristics in speaking the Hakka dialect and Mandarin, and following Chinese religious practices. The Hakka pay attention to Hakka dialect transmission to the young and use the dialect actively, and to the learning of Mandarin.

Chinese religious practices are kept, and convey a sense of identity and belonging to Engkilili. A major community celebration for the Hakka and other Chinese, the 10th day of the lunar new year celebrations for deity blessings, illustrates this sense of identification, an adherence to Chinese culture, and to the place Engkilili. The Hakka adapt to the wider environment around them as a minority living together with their numerically stronger Iban neighbours, showing a willingness to learn and speak Iban and inter-marry with Iban spouses. While adapting to the Iban, the Hakka have not lost their facility with the Hakka dialect and the mastery of Mandarin. This can be compared with the situation in Melaka where the Chinese Peranakan or Baba of Hokkien origin, who have acculturated to local circumstances, speak Baba Malay, and not Hokkien and Mandarin (Tan 2004). It can be said then that the Hakka in Engkilili represent an example of Chinese settlement and adaptation in Malaysia where the Hakka dialect is retained, and other languages, Mandarin and Iban are acquired.

Frequently referred to by other Chinese as *kejia* (guests) the Hakka are indeed no longer guests but have forged an adaptive and acculturated identity to Engkilili. The framework of analysis in this study has included Iban attitudes and interactions with the Hakka. The Iban acceptance of the Hakka as neighbours, the inter-marriages with the Hakka, and taking a keen interest in Chinese cultural practices such as the 10th day of the lunar new year celebrations for deity blessings, blur the ethnic boundaries between the Iban and Hakka. In other words, there are no rigid ethnic boundaries between the Iban and Hakka.

As a case study, this research has highlighted the historical and cultural experiences of a Chinese Hakka dialect group in Sarawak. More parallel studies are needed to show how the Chinese, and in particular the Hakka, live in a multi-ethnic and multi-linguistic environment to draw forth comparisons on Chinese cultural identity in Southeast Asia and beyond.

References

Beccari, Odoardo, 1986 [1904], *Wanderings in the Great Forests of Borneo*. Singapore: Oxford University Press.

Braudel, Fernand, "History and the Social Sciences: the longue duree", in Sarah Matthews trans., *On History*, pp. 26-27, 35-38, 47-48. Weidenfeld and Nicolson, 1980; in John Tosh ed., *Historians on History*, pp. 245-253. Essex: Pearson Education Limited, 2000.

Brooke, Charles, 1886 [1990], *Ten Years in Sarawak*. Singapore: Oxford University Press.

Carstens, Sharon A., 2005, *Histories, Cultures, Identities: Studies in Malaysian Chinese Worlds*. Singapore: National University of Singapore Press.

Constable, Nicole, ed., 1996, *Guest People, Hakka Identity in China and Abroad*. Seattle: University of Washington Press.

Chew, Daniel, 2004 [1990], *Chinese Pioneers on the Sarawak Frontier, 1841-1941*. Kuala Lumpur: Oxford University Press.

Choo, F. C., 2009, *Children of the Monkey God, The Story of a Chinese Hakka Family in Sarawak, Borneo, 1850-1965*. Tempe, Arizona: Third Millenium Publishing.

Department of Statistics, Malaysia, 2010, *Preliminary Count Report*. Kuala Lumpur: Department of Statistics.

District Profile Lubok Antu, 2010.

Huang, Ji Qin, 1999, "A History of the Engkilili Hakka Association", in *A Collection of Historical Writings concerning the Ethnic Chinese People in Sri Aman Division*, pp. 135-137. Sibu: Sarawak Chinese Cultural Association [in Chinese].

Heidhues, Mary Somers, 2003, *Golddiggers, Farmers and Traders in the "Chinese Districts" of West Kalimantan, Indonesia*. Ithaca, New York: Cornell Southeast Asia Program.

Jensen, Erik, 1974, *The Iban and their Religion*. London: Oxford.

Goh Kaw Sze and Tay Chek Pin, 2006, *Historical Essays on the Marup Fifteen Shares Kongsi*. Sibu: Sarawak Chinese Cultural Association [in Chinese].

Kee, Howe Yong, 2006, "Silence in history and the nation-state", in *American Ethnologist*, August 2006, Vol. 33, No. 3, pp. 462-473.

Kuhn, Philip A., 2008, *Chinese Among Others, Emigration in Modern Times*. Singapore: National University of Singapore Press.

Leach, Edmund, 1950, *Social Science Research in Sarawak: A Report on the Possibilities of a Social Economic Survey of Sarawak Presented to the Colonial Social Science Research Council*. London: Colonial Social Science Research Council.

Leach, Edmund, 1990, *Political Systems of Highland Borneo, A Study of Kachin Social Structure*. London: The Athlone Press.

Lembat, Gerunsin, 1994, "The Dynamics of Customary Law and Indigenous Identity: The Case of the Dayak of Sarawak", in *Sarawak Gazette*, April 1994, pp. 4-8.

Liu, Pak Khui, 1991, *The Gold Route of the Early Sarawak Chinese*. Kuching [in Chinese].

Pringle, Robert, 2010 [1970], *Rajahs and Rebels, The Ibans of Sarawak under Brooke Rule, 1841-1941*. Kota Samarahan: Universiti Malaysia Sarawak.

Rousseau, Jerome, 1990, *Central Borneo, Ethnic Identity and Social Life in a Stratified Society*. Oxford: Clarendon Press.

Sandin, Benedict, 1994, "Sources of Iban Traditional History", in Clifford Sather ed., *The Sarawak Museum Journal*, Special Monograph No. 7, December 1994, pp. 1-333.

Sarawak Gazette, 1870 –

Sri Aman Chung Hua Primary Schools' Academic Committee, 1998, *An Introduction to the Chung Hua Schools in Sri Aman, Sarawak*. Kuching [in Chinese].

Shi Bai Mu, "Bits and Pieces on the History of Engkilili Town", in *A Collection of Historical Writings Concerning the Ethnic Chinese People In Sri Aman Division*, pp. 123-131. Sibu: Sarawak Chinese Cultural Association [in Chinese].

Skinner, G. William, 1957, *Chinese Society in Thailand: An Analytical History*. Ithaca, New York: Cornell University Press.

Sutlive, Vinson, 1978, *The Iban of Sarawak, Chronicle of a Vanishing World*. Prospect Heights, Illinois: Waveland Press.

Tan, Chee Beng, 1988, *The Baba of Melaka, Culture and Identity of a Chinese Peranakan Community in Malaysia*. Petaling Jaya: Pelanduk.

Tan, Chee Beng, ed., 1990, "Editor's Introduction", in *Contributions to Southeast Asian Ethnography, The Preservation and Adaptation of Chinese Religious Expression in Southeast Asia*, pp. 3-4. Columbus, Ohio: Anthony R. Walker.

Tan, Chee Beng, 2004, *Chinese Overseas, Comparative Cultural Issues*. Hong Kong: Hong Kong University Press.

Tien Ju-Kang, 1953, *The Chinese of Sarawak: As Study of Social Structure*, Monographs in Social Anthropology No. 12. London: London School of Economics.

Turner, Victor, 1969, *The Ritual Process, Structure and Anti-Structure*. New York: Aldine de Gruyter.

Yuan, Bingling, 2000, *Chinese Democracies: A Study of the Chinese Kongsis of West Borneo, 1776-1884*. Leiden: Research School of Asian, African, and Amerindian Studies, CNWS, Universiteit Leiden.

Ward, A. B., 1996, *Rajah's Servant*, Cornell University Southeast Asia Program Data Program No. 61. Ithaca, New York: Cornell University Press.

Zhuo, Ruo Guo, 1999, "A Short History of the Engkilili Teochew Association", in *A Collection of Historical Writings Concerning the Ethnic Chinese People in Sri Aman Division*, pp. 135-137. Sibu: Sarawak Chinese Cultural Association [in Chinese].

The Hakka in Sabah before World War Two: Their Adaptation to New Environment, Challenges and the Forging of New Identity

二戰前沙巴客家所面對的環境適應，挑戰和新認同

Danny Wong Tze Ken[†]

Introduction

The Hakka are the largest of the five main Chinese dialect groups living in Sabah. Making up around 58%[1] of the Chinese, the Hakka first became the main dialect group in the state only in 1921. In spite of being numerically superior, the Hakka remained very much in the background compared to the other dialect groups and were not prominent in business, trade, or even as a social group. Instead, the group remained rural-based, land-based, and was hardly organized. This phenomenon persisted until the 1940s, and only began to change in the 1950s. This paper will look into the evolution and transformation of this dialect group in Sabah from one that remained in the background into a major dialect group, not only in terms of numbers but also economic and organizational strength. This paper argues that the examination of the development of a sub-ethnic group such as the Hakka dialect group is crucial for the understanding of ethnic relations in a multi-ethnic and multicultural country like Malaysia. The role of ethnic sub-groups in driving the direction of the ethnic inclinations has not received sufficient attention

---

† 黃子堅，馬來亞大學歷史系。

1 *Population and Housing Census of Malaysia 2000: Sabah*, Kuala Lumpur: Department of Statistics Malaysia, 2000.

thus far. This paper proposes that the study of sub-ethnic groups such as the Hakka may be able to provide glimpses into the resilience and dynamics of the larger ethnic group, hence providing information which may help in the promotion of a deeper understanding of an ethnic group within a multi-ethnic setting such as in the case of Malaysia. In the case of the Chinese in Malaysia, the study of sub-ethnic groups such as the Hakka will ensure that the existence of dialect groups will not be neglected.

This paper will also address the question of the development of Hakka identity in Sabah.[2] This is a very challenging question that has been taken for granted by both the Hakka and those who came to interact with them. Their recent domination in both numbers and substance has somehow blurred the vision of how Hakka identity was forged in Sabah. There seems to be little understanding that the present-day Hakka identity in Sabah has undergone many challenges and changes, and evolved in different forms over the years.

The attempt to examine the question of Hakka identity will also draw the discussion into the many challenges faced by the Hakka in Sabah which helped in the process of forming their identity. For this the discussion will be divided into four sections, each a situation or challenge faced by the Hakka in Sabah as they evolved into what they are today. The first is the question of migration; this is followed by an investigation into the pioneering spirit of the Hakka; the third is an examination of their role in trade and agriculture; and finally, the question of leadership among the Hakka in Sabah.

---

2 To date several works on the Chinese of Sabah have been published; they include Victor Purcell, *The Chinese in South-east Asia*, London: Oxford University Press (reprint), 1980; Han Sin Fong, *The Chinese in Sabah, East Malaysia*, Taipei: The Oriental Cultural Service, 1976; Danny Wong Tze Ken, *The Transformation of an Immigrant Society: A Study of the Chinese of Sabah*, London: Asean Academic Press, 1998 & "The Chinese in Sabah: an Overview", in Lee Kam Hing & Tan Chee Beng (eds.), *The Chinese in Malaysia*, Kuala Lumpur: Oxford University Press, 2000, pp. 382-406.

Hakka Migration to Sabah

Hakka mass migration to Sabah began about 1882 with the establishment of the North Borneo Company 北婆羅州公司 administration (commonly known as the Chartered Company又名查打公司) as it had been granted a royal charter by the British Parliament in 1881. Prior to that, some smaller groups of Hakka may have arrived, but went to the adjacent island of Labuan where a settlement had already existed since 1846;[3] some may have worked in the coal mines on the northern tip of the island. The Hakka who came to Labuan 納閩 probably came via the Straits Settlements 海峽殖民地, as the island was administered as part of that territory. Others may have come from China as the period between 1860 and the establishment of Chartered Company administration in 1881 corresponded with the mass exodus of Hakka from China, especially in the aftermath of the Taiping Rebellion 太平天國 (1850-1864). In 1882 the Chartered Company engaged Sir Walter Medhurst, a former British Consul 英國領事 at Shanghai, as the Commissioner of Immigration 移民總監 for North Borneo; his task was to bring suitable Chinese migrants into the state. The Medhurst scheme lasted from 1882 to 1885. Initially, Medhurst recruited his immigrants from Hong Kong, only to find that they were not really suitable as the state needed settlers who were able to work on the land. One bright spot that emerged from this not-so-successful venture was the introduction of the Hakka to North Borneo.

The Hakka who came to Sabah (North Borneo) were mainly from Guangdong province – from the Jiayingzhou 嘉應州 (Meizhou 梅州) and

---

3 For a study on the Chinese in Labuan, see Nicholas Tarling, "The Entrepot at Labuan and the Chinese", *Sabah Society Journal*, Vol. V, No. 2, 1970, pp. 101-116.

Huizhou 惠州 prefectures，the two main Hakka-dominated areas in the province，covering counties such as Mei Xian 梅縣, Zi Jing 紫金, Hui Yang 惠陽, Long Chuan 龍川, Bao An 寶安, Wu Hua 五華, and He Yuan 河源. Medhurst's call for migrants came at a time when many Hakka were looking for opportunities to emigrate abroad. There were many reasons for this; pull and push factors were clearly at play. Many of the Hakka lived in mountainous and hilly areas where life was harsh; others found the agriculture-based economy less rewarding. Better opportunities and the prospect of improving their livelihood in a foreign land, and stories of successful migrants or returnees also encouraged them to decide to go abroad. Another push factor was the effect of the aftermath of the fall of the Taiping Heavenly Kingdom 太平天國 (1850-1864), the peasant rebellion that originated from Guangxi and Guangdong provinces, and whose founder Hong Xiuquan 洪秀全 and his early supporters were Hakka. Hong was a native of Huaxian 花縣. The end of the Taiping rebellion saw many Hakka being implicated and hunted down by the Qing authority 清廷, so they were compelled to emigrate abroad.

In Sabah, Medhurst's scheme provided the Hakka with an opportunity to migrate to a new and unexplored land. The offer of free land in Sabah, something unimaginable in China, became the main draw. At least two groups of Hakka migrated under the Medhurst scheme. The first – the group initially deemed unsuitable by the Chartered Company as they were not settlers – comprised businessmen and migrants from the urban areas of Huizhou. There are no concrete data on the size of the group, but it is clear that many of these Hakkas settled in Sandakan 山打根, and later in the area known as Kebun Cina (Chinese orchards), just outside Sandakan town proper. According to an official report, "At the Karbom Cheena [sic.] river village, where a good many of the Company migrants are, there is a busy scene, men, women and children all working with that industry peculiar to the Chinese race. Rows of pineapples, sugar-cane, and bananas are planted, kitchen garden plots are all over the place ..."[4] They eventually founded the Tam Kung 譚公廟 temple and Chi Hwa 啓華 school in that area. This group of Hakka formed the nucleus of the Hakka community in Sandakan and, later, the east coast.

The second group of Hakka who came under the Medhurst scheme were Christians who were brought to Sabah as a result of negotiations between the Chartered Company and the Basel Missionary Society 巴色差會. The society, which had been working among the Hakka, was looking for opportunities to resettle the Hakka, particularly those who were Christians, abroad. This was part of the efforts to help those who had been implicated in the Taiping rebellion to escape as well as to offer opportunities to start life in a different land for those who hoped to leave the harsh living conditions in China for a better life elsewhere. The second group came in batches, beginning in 1882 when some families were settled in Kudat 古達, at the northern tip of the state. These new migrants were given land and were expected to settle in the state. A marked difference between the first and second groups was that the second group consisted of families, which was not necessarily the case for the first group. The plans to settle the Hakka were reported and each batch began to prosper.

Subsequent Hakka migration to the state came mainly via certain percentage arrangements as well as through individual efforts. Through all these emigration schemes the Hakka population began to increase so rapidly that by the time of the 1921 census the Hakka population was reported to have overtaken all the other dialect groups combined. This was a significant

---

4 *British North Borneo Herald* 《北婆羅州訊報》, May 1883.

development, making the Hakka the largest dialect group in Sabah since that date. Further immigration schemes of the Chartered Company helped to ensure that more Hakka came to Sabah. The most effective scheme was the Free Passage Scheme 免費移民計畫 introduced by the Company in 1921 to induce those settlers already in Sabah to bring their relations, at government expense. Upon arrival, these new immigrants either joined their relations or applied for land of their own. The implementation of this scheme benefited many, particularly those associated with the Basel Missionary Society as many of the existing settlers belonged to this group of Hakka. Between 1921 and 1941 the Free Passage Scheme brought in close to 10,000 settlers, of whom almost 100% were Hakka.[5]

Table 1: Chinese Population of Sabah in Censuses of 1911-1951

Chinese/Year	1911*	1921	1931	1951
Hakka	-NA-	18,153	27,424	44,505
Cantonese	-NA-	12,268	12,831	11,833
Hokkien	-NA-	4,022	4,634	7,336
Teochiew	-NA-	2,480	2,511	3,948
Hailam	-NA-	1,294	1,589	3,571
Other Chinese	-NA-	1,039	1,067	3,181
Total	27,801	39,256	50,056	74,374

*Breakdown figures of the various dialect groups were not available.
Source: L.W. Jones, *North Borneo: A Report on the Census of Population held on 4th July 1951*, London: University of London, 1953, p. 112.

Yet, despite being the largest dialect group, the Hakka remained very much in the background. It was not until the 1950s that the dialect group began to demonstrate leadership in almost all spheres of life and presence.

---

5 *North Borneo Annual and Administrative Reports* 《北婆羅州行政報告》, 1921-1940.

Yet, at the time when the Hakka established their numerical superiority, the community remained backward and were hardly in the mainstream. The following sections will look at the various conditions and aspects of the Hakka presence in Sabah in the hope of providing some explanation about their conditions even as the study continues to plot the development of this dialect group in Sabah.

Challenges of Being Pioneers 先驅者的挑戰

When the Hakka first arrived in North Borneo, they were settled mainly in the rural areas. Even though land was cleared for them to build their dwellings, they still had to clear the rest of the land for their agricultural activities. This was a daunting prospect. The Hakka, though very accustomed to hard work and known to be resolute in overcoming difficulties, were ill-prepared for the challenges of settling down in North Borneo. As rural dwellers, the challenge of the natural setting was daunting and hardly for those who were weak in resolve. Their lives in rural China did little to prepare them to face the dense, massive primary jungle that they had to clear. They had to first overcome the challenges of heat, to which they were unaccustomed. They also had to face the menace of tropical diseases, especially malaria and typhoid. The answer to these was not Western medicine but traditional Chinese medicine, administered from the few medicine halls that had been established in Sandakan, including Leong Lee Tong, Fui Chun Tong, Chin Pen Tong and Chew Sin Tong.[6] Casualty and mortality rates were high, though much lower than among the other ethnic groups, including the

---

6 Wolfgang Franke & Chen Tieh Fan (comp.), *Chinese Epigraphic Materials in Malaysia, Vol. III*, Kuala Lumpur: University of Malaya Press, pp. 1237-1245.

Javanese 爪哇人 who were imported to work on the estates, or Chinese recruited for the same purpose.

The perils of living in Borneo at that time were not confined to disease. Not a few Chinese were taken by crocodiles or swept by a sudden rise in river level while bathing or crossing rivers. Many also became victims of floods.

In the early days the Chinese, the Hakka included, were not exactly welcomed by the indigenous people. There were many incidents of Chinese attacked by indigenous people 土族, sometimes by organized groups. Most attacks came from sporadic groups of natives who were not happy with the presence of the Chinese. Most attacks took place at more isolated places, for instance, shops at isolated river curves, many miles away from the main human settlements. At the height of the Mat Salleh Uprising 末沙里造反 against the Chartered Company from 1894 to 1900, on no fewer than five occasions Chinese traders operating shops upriver or on isolated islands were murdered by the marauding followers of Mat Salleh.[7] However, the event that certainly had a direct influence on the Hakka was the massacre of Hakka Christians in Kudat by the followers of Mat Salleh in February 1900. The attack, which took place in the evening, ended with the rebels causing wanton damage to the Chinese houses and cattle in the Happy Valley 快樂谷. They moved hastily, firing thatch buildings as they ran, killing no fewer than ten of the vegetable gardeners, and did other damage which was estimated at about 2000 dollars.[8] This was a considerable sum at that time, but the most

---

7 The Mat Salleh rebellion against the Chartered Company started as Mohammad Salleh, a minor chieftain on Sugut Island, began to challenge the authority of the Company in 1894. The rebellion took the form of armed attacks on government installations and settlements, including the burning down of the Government Station on Gaya Island 加雅島 in 1897. The rebellion only ended in 1900 when the Company managed to destroy Mat Salleh's forces at Tambunan, including killing Mat Salleh. However, for several years after the end of the rebellion the remnants of Mat Salleh's men continued to conduct raids on government settlements 政府管轄地. For a study on the rebellion, see Ian Black, *A Gambling Style of Government*, Singapore: Oxford University Press, 1983.

8 *British North Borneo Herald*, 16 May 1900.

damaging effect of the attack was the loss of lives. The Hakka Christians called this event "San Fan Zhuo Luon" (山藩作亂 The Disturbance of the Barbarians) and it was strongly imprinted in the minds of the Hakka from Kudat; some of the victims' descendants still talk about it.[9] It was the most tragic event of family history that was well remembered by the later generations.

Even though these challenges and problems of pioneering did not have any direct bearing on the forging of Hakka identity, they nevertheless helped to toughen the Hakka in the face of adversity. This is a very important attribute normally associated with the Hakka which became a trademark of the Hakka in Sabah, who usually came to the forefront of the Chinese community when it was under threat. A very good example of this was during the Japanese occupation from 1942 to 1945, when the Hakka, especially those Hakka Christians living along Tuaran Road 斗亞蘭路, were the main supporters and sympathizers of the anti-Japanese Kinabalu Guerrillas 抗日神山游擊隊. The guerrillas launched an uprising against the Japanese garrison army 日本駐軍 in Jesselton 亞庇 (present-day Kota Kinabalu) on 9 October 1943. The uprising killed about 50 Japanese and the town was briefly in the hands of the guerrillas for a night. However, Japanese retribution was swift and harsh, resulting in massive arrests and executions. As a result, at least 80 families of the Hakka Christians who lived along Tuaran Road lost their sole breadwinner due to their involvement in the uprising.[10]

---

9 Personal communication with Reverend Pung Shong Khoon 馮尚宣牧師, a clergyman of the Basel Church whose grandfather was one of the victims; Also personal communication with Lee Chip Min of Basel Church, Likas congregation. The Lee family also lost their great grandfather to the attack.

10 See Danny Wong Tze Ken, "Kinabalu Guerrillas: The Inanam-Menggatal-Telipok Basel Church Connections", in Chong Tet Loi (ed.), *The Hakka Experiment in Sabah*, Kota Kinabalu: Sabah Theological Seminary, 2007, pp. 166-188; Danny Wong Tze Ken, "The Petagas War Memorial and the Creation of a Heroic Past in Sabah", *Journal of the Malaysian Branch of the Royal Asiatic Society*, Vol. 80, Part 2, No. 293, December 2007, pp. 19-32; Maxwell Hall, *Kinabalu Guerrillas*, Kuching: Borneo Literature Bureau, 1962.

The massive involvement of the Hakka in the Kinabalu Guerrillas 神山游擊隊, and the sacrifices they made as a result of Japanese military retribution, contributed to the strengthening of the community's sense of belonging 歸屬感 to their newly adopted homeland – in many ways this enhanced their identity not just as Chinese (perhaps Hakka), but also helped to forge an identity of being a Chinese in North Borneo (later, Sabah).

Hakka in Agriculture and Trade 客家與農商業

The economic well-being 經濟情況 of the Hakka migrants depended very much on the vocations of the early arrivals. Many of the Hakka came as labourers. Unlike the Chinese migrants in the Malay Peninsula who were mainly engaged in mining activities, those who came to North Borneo were mainly employed in the estates. Unfortunately, the stories of this group of people are hardly documented. There are very little data on those who came on their own as free labourers. Many could have been employed to work on the numerous estates 園丘 which sprang up in the state from the day the Chartered Company started to administer the country. Given the high mortality rate of the estate workers during the early days of Chartered Company rule, many simply perished. Others joined the labour lines of the company which constructed the railway between Weston 威士敦 and Jesselton 亞庇, as well as to Melalap 文那納. By the time the railway was in operation at the turn of the century (1900-1906), many of the surplus workers moved on to other jobs, but most remained in North Borneo. There is very little information on the Hakka immigrants, but it is likely that there was a sizeable number of them. One of relics of their existence was a Tai Pak Kung (Da Bo Gong 大伯公廟) temple at Petagas 必打加士, a small settlement outside Jesselton, along the railway, which was originally started in

1914. Even though the Tai Pak Kung temple was not unique to the Hakka, in Sabah it was strongly tied to the community. Others worked in the coal mines of Labuan, at least until 1911 when the mines ceased operation. The existence of Hakka among the coal miners is not proven by statistical data, but deduced from the fact that the first Hakka 黃天玉牧師 clergyman despatched by the Basel Missionary Society was Reverend Wong Tien Nyuk 黃天玉牧師, who initially worked among a group of Chinese coal miners in Labuan before being sent to Kudat.[11] One can only conclude that he was working among the Hakka miners.

The majority of the Hakka, however, were tied to the land as agriculturalists. Those who came via the arrangement between the Basel Missionary Society and the Chartered Company were placed in the many new settlements in the vicinity of Kudat, including Lauson 老山, Sikuati 西加地, Pinangsoo 檳榔樹, Tamalang 大壩 and Buk Buk 百百. On the west coast, along the Tuaran Road are settlements such as Inanam 下南南, Menggatal 孟家達, Telipok 德里卜, Tamparuli 擔波羅里 and Tuaran. Also on the west coast, along the railway line, are Papar, Membakut 王麻骨 and Beaufort 保佛; and in the interior 內陸, Tenom 丹南, Sapong 沙邦 and Melalap. In the latter, many of the Hakka were not Christians and were probably surplus from the railway labourers.

When the Hakka Christians migrated to North Borneo under one of the immigration-settlement schemes, one of the terms was that the new settlers would be given land. This was a great opportunity to own land, something which was becoming increasingly difficult in China at that time unless inherited. Many received up to 10 acres of land. This was a large piece of land for someone who previously had to work in communal or clan-owned lands.

---

11 *BCCM Centenary Magazine*, p. 20.

Thus such schemes gave the immigrants access to new wealth and new opportunities. Yet at the same time, the nature of the land granted also 'assigned' a person to living in a rural setting and strongly reliant on the land. While it seemed that these Hakka had clearly benefited from this arrangement – which resulted in many eventually becoming smallholders – it was not an occupation that would ensure immediate high returns. It would take the community another two to three generations of hard living in the rural areas before they were able to emerge from this rural and agricultural setting.

In spite of the community undergoing many changes throughout the first forty years of their presence in North Borneo from 1882 to 1920, most of the Hakka were still strongly engaged in agriculture-related activities as their primary occupation. This is evident from the marriage certificates of those who were married in the Basel churches between 1921 and 1931; most gave their profession as either gardener or agriculturist. Other occupations listed included clerk, merchant, tailor, technician, teacher, but their numbers were few. Nevertheless, some who gave their profession as gardener were also trained in other fields, as in the case of Tsen En Lok 曾恩祿, whose occupation, like many others, was listed as a gardener in Inanam at the time of his wedding. Tsen was a theologically trained Hakka who was also a qualified Chinese physician 中醫 who become the first catechist 傳道 and school master in the newly established Basel Church in Menggatal 孟家達, a new township two miles from Inanam, in 1930.[12] Tsen's case may suggest that some Hakka were willing to take up land as settlers despite having trained in other fields. In many ways it also shows the close ties between the Hakka and land ownership.

In spite of their rural and agricultural settings, not all Hakka were

---

12 See *BCCM Centenary Magazine*, p. 76.

disadvantaged, particularly those associated with Christian churches. Due to such links, especially the Basel, Anglican and Catholic churches, many Hakka Christians were able to gain access to Western education, which gave the community a head start in obtaining white-collar jobs; most of the early support staff in the administration were Hakka who had been able to obtain English education in the schools established by the missionary societies or churches. For instance, Li Chi On 李賜安, son of Hakka pioneer Lee Shiong Kong 李祥光, was first employed as a clerk in the civil administration before venturing into business.[13] Li had been educated in the mission's school in Hong Kong before coming to Sabah. But it was the later group of scholars from the Basel Church school system of Lok Yuk 樂育 and Sung Siew 雙修 and the Anglican school system which produced locally trained young people well-versed in English. Li Tet Phui 李德培, who rose to be a chief clerk in the Lands Office before the war, was a product of the mission-school English education.[14] Another example was Ho Yin Fook 何英福, who attended the Basel Church school in Inanam; he was able to join the government service in 1918 and rose to the rank of chief clerk shortly after the war.[15]

It was the same English education system that helped to produce Hakka Christian scholars who won state scholarships for tertiary education abroad. This gave the Hakka, particularly the Hakka Christians, a head start in obtaining professional training, hence providing them with opportunities for social mobility, rising out of their agricultural background. During the

---

13 *British North Borneo Herald*, 1 May 1900.

14 Li Tet Phui was chief clerk of the Lands Office in Jesselton. He later joined the Anglican Church of All Saints' Cathedral and was the church organist. He also served as a Lieutenant in the North Borneo Volunteer Force, one of the two Chinese appointed to the rank. Li was implicated in the Jesselton Uprising against the Japanese and was arrested and executed by the Japanese in January 1944. See Danny Wong Tze Ken, "Li Tet Phui", in Lee Kam Hing and Chow Mun Seong (comp.), *Biographical Dictionary of the Chinese in Malaysia*, Petaling Jaya: Pelanduk Publications, 1997, pp. 100-101.

15 Unpublished personal papers of Ho Yin Fook, Basel Church Menggatal.

Colonial Office administration era from 1946 to 1963 the leaders of the Chinese community were dominated by Hakka Christians who had received English education in the mission schools. Chung Chao Lung 鍾兆龍, Philip Lee Thau Sang 李道生, Ngui Ah Kui 魏亞貴 and Pang Tet Tshung 彭德聰[16] were all Hakka Christians who provided leadership to the Chinese community during the colonial era and the early years of independence. This was an unexpected achievement least expected by anyone who had any dealings with the Hakka at the turn of the twentieth century.

The Hakka were not prominent in business circles, at least for most of the first four decades of Chartered Company rule in North Borneo. Having confined themselves to working the land or earning wages in the estates, the Hakka were economically disadvantaged and seldom able to accumulate capital to venture into other fields, especially business and entrepreneurship. However, in the midst of this supposedly 'sea of farmers' were some Hakka individuals who took up the challenge to venture into business and commercially inclined industries. They were the pioneers who later served as examples for other Hakka to venture into business.

Due to the nature of their migration, most of the Hakka were agriculture-based. Thus it is not surprising that the pioneer Hakka businessmen and entrepreneurs in North Borneo first ventured into enterprises related to agricultural produce and land-based activities. In relation to this, two pioneering entrepreneurs are examined here: Lee Shiong Kong of Kudat and Liau Nyuk Kui 廖玉魁 of Sandakan. Lee Shiong Kong was born in Qing Yuan 清遠 county, Guangdong. His father was Li Chin Gao 李正高, one of the earliest theologically-trained Chinese Christian

---

16 For a discussion on the quality of these Hakka leaders see Edwin Lee, *The Towkays of Sabah: Chinese Leadership and Indigenous Challenge in the last Phase of British Rule*, Singapore: Singapore University Press, 1976, pp. 37-50.

missionaries of the Basel Mission working in Guangdong province. Like his father, Lee Shiong Kong also received theological training, and graduated from the Lilong Theological Seminary 李朗神學院. He first worked as a teacher in schools started by the Berlin Mission 巴臨差會, which had sponsored his studies. He then transferred his service to the Basel Mission and served in various Hakka counties in northeast Guangdong before moving to Hong Kong where he also taught in schools.

In 1888, in response to the British North Borneo (Chartered) Company's call for Chinese settlers, Lee Shiong Kong decided to move to North Borneo. He was the leader of a group of 300 Hakka Christians who came to Kudat that year. Many Hakka Christians were keen to migrate overseas in those years as they were the target of persecution by the Manchu government in China which linked them to the Taiping Rebellion 太平天國 (1850-1864). Lee Shiong Kong's father Li Chin Gao was a classmate of Hong Xiuquan 洪秀全, the leader of the Taiping Rebellion. The Hakka were also attracted by the Chartered Company's offer of land, something which was difficult to obtain in China.

Upon arriving in Kudat, Lee Shiong Kong set himself two goals: to be economically viable and to organize church and education for the Hakka Christians. One of his earliest tasks was to get the earlier batch of Hakka Christian immigrants who had arrived in 1882 to attend church, and organized classes for their children. It was Lee Shiong Kong and his colleague Wong Shuk Min 黃旭民 who requested the Basel Missionary Society to send a Chinese clergyman to pastor the Hakka Christians in Kudat.

In the sphere of business, Lee Shiong Kong first invested in land. He purchased 300 acres of land from the Chartered Company and planted coconut trees. Later, he also planted rubber. These two crops profited Lee Shiong Kong, making him one of the wealthier persons in Kudat. He is reputed to have devised methods for processing coconuts, including the best way to produce copra (dried coconut), which probably contributed to the success of his business.[17]

The extraction of coconut oil and the processing of copra resulted in the emergence of cottage industries making soap and candles, coconut oil and other coconut-related products. Large-scale coconut plantations were possible as many of the more successful settlers later acquired more land in larger blocks of 200 acres from the government in places such as Sikuati 西加地, Pitas 必打斯 and Langkon 朗坤. Lee Shiong Kong was also the co-proprietor of a grocery business called Chi Nam 志南, a joint venture with Chin Sam Loong 陳三龍, another pioneering Hakka businessman from Kudat. The Lee family later bought out Chin's share in the business and the latter moved to Jesselton where he engaged in a lucrative rubber-planting business.

Lee Shiong Kong passed away in 1921 at the age of 76. Among his offspring were Li Chi On 李賜安 and Li Su Lin 李賜寧, both prominent citizens of their respective communities in Jesselton and Kudat. While the business in Kudat was carried on by Li Su Lin, Li Chi On ventured to Jesselton (Kota Kinabalu) and started a commercial firm called Kong Hiap Hin & Co. 廣協興that became one of the biggest in North Borneo.

Over in Sandakan, the pioneering Hakka entrepreneurs were Ou Shizhu 歐世珠 and Liau Nyuk Kui 廖玉魁. Liau, who was of Bao On (Baoan 寶安) origin, started to develop the area that is known today as Kebun Cina.[18] In 1888 Liau bought about 17 acres of land in Kebun Cina with his savings and emerged at that time as probably the richest Hakka in town, at least in terms of landholding. On that plot of land Liau started planting coconut and, later,

17 *BCCM Centenary Magazine*, p. 18.
18 *British North Borneo Herald*, 1 May 1888.

rubber. He also ventured into planting chrysanthemums. Among the Chinese in Sandakan, the name Kebun Cina did not stick; the place is commonly known to the community as Ngiu Liao (牛寮 cow sheds). This was the contribution of Liau, who added animal husbandry by breeding cows, buffaloes and ponies. It was because the cows and buffaloes made such an impact that Kebun Cina obtained a new name. Liau did not breed cattle merely for meat; he also branched into hide processing or tanning which saw his products being exported to Hong Kong and Europe.

Incidentally, Kebun Cina borders the Beatrice Plantation that was started by William Pryer, the founder of Sandakan. In 1892 Pryer and a group of European officers started pony racing 賽馬 on the Beatrice Estate. This allowed Liau Nyuk Kui to participate in these races. Apart from his business activities, Liau was also involved in socio-religious activities; among his chief contributions were the founding of Chi Hwa School and the Hakka temple of Tam Kung Chu Miao, both situated in Kebun Cina.

Buoyed by Liau Nyuk Kui's success, a group of 14 well-to-do Hakka Christians from Hong Kong arrived in Sandakan in 1891. Their arrival was different from that of earlier Hakka who had mainly been either contract labourers or settlers. Immediately after their arrival they purchased land in the Kebun Cina area, and started engaging others to work on their land.[19]

It is evident that the Hakka's initial involvement in business was still strongly tied to the land. This situation persisted well into the first decade of the twentieth century. While many Hakka businessmen continued this relationship with agricultural produce, the second generation of Hakka businessmen began to venture beyond agricultural activities, and became fully committed in business, including trading and services. However, this

---

19 *British North Borneo Herald*, 1 April 1891.

transformation only became more prominent after World War II.

Organization and Leadership 組織與領袖

Even though the Hakka were conscious of their identity as distinct from other Chinese, this consciousness was not reflected in the dialect group's organizations. When the Hakka community in Sandakan set up the first Hakka organization in 1886, it was not called a Hakka association, but was called Ngo Cheng Hui Guan (Er Cheng Hui Guan 鵝城會館) representing those who originated from Hui Zhou in Guangdong. Later, to reflect the multi-dialect group nature of the Hakka people in North Borneo, the association changed its name to Yan Ho Hui Gun (Ngin Foh Fui Kon 人和 會館 in Hakka).[20] The word Hakka was not used. The leaders of the association, including Lam Man Ching 林文澄 and Liau Nyuk Kui, were businessmen, and they took the initiative to establish the Tam Kung temple to honour the Hakka folk deity of Tam Kung 譚公. Next to the temple was the Chi Hwa School, also started by the same leaders.

It is interesting to look at the leaders as they were clearly very diverse in outlook. For instance, Lam Man Ching,[21] who was acknowledged as one of the main leaders of Ngin Foh Fui Kon and a director of the Tam Kung temple, was a member of the Basel Church, the predominantly Hakka church. Thus, Lam Man Ching was not only an acknowledged leader of the Basel Church, but he was also a willing provider of such leadership. Lam was later appointed a Kapitan China 華人甲必丹 of Sandakan in 1915,

---

20 *Sandakan Hakka Association Centenary Anniversary, 1886-1986*, Sandakan: Sandakan Hakka Association, 1986, p. 43. [In Chinese]

21 For a short biographical note on Lam Man Ching, see my entry on Lam in Lee Kam Hing & Chow Mun Seong (eds.), *Biographical Dictionary of the Chinese in Malaysia*, pp. 79-80.

providing leadership to the entire Chinese community. He was the last pre-war Kapitan China. It is assumed that the leadership provided by the Ngin Foh Fui Kon leaders was acknowledged, or at least accepted, by the Hakka community, but it is also clear that the association may not have represented the entire community.

Other members of the Hakka community looked elsewhere for leadership. For the Hakka Christians who arrived via the migration schemes of the government and missionary societies or even churches, the church clergy were their acknowledged leaders. Due to the nature of their migration and settlement processes, for many years the group was settled within the same vicinity where they were provided with land, schools and churches, forming distinctive settlements of their own. The church became the focal point of their activities, and church leaders, both clergy and lay, became their natural leaders. This situation was very clear in the case of the first Hakka Christian settlement in Kudat where Basel Missionary Society clergy, most of whom were Austrians or Germans who spoke fluent Hakka, became the first group of acknowledged leaders. They were followed by the lay leaders from among the Hakka Christians themselves. The likes of Wong Shuk Ming and Lee Shiong Kong provided much of the local leadership. Later, when the Basel Mission finally sent a Chinese pastor, Reverend Wong Tian Nyuk, he became the acknowledged Hakka leader. There was no Hakka association in Kudat until just before World War II. In the same way, many of the Hakka Christians who arrived in Kudat decided to join the Anglican Church as the Basel Missionary Society was unable for several years to send a clergyman to work among them. The group, which began to grow rapidly, acknowledged Reverend Richard Richards, a Hakka-speaking priest, as their leader. Within the Basel Church, the foreign missionaries were still crucial in providing much of the early leadership to the Hakka community. In 1925 the Basel churches in North Borneo redefined the long-term relationship with the Basel Missionary Society and re-designated themselves as the Self-Established Basel Church of North Borneo 北婆羅洲巴色自立會, with the Chinese clergy taking over much of the role of the leaders – hence, inevitably placing them in the forefront of being leadership

In Sandakan, the absence of a Hakka Christian settlement resulted in the Hakka, including the Hakka Christians, acknowledging the Ngin Foh Fui Kon as the main Hakka association even though a Basel church was eventually established in that town in 1901, and the Anglican Church established a Hakka language service, with a Hakka-speaking priest.

When the west coast of Sabah was opened with the establishment of the town of Beaufort in 1896 and Jesselton in 1899, Hakka Christians were recruited to settle in the new areas. The first church using the Hakka dialect was started in Jesselton in 1905 when the Basel Church set up operations to care for the increasing number of Hakka Christians arriving in the newly established township. The first clergyman was Reverend Yap Hen Mu 葉賢模牧師. Later, new immigration schemes began to bring Christians, notably in 1913 when a large group of Hakka Christian families were brought to settle in the Inanam, Menggatal and Telipok area, along the Tuaran Road. This combination of the three Hakka rural settlements and those staying at the outskirts of Jesselton township helped to ensure that the Hakka became the dominant dialect group on the west coast, and Hakka the main Chinese dialect.

Yet, despite of this numerical superiority, it was not until 1940 that a Hakka association was established on the west coast – the Jesselton and West Coast Hakka Association (Ke Shu Gong Hui 西海岸客屬公會). Even then, its leader was a Basel Church pastor, and its executive committee was comprised almost entirely of Basel Church leaders. The establishment of the

Ngin Foh Fui Kon 人和會館 clearly acknowledged the further sub-division of the Hakka dialect group. The Hui Zhou (Fuijiu 惠州) consisted of those from Fuiyong (Huiyang 惠陽), Polo (Bo Luo 博羅), Fuijiu (Huizhou 惠州), whereas those from the Meizhou consisted of others like Ng Fah (Wu Hua 五華), Moi Yan (Meixian 梅縣). In the same way, the setting up of the Hakka Association in 1940 reflected this sub-division of the Hakka people. The Chinese name of the association was Ke Shu Gong Hui 客屬公會(common association of those belonging to the Hakka dialect group). In other words, even in 1940 the identity of the Hakka as it is understood today was only beginning to take shape. Prior to that date, Hakka identity was based on Hakka dialect and county of origin. While these two elements remained the mainstay of Hakka identity in Sabah, it was a gradual progression which reflected the multi-faceted character and background of the Hakka people in Sabah. This situation persisted long after the end of the war.

Conclusion

After more than 130 years of continuous presence in Sabah, the Hakka have emerged as the most important Chinese dialect group in the state. Their dominance of public life, as well as providing the uniqueness of Hakka identity as a characteristic of being a Chinese in Sabah, made it even more meaningful. However, such identification and uniqueness – as well as dominance – did not happen overnight. In fact, it could be considered a recent development, for the Hakka had remained very much in the background of public life in Sabah for the larger part of their existence in the state. Their dominance only became more apparent with the emergence of Hakka leaders as the political leaders of the Sabah Chinese since the late 1950s.

It is evident that in spite of their early arrival in the state, the Hakka were not organized in the manner they are today. Far from being known as a single dialect group, the term 'Hakka' was not even used commonly amongst the Hakka themselves for the larger part of their existence in the state even though the term was used by the British administration as a way of identifying the different dialect groups – as in the matter of identifying representatives – and the Hakka also identified themselves in this manner. However, when it came to organization, sub-dialect identification was probably more relevant at the time of their initial arrival in Sabah.

Hakka identity in Sabah was strongly tied to the land. Even though they had started to engage in business and other economic activities prior to World War II, the majority were still engaged in land-related activities, either as farmers or estate labourers. Thus, until the outbreak of the War the primary economic activities of the Hakka were farming and agriculture-based. This strong tie to the land also made the community more rural-based than the other Chinese dialect groups.

The pioneering businessmen and entrepreneurs discussed above were exceptions to the agriculture-oriented community at that time. Despite their negligible numbers compared to other dialect groups, especially the Hokkiens and the Teochius, they nevertheless formed the nucleus of Hakka businessmen who dared to venture beyond their 'traditionally defined' economic activities. The effect of this group of early businessmen and entrepreneurs is most apparent in the post-World War II era when larger numbers of Hakka began to engage in business enterprises. One research finding suggests that the percentage of Hakka in North Borneo involved in business and entrepreneurship increased from 2% for the first generation to about 11% for the third generation.[22] This figure has surely increased for the later generations.

This transformation from agriculture-based economic activities to business and entrepreneurship has been taking place within the Hakka community since the end of World War II, albeit at a slow pace. The large number of Hakka children who enrolled in the English-medium schools inevitably resulted in a major shift in the community's inclination to break their traditional ties with landholding, and venture into other occupations, including the civil service, professions and business ventures.

Today, the Hakka in North Borneo contribute about 60% of the state's Chinese population. This growth in number is significant in the sense that not only has the Hakka population grown many-fold from a mere 100 new arrivals in 1882, but it has actually outgrown other dialect groups to become the largest in the state. Another significant change that is visible today is that the Hakka have penetrated into all facets of life in North Borneo and, in many cases, dominated them. This demonstrates a transformation from a predominantly agricultural and rural-based community to a more urbanized one and, thus, less active in the agricultural sector. Now more than 70% of the Hakka are urban-based.[23] Present-day Hakka also make up significant numbers in the business community of Sabah and since the 1960s their leaders have dominated the local Chinese Chamber of Commerce. The Hakka community have also produced two chief ministers and a score of other politicians for the state.

---

22 R.D. Hill and Vo Min Shin, "Occupational and Spatial Mobility in an Overseas Chinese Agricultural Community: The Hakkas of Kudat, North Borneo, Malaysia", Unpublished paper, n.d.

23 *Population & Housing Census of Malaysia, 1991: State Population Report, North Borneo*, Kuala Lumpur: Department of Statistics Malaysia, 1995, p. 91.

Select References

BCCM Centenary Magazine 1882-1982. Kota Kinabalu: Basel Christian Church of Malaysia, 1983 [mostly in Chinese, with some pages in English and Malay].

Black, Ian, 1983, *A Gambling Style of Government*. Singapore: Oxford University Press.

British North Borneo Herald, 1 March 1883, May 1883, 1 Sept. 1884, 1 May 1888, 1 April 1891, 1 May 1900, 16 May 1900, 1 June 1915, 16 November 1928, 16 July 1929.

Franke, Wolfgang & Chen Tieh Fan (comp.), 1987, *Chinese Epigraphic Materials in Malaysia, Vol. III*. Kuala Lumpur: University of Malaya Press.

"Genealogy of the Lo Family: the Line of Nyit Sin Gong", Lo Vun Chen (comp.). Kudat, 1985 (unpublished).

Han Sin Fong, 1976, *The Chinese in Sabah, East Malaysia*. Taipei: The Oriental Cultural Service.

Hill, R. D. and Vo Min Shin, "Occupational and Spatial Mobility in an Overseas Chinese Agricultural Community: The Hakkas of Kudat, North Borneo, Malaysia". unpublished paper, n.d.

Jones, L.W., 1953, *North Borneo: A Report on the Census of Population held on 4th July, 1951*. London: University of London.

_____, 1966, *The Population of Borneo: A Study of the Peoples of Sarawak, North Borneo and Brunei*. London: University of London, The Athlone Press.

Lee, Edwin, 1976, *The Towkays of Sabah: Chinese Leadership and Indigenous Challenge in the last Phase of British Rule*. Singapore: Singapore University Press.

Lee Tak Vui, 1980, "The Hakka Mission in China in Relation to the Basel Christian Church of Malaysia". Graduation Exercise, B.Th., Trinity Theological College, Singapore.

Lutz, Jessie G. and Lutz, Rolland Ray, 1998, *Hakka Chinese Confront Protestant Christianity, 1850-1900*. London: M. E. Sharpe.

Niew Shong Tong, "A Brief History of the Hakka Immigrants in East Malaysia", *Asian Culture*, No. 17, June 1993, pp. 187-195 [in Chinese].

North Borneo Annual and Administrative Reports, 1921-1940.

Oades, Rizalino,1961, "Chinese Emigration through Hong Kong to North Borneo since 1880". MA dissertation, Hong Kong University.

Population and Housing Census of Malaysia 1991: North Borneo. Kuala Lumpur: Department of Statistics Malaysia, 1995.

Population and Housing Census of Malaysia 2000: Sabah. Kuala Lumpur: Department of Statistics Malaysia, 2000.

Purcell, Victor, 1980, *The Chinese in Southeast Asia*. London: Oxford University Press (reprint).

Sandakan Hakka Association Centenary Anniversary, 1886-1986. Sandakan: Sandakan Hakka Association, 1986 [in Chinese].

Secretariat File No. 1063, "Marriage Certificates of the Basel Church, 1921-1931". (Sabah State Archives)

Tarling, Nicholas, 1970, "The Entrepot at Labuan and the Chinese", *Sabah Society Journal*, Vol. V, No. 2, pp. 101-116.

Wong Tze Ken, Danny, 1977, "Lam Man Ching", in Lee Kam Hing & Chow Mun Seong eds., *Biographical Dictionary of the Chinese in Malaysia*, pp. 79-80. Petaling Jaya: Pelanduk Publications and Institute of Advanced Studies, University of Malaya.

_____, 1977, "Li Tet Phui", in Lee Kam Hing & Chow Mun Seong eds., *Biographical Dictionary of the Chinese in Malaysia*, pp. 100-101. Petaling Jaya: Pelanduk Publications and Institute of Advanced Studies, University of Malaya.

_____, 1998, *The Transformation of an Immigrant Society: A Study of the Chinese of North Borneo*. London: Asean Academic Press.

_____, 1999, "Chinese Migration to North Borneo before the Second World War", *Archipel*, No. 58, Vol. III, pp. 131-158.

_____, 2000, "The Chinese in Sabah: An Overview", in Lee Kam Hing & Tan Chee Beng eds., *The Chinese in Malaysia*, pp. 382-406. Kuala Lumpur: Oxford University Press.

_____, 2007, "The Petagas War Memorial and the Creation of a Heroic Past in Sabah", *Journal of the Malaysian Branch of the Royal Asiatic Society*, Vol. 80, Part 2, No. 293, December, pp. 19-32.

_____, 2007, "Kinabalu Guerrillas: The Inanam-Menggatal-Telipok Basel Church Connections", in Chong Tet Loi ed., *The Hakka Experiment in Sabah*, pp. 166-188. Kota Kinabalu: Sabah Theological Seminary.

國家圖書館出版品預行編目（CIP）資料

東南亞客家及其周邊 / 張維安編. -- 初版. -- 桃園縣中壢
市：中央大學出版中心；臺北市：遠流, 2013.09
　　面；　公分
　　部分內容為英文
　　ISBN 978-986-03-6855-0（平裝）

　　1. 客家　2. 東南亞

536.211　　　　　　　　　　　　　　　102008994

東南亞客家及其周邊

主編：張維安
執行編輯：許家泰
編輯協力：黃薰儀

出版單位：國立中央大學出版中心
　　　　　桃園市中壢區中大路300號

　　　　　遠流出版事業股份有限公司
　　　　　台北市南昌路二段81號6樓

發行單位／展售處：遠流出版事業股份有限公司
地址：台北市南昌路二段81號6樓
電話：(02) 23926899　傳真：(02) 23926658
劃撥帳號：0189456-1

著作權顧問：蕭雄淋律師
2013年9月 初版一刷
2018年6月 初版二刷
售價：新台幣350元

YL一遠流博識網 http://www.ylib.com　E-mail: ylib@ylib.com